SCHOOL AND PUBLIC LIBRARY MEDIA PROGRAMS

for Children and Young Adults

Advisory Committee

AUGUSTA BAKER
Formerly Coordinator of Children's Services
New York Public Library System
New York, New York

PHYLLIS LAND
Director, Division of Instructional Media
Indiana Department of Public Instruction
Indianapolis, Indiana

DR. JEAN LOWRIE
Director, School of Librarianship
Western Michigan University
Kalamazoo, Michigan

DR. CURTIS MAY
Director, Educational Resources Center
San Mateo County Schools
Redwood City, California

AMANDA RUDD
Deputy Director
Chicago Public Library
Chicago, Illinois

School and Public Library Media Programs
for Children and Young Adults

BY

D. Philip Baker

with a foreword by Augusta Baker

Gaylord Professional Publications
Syracuse, New York
1977

Library of Congress Cataloging in Publication Data

Baker, D   Philip, 1937-
    School and public library media programs for children and young adults.

    Includes index.
    1. Media programs (education). 2. Instructional materials center. 3. School libraries. 4. Public libraries. I. Title.
LB1028.4.B34   027.62′5   76-54919
ISBN 0-915794-09-8

© D. Philip Baker 1977

First published 1977 by
GAYLORD PROFESSIONAL PUBLICATIONS,
Syracuse, New York 13201

All rights reserved

Printed in the United States of America

This book is for the school library media specialists of the Stamford and Darien, Connecticut, Public Schools and the librarians of the Ferguson Public Library, Stamford, Connecticut. Their programs of excellence alone would fill many books. Thank you for demonstrating daily the meaning of excellence.

Contents

Foreword 9

Acknowledgements 17

PART I

Introduction 21

Characteristics of Exemplary Library Media Programs 28

Changing Expectations and Library Media Programs 44

PART II

Description of Library Media Programs for Children and Young Adults 71

PART III

Interpreting the Surveys; Implications for School and Public Library Programs 341

Afterword 361

APPENDIXES

A. Survey Instrument 369
B. School Library Media Programs Reported in this Study 377
C. Public Library Programs reported in this Study 385
D. Instructions to Site Visitors 391

Index 403

Foreword

Service to children and young people has been among the greatest strengths and glories of American libraries.

Back on the frontiers of early America the few precious books brought along the pioneer trails and waterways were eagerly shared with the young people—the Bible, of course, but also books of historical adventure, travel essays about the old world and the new that would inspire and broaden horizons. Books were scarce and treasured; they attracted the gifted and ambitious youngster to the office of the judge or lawyer, and to the minister's study. A little more accessible, perhaps, were the few books that were part of the intellectual resource of the teacher, in communities fortunate enough to have one. Books were viewed as precious personal possessions, the hallmarks and essential equipment of admired and influential adults.

The sharing of books through some form of communal library began early in this country. While Jefferson gave his collections to begin a library for Congress, and others gave theirs to begin or enhance the libraries of universities, Ben Franklin used his considerable talents to begin a library for the public in the City of Philadelphia. Other libraries were soon started in the population centers of the Northeast and Southeast. There was an informal secret sharing on some of the Southern plantations, too, despite the fact that it was expressly forbidden under slavery to teach a black child to read or to allow him exposure to books. The idea of better learning opportunities for children sustained the public library movement as it developed, and even gained tax support in community after community.

The mandating of tax-supported education which began in the 1850s siphoned off some momentum from public libraries for a time, but in the last quarter of the nineteenth century, community libraries found the schools to be a new stimulus to services to children and young people. Special departments provided service to children not only in the library itself but in classrooms, in hospitals, in orphanages, and even in homes. These blossomed in such places as Brooklyn, Boston, Hartford, Denver, and Cleveland. Child labor laws freed hundreds of thousands of children to *be* children before they had to take on adult responsibilities; millions more arrived in the two great immigrant waves of the late 1880s and early 1900s. The great public libraries with their instructional partners, the public schools, stood open to help them shake free from the ethnic ghettoes. Small town libraries, some of them housed through gifts of the most famous immigrant boy who ever read his way to fame and fortune, Andrew Carnegie, found in children their most responsive clientele.

Indeed, from the 1890s through the 1930s there developed a golden age of work with children and young people in libraries. Such pioneers as Carolyn Hewins in Hartford, Linda Eastman in Cleveland, and Anne Carroll Moore in New York enveloped the library world of children with story hours, creative dramatics, puppet shows, and other kinds of magic. They imported the best of English and European picture books, while creators of books for children here in the United States turned out a literature unparallelled in richness and variety. The story magazines of the late 1800s—the legendary St. Nicholas especially—provided a showcase and a living for such as Howard Pyle, Joel Chandler Harris, Frances Hodgeson Burnett, and Mary Mapes Dodge clear into the 1920s. Such diverse talents as those of Margaret Sidney and A. A. Milne fed the hunger of children for laughter and adventure. Publishing houses began to make a specialty of publishing for children about the end of World War I, when Macmillan, Stokes, Longmans Green, and Doubleday—quickly followed by others—began special departments to develop the talents of writers and artists as illustrators. New printing and art reproduction capabilities in Europe and America made beautiful color picture books possible.

A world of children's books came into being. It was a close-knit fraternity—more a sorority, perhaps—of editors, authors, critics, illustrators, librarians, and even booksellers who stimulated and monitored each other to the greater glory of books for children. Out of Bertha Mahony Miller's Bookshop for Boys and Girls in Boston came what is still the only magazine devoted to children's books, *The Horn Book;* May Massee, an outstanding librarian, became a brilliant editor and founded first a children's book department at Doubleday and then one at Viking Press; Anne Carroll Moore was a children's librarian who became as author, editor, and critic one of the most powerful influences on books for children; Frederic G. Melcher, devoted bookman and publisher, helped to found Children's Book Week and conceived the Newbery and Caldecott Medals for the best in children's literature. These were but a few of the personalities who made their lasting mark.

The excitement and creativity was for the most part among those concerned with books for children under fourteen years of age, and it was, therefore, associated with public library work since almost no grade schools had libraries of their own. Indeed, perhaps one reason for the enormous effectiveness of library work with children during the first fifty years of the century was that the elementary school curriculum was a pretty circumscribed, routine, and uninteresting affair. There was little room for departure into the individual interests or projects of pupils, and most schools did little to motivate or enhance the joy of learning. The progressive schools of the thirties set out to remedy this but their influence, probably due to the constraints of the Great Depression and the War, was slow in taking hold. For most children the public library's rooms in city branches and in small towns and their book services to teachers and classrooms provided the enrichment, the adventures in reading, and alternatives to lock-step learning for those fortunate enough to live in areas where there were good public libraries.

Meanwhile, growing numbers of young people continued up the education ladder through high school. Increasingly sophisticated high schools—taking their cue from the colleges and the great preparatory schools—established their own libraries as resources for continuous student use. Masses of high school students continued to use the public libraries as well, drawn by its longer open hours and a certain charm lent by its greater informality, its broader holdings, and its distance from teachers and classrooms.

Things began to change in the fifties. With the advent of federal aid to education, secondary schools improved their libraries greatly, and libraries at the elementary level were developed with unprecedented speed. School librarians felt the need to separate themselves from the influence and traditions of public library service in order to grow. Books and services imported from outside the school could never, they felt, be regarded by teachers and principals as an intrinsic part of the curriculum or the teacher's instructional method. Elementary school curriculum was changing as educators recognized the great foundational importance of the grade school and the learning habits established there, and librarians wanted to be a part of that change. Librarians hired to work for the school system, responsible to tne principal as members of his staff and trained and accredited as teachers felt that they must prove that they were different from the librarians of the past. Further, school library leaders envisioned changes in learning style which would greatly enhance the importance of the nonprint media. They recognized far earlier than most librarians in other types of libraries that the librarians of the future must be prepared to go beyond print, beyond film and recordings, to encompass all media that carries information and knowledge. They would need to be expert in how to purchase, organize, use and help others to use all of these other media.

The separation years were difficult and filled with resentments, personal antagonisms and cross purposes. School librarians split off to form a new division within the American Library Association in the early 1950s, and strivings by both public librarians serving children and young people and school librarians for role and identity brought about some extreme positions and a degree of isolation from each other. Some children's librarians in public libraries, noting the millions of dollars being allocated to the development of school libraries, vowed to turn their backs completely on teachers, children as students, and all school-related work. That would be the school librarians' province, and public library programs would be characterized exclusively by fun, cultural enrichment, and enjoyment. Equally foolish was the avowal of some school librarians that they were really not librarians at all but teachers of a special sort who happened to deal with materials. The indifference or outright distaste for children's programs on the part of some public library administrators did not help matters any.

At this point it is appropriate to say a word, perhaps, about semantics and what they have done to mislead us. Eager to show that they were not made in the outworn image of card-stamping, book-guarding librarians which was engrained in the hearts and minds of so many school board members, principals, parents, and teachers, school librarians decided in the sixties that they would be known henceforth as *media specialists,* presiding over media in a media center—instead of a library. There were good and compelling political and financial reasons for this: money was available for "media" and there was a need to dramatize the programs as innovative and entirely different from what had gone before under the name of "library." But the troubles were many. One was, and is, that most people incorrectly take "media" to mean audio and visual materials and equipment exclusively—not books at all. Another is that "media" does not convey much of anything to the great majority of people, including those in education. By rejecting the title *librarian*—even with its attendant disadvantage of the fading but still prevalent bun-headed image—school librarians put themselves in a kind of no-man's land.

There are welcome signs that leaders are now quietly and

wisely returning to the use of at least "library-media" to try to capture the best of both worlds and convey what they really are about. At a recent conference in Maryland of the International Association of School Librarians (associated with the World Confederation of Organizations of the Teaching Profession) Dr. Frances Henne, the brilliant conceptualizer and major influence in the school library field for more than forty years, and a chief proponent of school librarian as media specialist, stated that dropping "librarian" from the school librarian's title had been a major mistake and must now be rectified.

Well, where are we now? I believe, as does Phil Baker, one of the finest of the newer leaders in the school library field, that we are, we must—school and public librarians who serve children and youth—come together again, each bringing new strengths to a new and fully realized partnership. We are neither urging the merging of our agencies nor the elimination of either. Each has its special job to do. We are proponents, however, of genuine joint planning and in many more instances, joint carrying out of programs and services. We must enter into a new relationship to insure that just as adults of a given community—a locality, a state, or a nation—have access to different types of libraries to suit their needs, so children and young people must have a planned dove-tailed network of service outlets in various locations and geared to particular needs.

We are back, full circle, to emphasis where it should be: on the user, the child or youth whose access to information must be widened, and whose ability to use it developed. Artificial lines between what is enjoyment and what is learning, what is instruction and what is cultural, must be eliminated. Adherence to what is traditional "children's work" and avoidance of any and all formal teaching responsibility must be carefully re-examined by public librarians. Equally, school librarians must recognize that all exposure to books and the sight and sound media will not, need not, result in structured, visible, measurable learning and response. School librarians must become, in my view, more aware of the "affective domain"—the unstructured, perhaps delayed impact of library programs and materials on emotions, behavior and enduring values. Children's librarians in public libraries, on the other hand, must realize that they will not be totally absolved from accountability to the public; indicators, measures, of some persuasive kind that show that programs and services are valuable and effective are needed.

Public librarians as well as school librarians must accept responsibility to help audiovisually minded and nurtured youngsters to evaluate and be selective about what they see and hear. We must, all of us, help children to learn to express and communicate in *words* (other than "ya know, ya know") what they feel and think, remembering that not all response will be immediate or shared. We must try harder than ever to be adult models of humanistic behavior, good listeners and holders of high expectations for our clients. We must be ever ready to demonstrate the values for children *now* of the tried and true—the story hours and the reading aloud sessions—even while we add other program modes to them.

Both school and public librarians who serve children must become more adept at indirect influences they can exert through others who touch the lives of children: parents above all, but also teachers, social workers, recreation directors, and others. Public librarians and school librarians need to work hand-in-hand to develop ways in which to measure the impact, both short term and long range, of library materials and programs. Above all, both school and public librarians serving children must be more willing to cast themselves into roles as administrators, planners, conceptualizers with others whose decisions affect children in their communities. They must determine priorities, and persuade others to accept the right priorities. Both must fight the pressures from within themselves and externally to allow housekeeping chores to become the excuse not to do the extra planning and the extra work that good programs demand. People who desire only a routine and non-thinking way to earn a living should be eased out of the profession.

It is time now for school and public librarians to form a team to serve their common clientele. This effort must claim their whole attention, and their highest loyalty. This book has been carefully researched and written to document some of the best efforts that school and public libraries have been able to make for children; it is time now to see how the best of both can be reshaped into a total network of service—a network of thousands of good efforts and programs that complement each other and offer children the very best that librarians can offer.

Augusta Baker

New York
August 1976

Acknowledgements

My special thanks to the members of the Advisory Committee for this book. Their suggestions were always helpful, their criticisms kind, but to the point, and their conscientious work a great support. To Augusta Baker, whose knowledge about excellent library programs for children is unsurpassed, my gratitude. She provided invaluable help, thoughtful criticism, and perceptive advice. Finally, thanks to Virginia Mathews, friend and editor, for her great support and help—every step of the way.

Stamford, Connecticut D. PHILIP BAKER

PART I

Introduction

A watery unfriendly sun surrendered at last to a torrential rain more appropriate to April than November, on Thanksgiving Day, 1975. No lightening of this climatic mood could be found indoors either. The *New York Times* was filled with news of the miraculous rescue of New York City from bankruptcy. Close, very close; now, reprieved at eight percent interest!

On the front page, lower left, appeared a story about the severe economic pinch facing the nation's libraries. The facts were already well known to any librarian who had not chosen to sleep through the first five years of this decade. In New York City, library branches were closing, hours of service being reduced, librarians and aides discharged, bookmobiles taken off the streets, and fewer books and periodicals being purchased. Library disaster, just a part of other unhappy front page news.

Inflation, economic failure, social uncertainties, and a kind of political paralysis combine now to reinforce a harsh and newly learned lesson: that institutions, like individuals, are subject to every dislocation and trend of our times. They are not insulated from change and, in fact, seem perilously ill-equipped to cope with it.

In Atlanta, the director of that city's library system pointed out that "The worse times get, the more use the library gets."

For those uneasy about the economic future, anxiety mounts with his additional statement that "The best year in the history of this library was 1931." A new school of theoretical economics might posit that the fuller the public library reading rooms, the closer we are to the bottom of a business cycle. This would place libraries on line with auto production, housing starts, rolled steel processing, and savings statistics among those leading economic indicators that predict our future economic course. While this may be a nonsense notion, in times when the bizarre often becomes the norm, no idea should be overlooked completely.

Both schools and public libraries have proved particularly vulnerable to the economic troubles of this decade. Public library directors, desperate to prove the library's economic worth, have down-graded or closed down children's services often with the rationale that children and youth are being served by the schools. In schools, media center programs are phased out; professional and support staff join the unemployed work force and the brilliant promise of earlier times that media programs would lead children and teachers into a new educational era by curriculum reform, instructional innovation and the application of technology to learning, stands challenged nearly everywhere.

For political and social as well as economic reasons, public library and school media programs for children and young people are under siege. It is a tallying time and a public increasingly aware of such terms as accountability, management by objectives, and zero budgeting seeks specific answers to difficult questions. It demands proof that the media work; even that independent learning works.

For the remainder of this century at least, it is probable that meager economic resources will go first to those services perceived as most critical at the national, state, and local level. At the national level this will mean the maintenance of the defense establishment, debt servicing, and the like. All sorts of persons and groups may continue to quarrel with these priorities, but they are likely to remain priorities. At the state and local level available funds will go first to protection services: support for police, fire, sanitation, and hospitals. This is realistic, if in the opinion of many, shortsighted.

INTRODUCTION   23

Spending for our schools, our libraries, and other cultural institutions—even our ecological well being—may well be severely reduced for years to come. Accepting this grim picture, as contrasted to the plenteous days of the sixties, may cause some to give up the fight. Many of those now maintaining media programs may head either for the bunkers or the Land of Oz, whichever best suits individual reaction to crises. But others will stave off total collapse of program successfully because they will adapt to changed conditions and demands.

Each of us should remember that just as success is never final neither is defeat. An editorial in the November 17, 1975 issue of *New York* magazine stated it well, "We've Got To Help Ourselves." That is really the purpose of this book. Much of the planning and preparation for it have been built upon the expectation that for the remainder of this century the greatest resource that school media and public library programs will have to rely upon will be ourselves. Our response to the challenge must be adaptation of our programs to meet new realities and changing conditions.

If there is to be a mobilization to maintain and develop what we have gained in excellence in the education of our youth, it should not be directed toward securing greatly increased federal, state, and local spending to support media programs. There is no money for this. This does *not* mean that all efforts to secure that rightful portion of the public spending that is "ours" should cease. In fact, these efforts will undoubtedly have to be stepped up since more persons and institutions will be competing for a share of diminishing public revenues. It is discouraging to face the fact that we will have to spend more time and money to obtain whatever smaller share of public finance the profession is to utilize. Foolishness raised to reality it may be, but as a profession we must pursue this course, for the alternative is *no* money at all and that is clearly unacceptable.

Some people who have some confused and even dangerous notions about *basics* in educational and public insitutional programs are going to have a lot of influence in the period just ahead. It is best to accept now that any program not pulling its weight in terms of accomplishing specific goals is pushing its luck, and that many of the notions we have had about measuring the worth of programs will have to be adjusted or discarded.

Hopefully, this book will reflect a characteristic that is particularly American and recognized as such through our history: we are at our best when there are problems to be solved. The problems as always seem more apparent, and numerous, than the solutions. Another simple premise underlies this book: that just as the success of one individual or one program enriches each of us, so also each person's or program's failure diminishes each of us.

Our purpose in presenting a series of fifty programs in public libraries and school media centers that use media in creative or exemplary ways with children and young adults is to share successful programs and ideas among ourselves and with others. If some of these programs and ideas are adopted or adapted by others, or even just spark a totally new idea, then the book may be judged a success.

Many, even most, of the programs described are not unique or original. What makes them useful models is that each has an extraordinary aura of purpose and intent to fulfill some very specific goals. They can serve as a compass, providing direction for others. Thus, if they do not reflect the sometimes frantic drive of the sixties to innovate at all (or any) cost, they *do* reflect an identity and a sureness that is today badly needed. It is not our purpose to describe simply "how they do it good" in one place or other, but rather to explain why people decided to do a program, what their purpose was, and how they worked to achieve it. What went right and what went wrong are here too. The latter, after all, is sometimes more important than the former.

If this is a time for self-reliance, determination, and hope, it can come best from a sense of belief in ourselves. The programs described in this book show us doing our best. Each program recognizes that, as S. I. Hayakawa has put it, "The enemy of the young is boredom." However, the response of these programs to this has not been to provide distracting entertainment to invoke mindless reaction or to kill time.

INTRODUCTION

Each of these programs is imaginative. In each, though, imagination has been tied securely to experience, heightening insight and learning. These programs, whether located in public libraries or schools, recognize that an exemplary media program is not a haven for pampered misfits, nor a dumping ground for kids nobody else can deal with. Each recognizes the fact that an excellent media program must provide structure and experience without being rigid or limiting.

All the programs show a sound and fundamental belief in children and young people and the uniqueness of the human experience of discovery. One mark of any exemplary program is its ability to become more creative and productive by encompassing the beautiful curiosity of children and young people into itself; these programs do this.

Selections for inclusion in this book recognize that locally planned programs that respond to local needs are the best. Many have, of course, been adopted from other places and institutions. But they have been refined with sensitivity and intelligence to fit special needs.

A unifying factor is that each of the programs analyzed makes use of resources already available, or rearranges existing resources to accomplish specific goals. These resources range from the volunteer worker to a furry mammal, and each has a flavor of "can-do" and "make-do" without seeming martyred or parsimonious.

Each program deals, specifically, with a relationship between ideas and activities. However, the ideas and activities presented here are not those searching for definition; they are operational rather than theoretical. They have been constructed with an obvious degree of common sense about children as people. They are also common sense in that, in my estimation, they reflect the knack of seeing things as they are and doing things as they ought to be done.

These projects lack affectation and pretense. Their simplicity and clarity of purpose show up the activities of those who are doing less but saying more. While words may describe these programs, it is the ideas behind these words that identify them as exemplary.

Simplicity, though, does not mean casual planning or

fuzziness about the rightness of one's course. Pride, too, is visible in those who run programs—not the pride of arrogance, too often coupled with incompetence, but pride that comes from the satisfaction of truly doing well. It is the pride that results from taking ideas and making them living things. This kind of pride is wary of slogans and defies labels. It is, fortunately, still recognized instantly and it will exist as long as there is integrity. It is this integrity that commends these programs for the reader to consider and use.

Another criterion by which programs were selected for inclusion in this book was evidence of their having worked effectively with components that are frequently oversold for their supposed impact on learning. Television provides the best example. No one has discovered an inexpensive way of incorporating video into any school media or public library program. It is costly—costly in terms of personnel, costly in terms of equipment, and costly in terms of the time it takes to run it well. While many schools and public libraries have shown creative (and cost-saving) ways of using support staff or children to operate video programs, they remain generally, high cost programs. The promise that video communication will revolutionize instruction and improve teaching remains largely a promise. Probably there is no area in which schools and public libraries have been more the victim of their own erroneous preformed conclusions. For most, the experience of using video programming as part of the mediated approach to learning or experience has been less than satisfying.

Yet, only a fool would ignore the overwhelming evidence that television has a greater impact on the learning and thinking of American youth than any other communication medium. We may respond to this evidence with emotions ranging from frustration to denial. We may blame television for the decline in S.A.T. scores, for the inability of our youth to communicate, orally or by writing; we may blame it for its frequent mindlessness and vulgarity, and for its preoccupation with violence and destruction. It makes no difference; television remains the single most pervasive force in our culture. It outranks the family as a communicator of values and ethics and a code of living. It far outstrips in influence the institutions that have provided cohesiveness of tradition so important to our culture. Television communicates more information and learning to youth than any educational institution.

Any book that would deal realistically with media programs for young persons must consider television and its role in media programming. Hopefully, the video programs presented in this book do fulfill the criteria of simplicity, effectiveness and integrity. Granted that it is not possible to have any sort of video program without some extraordinary expenditure, the programs reported do reflect an understanding of how children learn best and a compelling interest in stimulating the creativity that is inherent in every child.

The programs included in the book represent a wide geographic range. This was not a criterion for inclusion, but it does add a useful dimension.

Wherever possible, an effort was made to select programs that used professionals, support personnel, and volunteers in effective combinations to advance the stated goals.

On the initial survey instrument, several questions were asked about the facility (or facilities) that housed the program. In the final analysis though, the physical facility—its newness, convenience, and equipment—was not of primary importance to the impact of the program. This may reflect my own bias that American architecture is too often just silly exhibitionism. Visits to many schools, to a large number of new public libraries, and to many new junior colleges reinforce a suspicion that architects, frequently working hand in hand with members of our own profession, are too often preoccupied with building monuments, which express their own misconceptions about libraries.

Other sections of the survey contained questions about budget, personnel, innovations, and recognition. All these factors were reviewed carefully. It was, finally, the program that worked because it was well conceived, consistently carried out, and reasonably well evaluated that eventually found its way into this book about exemplary media programs.

Characteristics of Exemplary Library Media Programs

In *Precious Bane*, a novel which fuses beautifully the elements of nature and man, Mary Webb has the mother say to her children "You must harness your dreams before you ride them." I have always liked this homely advice which seems somehow inappropriate to an era which appears to be so willfully embarked upon exactly the opposite course. Pat sayings cannot provide specific directions or easy answers to complex problems, but if they make us pause to gain perspective on an idea or expectation, they serve a useful purpose. So it is with the media.

Media! The very word conjures up visions of supergraphics, insistent newspaper headlines, the disaster and disarray exposed on the nightly television newscasts. The media are—in their audio and visual impact—clamorous, insistent, unceasing and immediate. By the vast majority, the media and their content are accepted uncritically, talked about and chuckled with; by a relatively small minority they are worried over, editorialized about, warned against, deplored, and, usually, accepted with resignation. A few treat the media with aloof disdain, but in this decade political careers have been made, and broken, by the simple turn of the television switch or the banner news headline. The increasing power of the media to shape our thinking and mold our opinions is a phenomenon of the late twentieth century.

Marshall McLuhan told us in the sixties that the "Medium is the message." No one was absolutely certain what he meant. There exists still, widespread confusion between the message and the messenger. Television and the press are blamed for inflaming crowds, creating scandals, and other misdeeds. Yet it is perfectly clear that neither television nor the newspapers created Watergate, Viet Nam, or natural disasters. As much as they mold, the media still serve to reflect what we are, what we do and what happens to us. No one can be certain where the truth lies.

No one knows what most Americans really think or feel about media. Feelings are difficult to define because they are shaped by the experience of the immediate past and the anticipation of the near future and both of these are ruled as much by fancy as by reason. Yet, most of us believe that only in the present may reality be found. One revolutionary concept that the media force us to confront, is that the *present* really is the past, and the future, programmed by computers and filled with bionic miracles, remains an uncomfortable threat to most.

Perhaps this is the reason for a growing, though poorly articulated, fear in this culture today, a fear that finds its focus in the media. It mushrooms in widely scattered places and assumes a variety of shapes and postures. It may be expressed as the fear of being manipulated, used, "brainwashed," *changed*. Reaction to this may take the form of attempts to censor books that deal with the biological and anthropological origins of man; it may be vocal reactions to the more petty excesses of "liberation movements"; or it may be the picketing of the pornographic theatre by the local league for decency. Whatever the mood, or its expression, it is often based on fear—fear of something only dimly perceived and but vaguely understood.

Again and again—in books, in editorials, on film and television, in articles and in public debate, as a nation and as a culture we have tried to define the role media play in shaping our lives and our destinies. If a talent for consensus remains a peculiar hallmark of this nation, we have failed thus far in our efforts regarding the media. For as yet we have no shared notion, no recognized "common wisdom," about what is positive and what is negative, and how much is too much of the media.

It may be for the best that we have yet to find consensus. This might only curb troublesome thinking and thinking about the media is required. Since, too, there will always be a gap between expectations and reality, we may never reach a shared opinion on the worth or value of the media to our lives. Media reflect us; they are what we are, and since we are constantly changing in a culture in which the lines between future and the present are blurred, perhaps no ultimate definition will ever be possible.

As with many other issues of the times, what we deal with here is complex. Are media a good or bad influence on our lives? There is no answer now, nor is there likely to be in our lifetime. All the heavy thinkers in the world concentrating on this single question will not provide an answer acceptable to most persons. Our approach, though, can not be simply to ignore the matter. No course could be more perilous or shortsighted. Rather, our efforts must go toward managing the media so that they fulfill, as nearly as possible, some reasonable expectations of positive contributions to the development and progress of society. Thus, the challenge!

If we accept this challenge, the possibilities for effectively using media in productive and significant ways are limited only by our own imaginations. Nothing else—lack of money, personnel, or other resources need prevent the excellent application of the media to programs serving children and young persons in schools and public libraries.

Media use must not be a process of searching for definitions. Our efforts to use media well should be founded on a commitment to make their application to learning operational rather than theoretical, specific rather than abstract. It is a passion for the abstract that has so undermined the credibility of many of the leading thinkers about the role of media in learning.

Most of us would probably accept the dictum that the information we receive and the attitudes and activities this information engenders cannot be separated. Paul Ehrlich, a gifted writer and creative social thinker, perceives this when he states that, "Most of the supposedly extremely technical problems are just not that technical. . . . People can easily grasp enough of the facts to draw their own conclusions." Ehrlich also downplays the role of experts, stating that "There isn't one serious question today that doesn't have experts lined up on either side of it." This profusion of experts—on every issue—has led in recent years to some very incoherent applications of knowledge. Ehrlich has more important advice. He says that "People have got to learn how to make their own evaluations rather than look to 'experts.'" Ehrlich equates this with survival, believe him! This process of providing the tools (information) for decision making cannot be arrogated simply to the schools; it is too much to expect from an already overburdened public education system. Excellent use of media should provide access to necessary information, helping persons make well informed decisions from alternative possibilities.

The media have been the trigger for much debate over how best to apply knowledge and to organize information. This discussion of issues and choices has often been frustrating. And the debate has been disillusioning too, for we have found that many decisions about issues are not ours to make. Much of this discussion has had the substance and sense of planning for the future by breaking open fortune cookies. In such an atmosphere the primary requisite for all players has been to leave your wits at home.

The American Association of School Librarians (AASL) and the Association for Educational Communications and Technology (AECT) deserve credit for their efforts to explain that people who work with media are not just combinations of astrologers and court jesters. The two associations, primarily through the *Standards For School Media Programs* issued in 1969 and *Media Programs: District and School* issued in 1975, have forcefully addressed the fact that the excellent application of media to learning is probably the fundamental issue facing any agency that is in any way concerned with how people learn.

Other realities face us as well. We now believe that by age

five, before he enters formal schooling, a child has learned a language, can imagine the unknown, can create music, poetry, art and has learned well over fifty percent of all that he will ever learn. It is the responsibility of education to help him to sort out, organize, and put these learnings together in usable form.

We accept increasingly the idea that education is a matter of life-long necessity. Accepting these realities, though, means change and change threatens: our power, our security, our success, our adjustment to life. It frightens us because it is so limitless. It severs our connections with the past, sometimes even with the present. Alvin Toffler and William Thompson, among others, have told us that a problem with perceiving time is the quality of invisibility about the events that shape time. The pace of change has become so rapid that we actually witness it, while the present is so transient that it seems invisible. Indeed, the old injunction to "look around you, you'll see what I mean" is inoperable, for now when we say this we are not seeing the present, but the past. It takes a great deal more imagination than most of us possess to "simply see" what is going on. The concern of this book though is not futurism which, while stimulating and provocative to consider, is not our focus.

It is a fundamental purpose of this book, however, to help those who work in information programs with children and young persons to nurture as the end product of their efforts persons who will find pleasure in the learning process, who will want to explore and discover in an effort to develop ideas and values. Such people will be able to develop self esteem sufficient to allow them to function as capable and contributing citizens. By learning how to process, evaluate, and use information young people may develop the resources to be reasonably secure in a world that never can be fully understood or controlled. These goals are not idealistic—they are real, immediate, and vital.

From a secure personal base should come a deeper sense of social commitment. The ability of media to humanize learning and reinforce people to people contact must be emphasized over the technological capacity of media. We must create media programs that will promote the development of critical thinking, and the desire to learn throughout life. Margaret Mead has expressed this as the need to create new adult models who can teach children not what to learn, but how to learn; not what they should be committed to but the value of commitment.

It is a sad distinction of our times that the smaller our world has become, the more we seem to have barricaded ourselves from thoughts or ideas that are difficult or different. The labels or convenient definitions, which served us for so long as insulation, no longer work. The media has had much to do with bringing us to this point, and our ability now to master their use will have direct bearing on our future course.

The process of managing information, and applying it to learning must not be allowed to lead us into a maze in which the more we discover the greater our sense of futility over what we have learned. The theoretical uses of media and their practical management should be utilized to give structure and support to humans seeking answers. They should provide intellectual support for intuitive feelings. They should help us become keen observers, to recognize change and how best to manage it. They should help us relate with intelligence and compassion to a world outside of ourselves.

Indeed, the most basic skill may be the skill of relating well to others. The media should help us to understand and accept that the absence of absolute answers to problems or their definitions should not lead to a paralysis of individual or group action. To guide implies setting the course or direction and proceeding correctly along it. Good application of media should provide this kind of guidance, but it may show us too that perhaps the most we can expect from knowledge is heightened understanding rather than specific direction. There are today infinite varieties and expressions of knowledge and truth. But there are constants, and it is some of these constants with which this book deals.

The concept of exemplary programs is difficult to define satisfactorily. What makes something exemplary? Is it money? A personality on a staff? Leadership by a director? Exciting facility? High achievement test scores? Publicity?

Yes, these are often present in exemplary programs, but it is a sum greater than any of these single parts we seek to define. In fact, there are no words describing exactly what exemplary means. Describing something exemplary is akin to measuring outer space, an impossible task. But, experience shows that nearly everyone knows, at once, when they find excellence. It is outlined with the same blinding clarity by which objects are seen during a lightning flash. Class, style, integrity, character—each of these words describes being exemplary but they do not quite satisfy as definitions. Being exemplary is having these qualities, and more.

And the use of research to establish what is exemplary presents as many problems as solutions. While the truism that research is only a systematic way of proving what we already know is too simplistic, there is much truth in it. Research as systematic answer-providing analysis is too strict a master for our purposes in this book.

All of this, by the way, is not an attempt to avoid describing how and in what ways programs described in this book as exemplary deserve to be called so. Certainly, more than intuition, blind instinct and a search for clues and definitions motivated their selection.

Basic to the selection of these programs is a belief that people need models to pattern improvements after. Each of us may have an ideal, a goal to achieve, but the chances of accomplishing this satisfactorily are diminished without patterns and encouragement to look beyond what we already know. This "exploring" process may lead to rejection or adoption of what we discover. For most though, *adaptation* of a model to a mode that best suits individual styles or needs will be the result.

For this book, definite criteria were established to define what is exemplary. To some extent these criteria were predetermined and to some extent these were shaped by the commonalities we "found." One, was that exemplary programs involve staff in ways that heighten their sense of personal and professional value. And small groups of dedicated people who truly want to accomplish something will do so; they can make a program exemplary. This is a value to be searched out, identified and emulated.

Secondly, many of the exemplary programs described in this book involve a reward of one kind or another. Where reward awaits, there is a heightened will to innovate. It is not necessary that this reward be financial or material. In fact, the reward may be internalized and almost psychic. But it must be specific and include personal recognition for a job well done; a task accomplished. The reward reflects caring and concern and underlies high personal and professional expectations that make people want to achieve still more.

A third criterion was that the programs described in this book addressed themselves to the development and learning of some basic skills. It is with reluctance that I use the word "basic"; it is a word used inappropriately and improperly so often these days. But basic skills are important. And the complex of skills called "reading" is still the *most* important. Undeniably, necessary information and knowledge can come to us through a variety of visual or auditory experiences. But we must not permit the delusion that reading, in the sense of print literacy, is no longer essential. Rather than eliminating the need to read, the information explosion makes it far more important than ever that everyone read as skillfully as possible, with the greatest speed and comprehension.

Sound attention, then, to fundamental learning skills should be present in exemplary media programs; but so also should opportunities to develop good attitudes, values, and respect for new ideas. In accomplishing these goals, exemplary programs do not treat the cognitive and affective "domains" as though they were separate and mutually exclusive. They are not, and learning to obey rules, respect authority, and care about the rights of others can occur simultaneously with the learning of skills and subject matter. In fact, exemplary programs demonstrate understanding of how to relate the two, increasing the excellence of the program. Enjoyment and discipline are combined together to heighten motivation.

As a fourth criterion, we found that exemplary programs contain within them a high element of appreciation and enjoyment, increased because they are shared by everyone involved with the program. Children and young people participating in exemplary programs develop and maintain high levels of interest and involvement. They display a strong personal commitment, which they share with professionals, to the success of the program.

Exemplary programs also include clear, specific and agreed-upon methods to provide discipline, not a discipline of repression and imposed values, but one developed by a consensus that permits each individual to make a maximum personal contribution by working with others. This kind of discipline requires good program management, management that is responsive to the needs of children and staff, yet capable of making decisions and implementing them with vigor and tact. This kind of management leads, but also shares. It defines and provides strategies by which goals and objectives are established, but enlists the involvement of everyone in their continuous development and in their achievement. Programs exhibiting these qualities met a fifth criterion for selection.

We found, sixth, that exemplary programs have a built-in resiliency and flexibility that permits them to meet and cope with setbacks, making defeats temporary. To judge the true value of some media programs, attention must be given to understanding how the program worked to overcome failure, to find success. Exemplary programs seem to have a built-in capability to change their course or direction without altering substantially their intent or purpose. They exhibit that to achieve one goal it may be necessary to use several methods.

A seventh criterion by which a media program was evaluated was its adaptability or adoptability to other institutions or individuals with some predictable degree of success: in other words, its value as a model. Essential to this is the establishment of program goals and objectives that are definable, obtainable and measurable. Essential, too, is good record-keeping in both narrative and itemized form. These records, far from restraining or entangling successful media programs in a web of red tape or duplication, help tremendously in evolving an excellent program and finally in its evaluation.

An eighth criterion established that a characteristic of

exemplary programs is their ability to establish a "personality," generating their own mystique, while at the same time becoming integrated into a larger program in ways that support and reinforce its overall purpose—service to clients.

This criterion leads to the ninth, basic factor of excellence found in the case surveys. Because of its integration with an overall program the exemplary media program does not create an elitist group, whose purposes and directions are separate and set apart from those who run the on-going program. Rather, the exemplary program is the result of the widest possible staff and participant involvement in its planning. And once this planning is accomplished, continuing participation and evaluation by participants and staff is essential. Many sound programs achieve initial success, then die, because their separateness promotes staff alienation and generates a wish that they fail.

A tenth criterion. Is it necessary to state again that any program must fill a need? Apparently, yes! Too often programs in the past were devised by persons who failed to establish any *need* or purpose for them. This is like racing a car engine in neutral, in the vain hope that noise and thrust will move it! The excellent program must always be one that is *needed* and therefore accepted with enthusiasm. Regrettably, many a project has been begun because there were excess funds or staff available for a certain category of program—a condition which exists far less today than it did ten years ago. "Greed before Need" is an almost sure recipe for a mindless, pointless exercise. Frequently in an attempt to establish their credibility these programs were labeled "exemplary," "innovative" or "lighthouse." In fact, these labels often separated the programs from their users and those expected to emulate them. Today, the ghosts of these programs haunt our attempts to innovate or provide models—they are a difficult legacy to overcome.

Tied closely to the requirement to assess need is the commitment to evaluate and measure program effectiveness. Performance evaluation by measuring achievement against stated objectives is required now for many school media programs. As is frequently true of new movements oriented strongly toward salvation (and at its worst, measurement is sometimes confused with salvation), our initial efforts to measure, assess, and evaluate programs have often made us appear foolish. Our use of management by objective systems, performance budgeting systems, and other management systems has sometimes lead us astray. Too often we have become fascinated with wrong variables and accordingly developed programs around invalid expectations. In the hands of the wrong personnel these necessary tools can be positively destructive. However, having survived the excesses it is probable that we shall arrive eventually at methods of program evaluation that are valid as well as comfortable to use.

Evaluation is something that anyone with common sense and professional integrity does. Each of us evaluates our actions, programs, the consequences of our decisions several times during any normal day. Why did I do that? is, after all, a pretty basic evaluation mode. The relevant question to ask is not *what* to evaluate, but *how* to evaluate effectively and purposefully so that a program or person may be improved or made more effective. Evaluation systems devised by theorists and imposed externally (usually from above) are guaranteed to achieve the same effect as throwing a stone to a drowning man. The statement of program need, its justification, and the ordering of evaluative criteria developed by the participants and staff must be structured internally into the program *before* it is set into motion.

No media program can be guaranteed success through careful needs assessment, goal setting, developing measurable objectives, or other evaluative procedures. Failure, however, is guaranteed if these are ignored or overlooked. These are the factors that provide the internal compass by which any individual or program finds direction.

A willingness to admit error or misdirection must be built into any evaluative system. While such admissions by people about programs they devise and operate are painful, they are often necessary. It is said that the true measure of successful persons is not how they handle their successes but rather how they deal with their failures. Media programs are no different;

when the evaluative process finds mistakes or weakness, exemplary programs will respond in a positive way by applying their own corrective measures. This response is internalized and almost axiomatic to excellence. The ability to deal with failure by reassessing and reevaluating must be contained within any exemplary program.

These appear as the most distinct and apparent criteria by which programs selected for this book were measured and evaluated. Doubtless, other important facts were overlooked or given less weight, but it was on the foregoing that most decisions to include or exclude were made.

Looking toward the Future

While the intent of this book is not to range over the impact of an "anticipated" future on media programs for children and young adults, the future (no matter how unpredictable or uncertain) must receive some attention. It is necessary in thinking about what we want media programs to be.

It may be that the explosive growth of astrological forecasting and a preoccupation with finding out what lies ahead is our rather pathetic reaction to the realization that indeed we cannot predict the future. We do not like to acknowledge this; it runs counter to the uniquely American belief that we can, and do, *control* the future.

The American tradition in this regard is firmly rooted in our successful applications of science and technology to control (and in that sense predict) the future course of history. At exactly what precise moment this basic tenet of The American Dream was rendered inoperable is a matter of conjecture. The splitting of the atom; the growth of rootless, anonymous urban masses; the disintegration of the ability of our political, economic and social institutions to confront the issues that force the process by which change is accommodated; the Vietnamese quagmire which so brutally exposed these same failings: all contributed. These are only some of the events of the past thirty years that social philosophers have cited to explain our present transitional society.

Another reaction to future fear is an ardent interest in returning to the past. The current American concern to recapture the past, in dress, entertainment, and other ways reflects this. An excess of nostalgia that forms a desire to turn back in time and mood may be associated with a fear of what lies ahead. If in the past we have overindulged our desire or need to predict and control the future, we must now take care that we do not uncritically accept the past as good or take refuge from reality in it. If it does assume this dimension, nostalgia is not a harmless whimsy; it becomes a trap.

New and better ways must be found to deal with pressing issues, before they overwhelm us. Some attempt to deal with change by helping people think about some solutions to the monumental problems before us must be undertaken. In a sense, seen in total, the issues facing us are so overwhelming that we lose sight of the central, ultimate issue: survival of the human race. For most, this is simply too all-encompassing in its finality to cope with, and so we quantify into elements, breaking down issues into more manageable parts such as ecology, energy use, population, food production, and economic growth.

It is likely that most of these social, political, and economic problems are entirely too difficult to assemble into soluble entities. Perhaps they are not even soluble in the classic sense that answers will be given. Our greatest need may well be for information that points to the alternatives for living with or managing global problems in the most effective or the least disastrous way. Both the quantitative and qualitative flow of information will be critical in supplying the examples, options, and models that will govern our choices. Our schools, our libraries, and other institutions have a major role to play in getting this information to people.

It may well be that future school and public library media programs will best serve their purpose simply by being responsive, helping people cope with and process information. By now, most educators (and I include the public librarian as an educator) have accepted what was once a radical educational theory: that it is not *what* we learn but *how* we learn that is important. During the past decade acceptance of this doctrine has resulted in some far reaching and fundamental changes affecting teaching and learning everywhere. That it has also led to some aberrations and excesses cannot deny its basic soundness.

All of this means that the school and the public library face significantly altered methods of doing their jobs, and change is threatening to any institution; for self-preservation and maintenance of the status quo are too often its primary goal. *Both* institutions will have to accept responsibility for helping children and young persons, as well as the adults who model life roles and behaviors for them, learn *how* to learn. Access to an all-out information supply should help individuals clarify values, ask the right questions, and be resourceful in applying the best possible information toward the management of their lives.

For years, school and public libraries have reached out, seeking to improve service by expanding the information base for people to use. It requires no radical change in our professional orientation to adapt these attitudes to new and different needs. Technology will, in one sense, continue to advance civilization. But, if the trends of the past thirty years are read properly, these advances will probably cause increasing social problems, group tensions, and still more pressures on individuals trying to adjust to rapidly changing conditions. School and public libraries must develop those programs that will humanize technology so that it may be used by individuals, not elite groups.

Careful thought must go to creating programs that serve these new user needs. Undoubtedly, continuing knowledge expansion with computers playing an ever-growing role in shaping our living and learning styles can be predicted safely. Imagine future presidential debates about how to control vast data banks of information or who shall have access to them. What is now only a matter of intellectual concern will probably emerge as a clear political issue in this decade or the next. The biological revolution will doubtless continue as well. Soon the "average" American must become informed about the issues governing nonsexual reproduction. And continuing changes in the work ethic will come as we pass into increasing automation, moving ever more from a production to a consumption society; and these changes will create new information demands by people.

Truly, issues that will command our attention for the remainder of this century are impossible to number, even imagine. If media programs in schools and public libraries are to come anywhere near fulfilling their potential role of improving the flow of information so that persons may make intelligent informed decisions about issues we cannot now even anticipate, they must face the future now.

Formerly, what was seen as a trend with possible economic, social, or political consequences emerged slowly. Now, these trends manifest with greater rapidity than ever before. Indeed the rapidity of this process makes change the single greatest constant of our lives today.

A basic premise of this book is that if the profession is to deal successfully with these challenges we must rely to a great extent on our own resources. We've got to help ourselves to survive, to grow, and to extend our influence and ability to help the public develop those attitudes and abilities that will allow them to manage change.

Someone once said "Make no little plans. . . . They have no power to stir men's blood—make big plans and perhaps down through the ages they can be a living and breathing thing." In a sense, this book rejects this notion. Not that there is not a great need for creative and imaginative thinking; we need it badly. And certainly, only if sound long-range plans exist can short-term successes be transformed into lasting good results. It is, however, a premise of this book that along with the search for the grand idea must go a more personal need to observe, select, modify, or assimilate those ideas and programs that stimulate personal and professional growth.

Change does not have to be threatening or disheartening. It is still possible for individuals to become involved in the process of change without being demolished by it. Given the proper resources (often very minimal in nature), the proper involvement of persons, some well defined goals, and some reasonable rewards, people can and do respond quite rationally to change. The media program that helps persons cope with these changes will be the effective program of the future. Its attributes and patterns of service will be observable in the programs described in this book.

Changing Expectations
and Library Media Programs

Children and media! Everyone, it seems, has an opinion about this combination. As a conference topic or journal article it is an unbeatable attention getter. It provokes endless discussion and there are as many theories, judgments, and notions on the topic as there are varieties of media.

The effects of media on children's lives are a matter of special concern to anyone who works in education, libraries, or communications. Some express this concern as little more than an oversimplified condemnation of the negative impact of television in helping to create a nonreading society. For others, this concern has led to attempts to marry the learning theories of Piaget, the Swiss learning theorist, to media use by children in an effort to develop new learning theories. Thus are whole new schools of educational theory developed and visited upon the teaching profession.

For others, the approach to the topic is an attempt to build around media use a series of taxonomies of learning theories or even personal behaviors. This approach seeks to collect knowledge and arrange it in various classifications. So much time is spent in trying to fit the kinds of media experiences to the varieties of learning theories available that we frequently end up with nonsense or, at best, half-sense, ideas formed more from emotion and wishes than logic or rational thinking. And all the theorizing in the world will not get us where we want to be in terms of providing media programs that are excellent and appropriate.

However far apart school media programs and public library programs may be in some respects, they need to share some common understandings and perceptions about the place of media in their programs for children. It should not be necessary to state that learning (and teaching) is not the exclusive responsibility of the schools. But that point needs special emphasis. Indeed, the time children spend in schools is very brief: somewhere around seven percent of all living hours by age thirteen; a little more than eight percent by the age of seventeen. There is an increasing amount of discovering and learning taking place totally outside the bounds of what we define traditionally as a school. And the media are now basic carriers of such learning. The remainder of this century will see this process accelerate and affect people of all ages, occupations, and living conditions. The media, in this context, offer the information profession an extraordinary opportunity to transcend the limitations of the past and shape the ways by which people come into contact with, assimilate, and use information.

We need to be much more effective in impressing on public policy makers the fact that access to a wide and varied array of media is *not* a frill or a supportive learning activity in any setting. Investments in these programs are just that, investments—rather than expenditures. Too often librarians plead for support for media program while failing to project them as the sound investment in the future that they are.

If we accept the fact that learning now and in the future will be more than the exposure of the child to a "teacher" personality or to the single dimension of any one medium or format in any limited time or place, then the cooperative and mutually reinforcing roles of public library and school media programs become clear and specific.

It is not possible to incorporate here all the legitimate concerns and demands for equal access to information and knowledge by all the age groupings in this country. Our concern is with the youth, the child from three years to eighteen years. How do media programs contribute to the learning of children? How will media programs help to deliver the good educational results that we continue to expect for our young people?

A brief review of Jean Piaget's thinking may help us answer these questions. Piaget has defined for us some generally accepted learning theories: Children start with a sensory-motor period, a period from birth to age two, during which the major learning is through the senses and the motor responses to things sensed; from age two to seven the child experiences a period termed "pre-operational," during which he begins to deal with the one-to-one relationship of experiencing and knowing; this is followed, in turn, by a phase termed "concrete operational," in which, from about the age of seven through the age of eleven, the child finds himself able to deal with two relationships or properties at the same time; and finally, he arrives at the capability—after eleven for most children—for abstract thinking, when the need to handle or manipulate concrete materials to encourage thinking is no longer necessary to start the process.

Of course, this simplified restatement of Piaget's learning theories does not fit each child exactly. A host of other contributing factors may impede or speed up development, but every school media professional or public librarian who works with children will deal, more or less, with children who fit this pattern. Later in this book, we will describe some media programs planned for the exceptional child, the child who falls far outside these norms. However, since most of our effort on a day-to-day basis is with the normal or norm-fitting child, he is the main focus of this book.

The parent, who in our complex society, gives over the education of a child to various institutions has legitimate and understandable concerns about just what those institutions will do with that child. In the recent past, parents and schools have frequently been in dispute about how well the institution does the job of educating children.

In many communities this translates into "who shall control the schools?" While the public library has remained apart from this confrontation, this situation will probably not continue. What will probably emerge is a much more important issue: Who shall control the variety and kinds of information that are to be made available to children as they learn? This is a matter that directly involves the public library. We must be alert not to allow institutional goals of self-preservation or political expedience to circumvent our best efforts to provide the appropriate answers to this question. The status quo will not do and our professional response must be imaginative and creative, displaying a willingness to accept new responsibilities for information management.

Throughout history, the ability of humans to react, respond, and progress has been refined and defined generally through an institutional process. Some have rebelled, but the majority of people seek and need the comfort and support of the institution in its religious, political, or educational form. It is doubtful when all the sound and fury that accompanies change clears away that humans will be much different in their basic needs and expectations; yet the social and economic conditions with which they must cope will be much changed.

It is likely then that the impact of institutions, (especially schools and libraries) on the learning of children will remain reasonably constant. It is not a premise of this book that our institutions will crumble and collapse in the face of a vastly changed society. Rather, we assume that they will respond to the demands of change and that they will accommodate to it. It is the manner by which they achieve this accommodation and the methods by which they adapt themselves and their programs that they should properly concern us.

The need of children to learn and the patterns in which they learn remain to a remarkable extent constant and unchanging. From birth, the human being is quite able to function as an entity. Physical growth, cultural impact, biological considerations, environmental considerations, and technological factors can, in a positive or negative sense, affect the learning process, but they cannot totally alter what is actually a *natural* process of intellectual development.

Unfortunately, too many of our institutions have intervened improperly in this process, proving to be repressive and regimented, indeed self-righteous in their imposition of style and method on those given to them for nurturing. Those who would in desperation destroy these institutions, though, fail to perceive yet another verity: that changes in institutions follow rather than lead changes in society. It is our present inability to institutionalize the use of media as positive agents that really should most concern us.

This is true of all the media that convey information and shape knowledge for children. Television, the cassette tape, the recording, the filmstrip, the 16mm film, the piece of realia—the nonprint media are not in themselves evil, destructive, or harmful to children. Rather, it is our use of them that may provoke bad or unanticipated results. Likewise, the belief that their mere existence will enhance learning, promote inquiry, lead to heightened awareness or any of the other virtues that the purveyors of the nonprint media would have us accept uncritically, is equally unsupportable.

Perhaps, in the past decade, too many influential persons became hooked on the notion that the "media" would become the salvation of learning. All too many embraced the media as a "cop-out"—a means of handling "difficult" students or unfamiliar content. The idea that if something is good, more must be better is a pronounced symptom of this approach to media use with children. This led, in the most uncontrolled cases, to large quantities and collections of nonprint media which were supposed to insure that through exposure to them every child would "learn" something. The proof of research today bears out what common sense would have told us had we but listened: there is no mechanical gadget, no piece of software, no form of building, no type of teacher, no mediated instructional program that will *guarantee* that a child will learn. The media, used separately or in combinations with other resources, can and do have a positive effect on the learning of children. And the media can improve the ability of children to react with intelligence and discrimintion to the information that saturates their existence from birth.

There is no secret, however, about what really makes a child want to learn. For learning to occur, a child must become personally involved in the process. Whatever innate talents

CHANGING EXPECTATIONS

and interests are present must be stimulated and activated. To learn, a child must work toward some specific and well-defined goals. Such goals usually cannot be imposed but are the product of an internal process by which the child sifts and selects alternatives. The right *choice* of alternatives is at the heart of successful education. The child is involved at every step of the way. A teacher may reflect, direct, suggest, perhaps order, if necessary, so that choices are available to be considered and selected. It is crucial that the teacher (and I include here media specialist, librarian, *and* parent) understand the needs and interests of children and how they learn. We cannot ignore, for long, the fact that it is the child around whom the learning program must be organized.

Part of this understanding lies in accepting that any program that will help children learn must include mastering of basic skills. One can theorize with charts and films of muscle movements and of properties of water to understand how individuals swim. The only way people *learn* to swim however is by putting their bodies in water and moving their muscles in such a way that the body moves on top of and through the water. Yes, we master skills only by doing them.

Many who have been disappointed by the gap between the promise of mediated learning and its delivery have not understood the need for basics in helping the child learn. Mastering basics does not have to mean "lockstep" teaching and learning that is destructive to individuality; it need not destroy creativity, or the spontaneity of response necessary to the process of problem solving. The assimilation of basics can be personalized to involve the learner. It can, and does, provide the tools for innovative thinking.

The most overworked word of our times must be "relevance." But despite its tiresome repetition it is an important factor in learning. The last decade showed just how many of our institutional programs were not relevant. The challenge to force them into relevance convulsed America. Too often, though, basic learning skills—like listening, speaking clearly, reading, and writing—got tagged "irrelevant" in the dash for innovation that somehow became confused with the word "relevance."

Attention to basic skills is essential to creative, personalized learning. The inability to communicate, effectively, because basic skills have been neglected, is responsible for the frightening reading, speaking, or writing "competence gap" noted in an increasing number of American young people.

An excellent media program can provide for better communications and improved understandings among children, parents, professionals, and the community. It can clarify adult understanding of what children need, and help children to understand and accept responsibility for becoming personally involved in the process of their education.

Excellent media programs can help educational institutions become true learning centers. They can help children to understand that a positive self-identity, personal satisfaction, and a sense of accomplishment are rewards earned by honest and hard effort. They can help us *persuade* children that learning is important, but requires a discipline that can be satisfying as well as relevant.

All this, and more, the media program can accomplish if used with intelligence, sensibility, and restraint. In and of themselves, the media can accomplish nothing. It is our ability to *manage* the media with concern for excellent results, and realistic expectations of what they can and cannot do that will make them effective learning resources and teaching tools.

These concerns and considerations about using the media effectively with children should be shared by public schools and public libraries in their institutional roles. *Shared* institutional responsibilities for the learning of children are a central concern of this book. We must have the fullest possible cooperation in planning and implementing media programs between the public schools and public libraries. The failure of media programs in one institution can only diminish the potential for development in the other. And the success of media programs in either one will enhance the effectiveness for both. The need for cooperation and working together is fundamental at the administrative planning level and at the level of program implementation. This procedure should receive a much higher priority than it has thus far.

This is *not* to say that school media programs and public library programs using media with children should merge into one program operation. There are many distinct and unique areas of responsibility that are handled better by one institution than the other. These programs will probably blend more thoroughly as the organization of schools and community agencies shifts in the not-too-distant future, but for now they will be maintained. In terms of service to children both institutions have overlapping and mutually reinforcing responsibilities and concerns.

It appears that the actual role of *service* to children by the school media program has undergone an evolutionary change with revolutionary consequences. *Media Programs, District and School,* the guidelines for school media programs developed jointly by the American Association of School Librarians and the Association for Educational Communications and Technology and issued in 1975, contains many extraordinary statements about the purpose and intent of a media program in a school. For example, "Program (media) elements and staff requirements are both influenced by and contribute to the overall instructional strategies of the school. ... It [the media program] provides curriculum design with broad alternatives in content, method and level of participation that require sophisticated uses of media and facilities.... It recognizes and helps to establish instructional programs based on individual programs at varying rates and in different intensities that in turn may require reallocation and expansion of media resources and a larger media staff to work as members of teaching-learning teams."

While many members of the profession have expressed apprehension, even anger, with the "jargon" contained in the guidelines, no one has apparently challenged seriously the revolutionary thesis stated in them that the school media specialist is actually a very special teacher whose instructional impact reaches throughout a building in various and varied program forms. Even more revolutionary, in light of our traditional views of what a librarian is, or does, is the assertion that the school media specialist must become adept at consulting with and even directing other professionals as learning management teams that seek the best methods and programs to insure individual learning.

If we accept this definition of role, the school media specialist can hardly be termed a "service" person merely "supporting" the work of other teachers and providing them with "supplemental" or "enrichment" materials. Such a description is much too passive for the activities declared to be the province of the media specialist in these guidelines. Their focus is instructional change, building level staff development, and better use of educational technology. The building media specialist is hereby expected to be competent to manage all the resources of materials, equipment, and personnel that will initiate and sustain educational innovation and change.

Implicit too is the concept that the school media specialist, working within the instructional program must place a first priority on work with teachers. While it is possible that direct service to children by school media professionals can be combined with effective instructional leadership at the building level, it seems an increasingly dim hope in this time of drastic staff cuts.

It is reasonable to assume, therefore, that if the 1975 guidelines are followed the individual media specialist will spend less time in direct contact with children. This has extraordinary implications for the profession. These implications range from consideration of the methods whereby media specialists are prepared by graduate library programs and the kinds of facilities that are designed and operated within buildings to the rapidly emerging difference between the media center and a media program.

The preoccupation of school media programs with staff development, curriculum design, and instructional innovation is not now shared by public libraries; there has been no need. The public library concept of service to children, while undergoing some changes, has remained relatively unchanged. Public libraries have been insulated to a large extent from the sharper conflicts and controversies that have preoccupied those in public education for the past decade or more, including busing, budget control, parent control, and other

CHANGING EXPECTATIONS

issues. This does not mean that a large number of public library institutions and the professionals who work in them have not been on the very cutting edge of change for the past decade. It means merely that the forces that have so affected (and afflicted) public education in our recent history have not had the direct impact on the public library as an institution as they have on the school as an institution.

Public libraries have, however, undergone profound changes in role definitions, and these changes are reflected in their programs serving young people. Programs of out-reach to children and new methods and services to involve children and young adults in library programs are now carried on by many public libraries and their personnel. But there is still a huge, untapped potential.

It is this potential for reaching out and interacting with children in a variety of locations, and in several ways, that will most contribute to the growing need for excellent media programs for children through public libraries. Program contact with children has been one of the outstanding successes of the American public library system. But now in some ways, like the school media professional, children's and young adult librarians are working more with influencing adults who work *with* children in order to expand and reinforce their effectiveness. Parents, youth leaders, community center personnel, day care personnel, and others are good examples.

This history of success should be expanded with new programs, into new areas. The public library must visualize its service contacts with children and adults who relate to them in imaginative and innovative ways. Early learning centers, day care operations, nursery schools, neighborhood youth centers—the contact possibilities are limited only by our own inability to imagine where the public library program may go in its search to serve young people. Many of the examples provided in this book show how far along many public libraries are in this effort.

A "body count" used to prove direct contact with children has always been, like numbers of books circulated, a faulty measure of the worth of a program. The value of a program must, after all, reflect the growth of learning, intellectual development, positive self-image, or the achievement of whatever objectives were established for it at the start. The "numbers" approach to assessing program worth is, at best, one of several yardsticks—a facile but often misleading one. The number of children sitting in or present at an area at any given time is a foolish way to measure program effectiveness.

If contact with children provides us with some indication of how professionals will use their time on-the-job, it also raises the entire issue of how the subprofessional and the volunteer will best make their contribution to media programs in both institutions.

Neither the school media specialist nor the children's or young adult public librarian should react defensively to the fact that if his job is to be done well some aspect of direct service to children may have to be done through other adults and agencies. It is probable that in both school media and public library media programs paraprofessionals or volunteers will assume more direct work or contact with children, while the professional assumes a more direct learning-management role.

The rapid process of unionization in most school systems and in many large public library systems demonstrates clearly one overriding concern of professionals: that their jobs be protected from takeovers by paraprofessionals or volunteers. It is unrealistic, however, given the overwhelming economic evidence now available, not to suppose that the next twenty-five years will see a continuing and growing utilization of less expensive personnel working in many aspects of public education and public librarianship. How witless must one be to argue seriously that it takes professionally trained personnel to perform dozens of tasks that can be done just as well by others less highly trained. For example, the growing availability and quality of cataloging and processing services and aids means that at last the school media specialist (who is too often expected to perform all the tasks) can be freed from what has always been the unprofessional task of clerical routine. There are, unfortunately, professionals in both schools and public libraries who have come to rely on having too much clerical work to do to hide the fact that they are neither capable of nor motivated to work well with children or other professionals. These attitudes can be modified or changed through staff development programs designed to help professionals change and improve.

It is likewise indefensible to maintain that only a certified or trained professional may tell stories to children in a public library. Not so long ago this was considered the epitome of the professional task. Now, training others with an aptitude for this—Spanish-speaking mothers in an Hispanic community for instance—is recognized as "professional" too. As professionals, our key obligation is to be alert that resources are used with children so that they will have the greatest impact for achievement of whatever learning/development objectives we have established. Assessments of priorities, goals, and needs must dictate how programs are organized and carried out. This will require better management skills than most professionals now possess.

Cooperative management—of information, of programs, of services, of staffing—this is the issue that school and public librarians must deal with as they identify the roles they are to share and those that will be filled separately but complementarily.

Effective media programs that involve children and the community offer unprecedented opportunity for a creative children's media network within the community. Already, some excellent media programs for children are done on a shared, cooperating basis between schools and public libraries.

Attitudes and preferences about *who* shall serve the child and in what ways are important concerns, but debate about this is often bitter, unproductive, and confusing. We must not allow this to happen (or continue, if that is the case) for both the school and public library have much of importance to contribute.

This book assumes no position on the mischievous issue of whether the *facilities* of a school and a public library should be shared jointly. The instant this issue is raised, all defenses go up. Rather than survey what might be best for a community, its children and their *right* of access to excellent information programs, our reaction is nearly always: "It can't be done! We can't serve two masters." These old chestnuts, and others as irrelevant, are cited to evade and obscure the real issue. This is, that for some communities it might make the very best of sense to combine facilities, personnel, and programs into one truly excellent multisited informational media program available for all children. For other communities, a single, merged administrative unit would make no sense at all and, in fact, would damage already excellent ongoing programs now available. But separately administered units could still be forged into an open access child-oriented "local" information network all the same.

Current discussions of networking or other proposals whereby school media programs, public, special, and academic libraries will share with and contribute to the free and constant flow of information present a real possibility to promote the kinds of changes being asked of libraries.

It is important—essential, that these networks be planned for *people* and not to satisfy the "people-proof" information systems experts. They must be geared to provide the informational alternatives most people will need to respond rationally and sensitively to the decisions of life. It is all too possible that the *politics* of networking will transform the network into simply another barrier for keeping people from the information diversity they must have. If the profession allows this to happen we shall have lost one of the greatest opportunities for service ever presented to us.

The economics of communication will probably force other equally important shared professional concerns and programs. The need for individuals to learn, in schools (at all levels), in libraries, on the job, in outreach programs, in child-care centers, in homes, and in golden-age clubs, to name but some, will also accelerate. These demands for increased individualized learning opportunities will multiply the need for media services. Attention to the economic and financial implications of mass communication must occupy a great deal more of our thinking and planning than it has previously. But so too must the economics of one-to-one communication be considered. As a theoretical concept, how to communicate frequently overshadows the more important concern for librarians which is what is to be communicated and in what format. Our attention to this issue as professionals is generally uncoordinated, inadequate and unsatisfactory.

Another concern to be shared by public librarians and school media specialists is the growing insistence of the courts and legislative branches of government that children must have equal access to educational opportunity. The ability of a more affluent community to support a rich and varied learning program cannot be used, in reverse, to deny the child who lives in a community less able to support this process. Equal opportunity and equal education thus become one single right.

It is logical, in fact necessary, to extend the concept that access to equal education is a right, not a privilege, to all those institutions (formal and informal), including public libraries, that in one way or another educate. *Equal access* for children to quality education and information programs may prove to be the most profound reshaper of the American political and social order in our history. Its implication for all media and information programs is inescapable and fundamental.

This single issue could provide the nucleus around which future school and public library media programs may cluster. While this will create many complex problems, it could also mandate the development of a coherent, logical, and enlightened national policy of access to information, providing new organizational modes for improved media programs. It should be our top priority to *make* this happen.

In any event, the time has come for closer cooperation and reinforcing alliances among schools, public libraries, and the homes from which come the children touched by these media-information programs. Planning for this should preoccupy our time and effort, now! This planning could permit us to create excellent media-information programs for children and youth that would enrich the entire community, improve the quality of life, and help enlist some needed adult models. The timing is too right, and the need too great to allow the concept to get bogged down in "territorial imperatives" and endless debate over whose facility should be used.

The education of teachers and their personal development and self-fulfillment, as well as the education of children, present school media and public library programs with unprecedented opportunities and almost limitless possibilities to work together. Just as the young learner faces a school environment that is startlingly different from that of twenty-five years ago, so does the teacher.

Past definitions of a "teacher," a "class," a "curriculum," a "school," like those of "library," "literacy," and dozens of other message- and image-provoking words no longer serve today. New meanings must be created for old words, while traditional values are maintained for new activities. Although we envision the school media program as a major contributor to the process of developing new teacher capabilities, attitudes, and aptitudes, it is obvious that other agencies and influences will be at work too.

It is possible that as much as fifty percent of what the teacher does today in schools will be abandoned by the end of this century or earlier. It is probable that the school (or learning center) of the future will be planned, designed, and built as a *community* learning and recreational center operative year-round, open day and night, and prepared and equipped to serve an almost unlimited variety of activities for people of all ages and backgrounds. If this is so, then it is obvious that the business of educating the educators cannot be left only to themselves.

Already, cooperative staff development programs between universities and local schools are in operation throughout this country. The public library should exercise its central and growing concern for continuing adult education within the community and assert its role in preparing the teacher as a community resource. If the school of the future is to be "no" school or the "anywhere" school, then public library programs must contribute their proper resources. After all, it remains true that to influence one child to change for the better is good; but to influence one teacher of children to change for the better means that each child that teacher touches and influences may potentially be changed in the same manner.

The notion that attitudes about learning, teaching, and education are a legitimate concern of public library programs has too often been overlooked. If we have learned nothing else in this past decade, we have learned that the media have an awesome capacity to shape social attitudes. If the media are information carriers and if the public library and the school media program are truly in the business of the management and dissemination of information, then both must be more concerned about coordinated service to meet the public need. The right to information to enable good decision making is so fundamental to our continued progress as a nation that it must have the highest planning priority.

The issue will be the ability of libraries and the people who direct them to develop necessary new sets of priorities, to govern their actions for the remainder of this century, and beyond. Here is a responsibility to be shared specifically by school media and public library programs. Those who organize, channel, and disseminate information will shape and control our society to an unprecedented degree. This is not a matter of futuristic predictions; it is here and now.

Imagine the information programs that will evolve from a technology that for the writer-creator means selling not just the rights to hard-cover, soft-cover, and foreign editions, as well as movie rights to a property, but also video tape rights, disc club rights, microfilm rights, and who knows what else from a single property.

Media will extend and accentuate the potency of any given idea, value, or view, and specific product demand can be explosive; in a few days, millions of people saw the movie *All The President's Men*. Such is the potential for mass exposure that media brings to this culture.

The frustration for most people, though, is their inability to control, or even manage, the information that so incessantly intrudes upon them. Much of this information is superficial, unrelated, even contradictory. And these fragments of information lessen our ability as individuals or groups to put things together in useful ways or act reasonably effectively.

No one would debate any more the fact that community and family characteristics have a tremendous bearing on how students perform. In our crisis-oriented rush to discover theoretical explanations for human behavior we ignore the simple truth that no matter how excellent an educational program may be, there is still a far greater impact by the family (positive or negative) upon the child's performance than by the school itself. Has not a concern with the family and the community always been at the heart of any decent public library program? This can hardly be considered new and revolutionary. What would be new, and revolutionary, would be the right kind of cooperation between the school media programs and the public libraries—a sharing of responsibility by two strong well developed agencies, each with a great deal to contribute to the partnership. Together, both must focus on the criticial national problems: disintegration of family life; the social alienation of large segments of our society, an alienation whose roots lie in such divergent causes as age, economic status, or condition of birth. The proper function of the school and the public library is to educate in the largest possible sense and we should get on with the task.

Quite aside from, and in addition to, all of the above, we know that the economic facts of life will dictate increasing cooperation between institutions. We had better make sure that economies sought by fiscal authorities take a professionally acceptable form.

The financial crisis, caused primarily by costs for services that rise faster than our economy can generate revenue to pay for them, will be with us for the remainder of this century. The cooperation we need so much may be forced, for all the wrong reasons, upon the media profession by those who control spending of the public revenues. The imperative for united action has never been more obvious and the media programs provided by schools and public libraries present many excellent possibilities to respond to this challenge by providing better services for more persons.

Hovering insistently on the fringes of all of this are the possibilities of cable television programming (CATV), multinational communication by satellite, and computer assisted instruction modes—the precursors of a whole new generation of sophisticated information transmission.

Most of us, when we think of information transmission visualize physical entities and ascribe concrete properties to them. Rather we must visualize the possibility that we shall soon enter an era in which any human being on the face of the earth can be in constant communication with any other human being on the face of the earth, or with any organizations, anyplace.

The hand-held math calculator is here to stay because it works! It satisfies a need, it is efficient. Its success provides us with one of the few perfectly clear examples of free market capitalism at work in recent years, of technology harnessed to serve humans. Research and development constantly improve the quality of the product; not only does the instrument serve a need, but there is status to be had in owning and showing it, and the highly competitive market has both lowered cost and improved product.

Other examples could be provided. But its importance to us in the information world is that someday, soon, communication linkups between humans and information banks may well undergo this same revolutionary, yet traditional process. The improvement and miniaturization of communication could mean that every human might carry on his person a device that would permit access to any information wished for or needed. Define then, what is a school? What is a public library? What is a media program?

The consequences of who is to control the access to media—which are both data base and delivery system—should figure largely in our planning for the future. Neither the "plan" of the *National Commission on Libraries and Information Science* nor *Media Programs; District and School* show real comprehension of the dimensions of these revolutionary changes.

Joint planning between the school media program and the public library must take into account a shared sense of obligation to make more humane the process of information exchange and assimilation by humans. If we allow ourselves to accept the idea that technology must, in one way or another, increase our alienation and sense of helplessness, then we shall start this process from behind. It is not a natural consequence of the application of technology that people should be threatened by it. Even though, as media professionals, we may see but dimly our special role in humanizing the technology of information and communication so that it may serve the advancement of humankind, we are still leagues ahead of most others in our understanding of the management of this process.

As technology truly comes into the living room, the traditional service concerns of the public library and the school media program will take on new scope. After all, someone has got to be the conduit between the mass of information available and the individual's need to assimilate that portion of it he requires without his being utterly overwhelmed. Who is better able to do this than we?

The point is that media programs, no matter where they may be housed physically or out of what "public pocketbook" they may be supported, must work hard at devising programs and using personnel in ways that will guarantee they will be more than a mere switching station, serving to receive and redistribute a series of sensory inputs and stimuli.

If we react in creative, energetic, and purposeful ways to these challenges, then we create our own enlarged service mission. We know now that the facility which houses a media program has little direct bearing on how a child will learn. So too do we know, even if we do not always accept it, that we cannot teach a child or any adult to learn. Learning is a process initiated by the learner as the result of stimuli that provoke reactions; there is potential for it in all persons. The media can enhance this process, but how it is to be done will be of the highest importance for the remainder of this century—and beyond.

For instance, it is hard to imagine Americans spending any more time watching television than they do now, but this will probably happen.

In a recent article entitled "Children of Television" Nancy Larrick points out that to most children television has become the baby sitter, teacher, and parent substitute. The impact of television in establishing a child's desires, values, and lifestyle is pervasive, nearly total for many children.

The reaction thus far to the impact of television on children's learning has been in many instances particularly foolish. Television need not inhibit the motivation of a child to read, or think, or create. That it may have this impact is not so much the fault of television but rather reflects the attitudes and actions of parents, teachers, and other adults who come into some sort of sustained contact with children. Their abdication from their responsibility to shape the ability of children to seek out solutions, to consider alternatives in reaching decisions, to bring to bear imagination and creativity cannot be blamed on television.

Dr. Larrick identified certain characteristics of the children of television. Among these are: they seem to thrive on noise, strife, and confusion; they get less sleep; they have little respect for adults; they regard school as irrelevant; they are filled with hostility and prone to poor interpersonal relations. Anticooperative values are a dominant response for many of these children. These are hardly the values we would endorse as being productive to a sustained process of responsible human growth; but is television alone projecting them?

Television can contribute much toward the ability of the child to manage learning with a degree of sophistication, a seriousness of purpose, and an intellectual comprehension that should gladden the heart of the most traditional educator. Exposure to television does not have to lead to alienation, the destruction of cultural values, mindless reaction to learning situations, or witless response to intellectual demands. If the professional managers of media allow this to happen, if they continue to simply react to the *threat* of television allowed to run amuck and unmanaged in the lives of children, then all of our most negative thoughts about television's impact on children will become self-fulfilling. This is not necessary, but it can happen.

The consequences of our failure as a profession to master the media, to provide for it within a framework of rationality, discipline, and humaneness are unacceptable. The evidence is ample, if often subjective, that the multiplier affect is at work concerning those social forces alienating us from each other, impeding our progress toward finding acceptable ways of managing the forces that confront us. Our soundest instincts tell us that to manage, to cope, and to move ahead with any sense of purpose humans must first want to or be made to cooperate.

Social psychologists looking at the recent past have written about the phenomenal rapidity and proliferation of technological change, while reflecting that the rate of human reactions to these changes remain as constant and as specifically patterned as they were 2,000 years ago. Old habits, old ways, and old ideas confront revolutionary changes that render some changes obsolete before we even realize they have happened.

Don Ely, one of the more creative and secure of the media futurists, uses some descriptors about what media programs should be which hopefully will influence the thinking of media program planners. This future is already here. If we want to insure that media programs of the future are more than a gathering in of bits and pieces of information received, shared, and dispensed as needed, we must have reinforced cooperative planning and programs between schools and public libraries. The following concepts and practices should help in this planning.

Says Ely, media programs should grant **access** to the widest number of persons to permit them to participate fully in the process of education and the process of learning. This means a great **diversity** of learning material and situations. The learning process begins at the earliest possible moment (birth) and continues, often until the termination of physical life. In a nonmetaphysical sense, the person born today will have a number of "incarnations" (of role, job, and location) during his life span. It must be the concern of all media programs to guarantee this person the access to the diversity of information that will allow him to acquire the skills and competence necessary to survive these transitions.

None of this will take place until there is **cooperation** in depth among all institutions responsible for media programs. Regional groupings, multi-use facilities for a variety of public needs and other cooperative ventures are coming and they will be imposed upon us unless we show the intelligence and the will to shape our own methods of cooperation and participation.

Participation should flow naturally from this cooperation. The issue today is not whether the community is to have a direct voice in deciding issues that it must deal with but rather how to guarantee that this participation will be informed, productive, and responsible instead of divisive and destructive. All public institutions need to develop their ability to react more specifically and quickly to the needs of the individual as opposed to the feelings of the group. The product of the information explosion delivered to the individual, in exactly the format and content he wishes, offers media programs their most exciting opportunity to pioneer in cooperative ways for the public good. The fight for survival becomes thus an exciting affirmation of life.

For children, media programs should continue to focus as specifically as possible on helping to develop the natural curiosity and desire to learn that is present in everyone. This means, in the classic sense of John Dewey, dealing with the child as a whole. It means accepting the fact that children are excited by learning, and capable of creativity and comprehension beyond what we have believed.

The need for adults to serve as positive behavior models for young children has never been greater. While machines and technology may receive, organize, and deliver to children a bewildering array of information, they cannot provide the one activating ingredient that gives it all reason and relationship. This essential ingredient is the interaction of humans with humans, of children with adults. This interaction causes us to weigh and evaluate, to think critically and objectively, to appreciate and to understand the consequences of actions taken, or not taken.

Media programs must not permit themselves to become equated with the excesses of what, for want of a better term, is referred to as the new permissive era. We have allowed the burden of this failure to be "laid upon us"—unfairly. Media programs are not synonymous with this lack of discipline, lack of self-control, and responsibility for one's actions.

George Gallup has pointed out that most children today have not been taught and do not understand why society has to have rules and why these rules have to be obeyed.

Institutions and individuals are joint victims of people who feel that they need not obey rules or that discipline impairs creativity and learning. There are many causative factors. But, in a land where everything is possible, nothing is possible. Without rules (laws) there can be no civilization.

It is why rules are necessary that needs to be transmitted to young children. Imposed discipline of the barracks variety is not the answer, but the alternative, a society where a lack of respect for authority is a way of life cannot be tolerated either.

Future events for human beings mandate the necessity to cooperate and this provides media programs with tremendous opportunities. Media programs can help children to develop the intellectual disciplines that will permit them to acquire important knowledge and skills. They can help children perceive and compare alternative courses of action, while understanding the consequences of those actions. Involvement, relevancy, and a host of other descriptive words may be used to point out correctly the attitudes children need in order to learn. Each of these is valid, but the most important need for the child remains the need to learn how to use the mind effectively in solving problems.

The media specialist, as information manager, public librarian, school media specialist, or instructional technologist must have more than the talent to amuse. This approach to the education of children has probably caused real damage to the many on whom it has been inflicted. It has made mockery of the notion that the media specialist is a highly skilled teacher and learning innovator; it has relegated many media programs in schools and public libraries to being little more than an in-one-eye and out-the-other routine. Further, it has misled the public as to what the true intent and purpose of media programs for children are. Learning, whether through a nonprint or print medium is sometimes dull and boring. Life itself is sometimes dull and boring. The more creative and fertile our imaginations and thinking, the less likely is life or learning to be dull or boring. Yet, to stimulate the one, the consequences of the other must be experienced.

As of now, the impact and consequence of media programs for children have not been as far reaching or as revolutionary as their most zealous sponsors would like to believe. Likewise, they have not been as destructive as their more vocal detractors would prefer to believe. Excesses in support or condemnation for either position are, for now at least, incorrect. The true consequence of media programs that relate to and influence the learning of children is not yet understood. We are on the threshold of a new era and it summons us incessantly ahead.

To achieve success requires profound changes in our attitudes and abilities as professionals and as people. It means implementing the concept of cooperative educational communities involving a wide variety of public institutions, of which schools and public libraries will be only two members.

PART II

Description of Library Media Programs for Children and Young Adults

The program reports which follow are arranged by state. Within the state, school and public library programs are described separately. In cases where budget figures are used unless otherwise noted they refer to FY 1975-76. In those programs where budget is not an important consideration in operating the program, it is omitted. All references to statistics, services, programs, or procedures are accurate (as reported) until July 1, 1976.

SARATOGA SCHOOL
Saratoga, California

Staff
Professional: 1
Support: 1
Volunteer: 20

Budget (1975-1976)
Print: $1,300
Nonprint: 1,000
Equipment: 500
(PTA Production Materials: $600)

Target Population: 420 children, K-6

Sometimes, a media program does its job with such consistent excellence that it is taken for granted. The Saratoga school media program is never taken for granted, but everyone it involves knows it to be a program performing always at a high level of excellence.

Program planning was done carefully, with clearly stated goals. In 1968, *parents* concerned about the need for more varied learning materials talked with the principal about the school's limitations. The need to relate learning to materials, staff, and facility was recognized immediately. This planning group was quick to involve children and professional staff in preparing for a media program. Their involvement is one specific factor in creating the excellent media program that resulted.

Condemnation of the school building in 1970 for failing to meet California earthquake standards presented the planning group with an opportunity to act. When the school building was condemned, the Facility Study Committee met with architects planning the renovation and had their plan for a media center incorporated into the building.

The establishment of school goals occurs too often in a vacuum, to be revealed piecemeal to a wary public concerned more often with cost rather than with accomplishment. The Saratoga experience proves this does not have to happen.

Applying for an ESEA Title II, Phase 2 grant helped to focus this planning process. In California these special competitive

Title II Grants were used to upgrade school library-media programs. The Saratoga application represented continuing cooperation of teachers, parents, and students, and this was a factor in the State's decision to give a $59,000 grant to the school. This grant helped to provide a book collection of twenty volumes per student, and a fifty-title periodical collection as well as an array of nonprint items including filmstrips, film loops, michrofiche, slides, transparencies, maps, globe, and study prints.

The use of special purpose funds to upgrade materials collections is common. Uncommon though is the careful planning that governed the expenditure of the funds. Purchase of the materials followed the identification of learning program needs within the school. The school community and the local community together assessed these needs and established priorities that made spending the grant monies relevant and realistic.

It was considered as fact from the start that a media program support component was necessary to meet effectively identified instructional needs. The first of these was the need for an individualized learning program to help children with varied learning abilities and achievements to learn at an individually prescribed pace. The second identified was the need for increased understanding and appreciation of other cultures by Saratoga students. The school contained a minority enrollment, less than five percent; thus media would become the most important element in teaching these understandings.

Community involvement in the media program was achieved with the third priority need identified: developing an understanding of people's interdependence with nature. The project application stated that ninety percent of the community residents responding to a survey believed that the schools should provide instruction in the need for restoring and preserving our natural resources and in the ways such restoration and preservation could be accomplished.

Former students from the Saratoga School helped establish a fourth priority need. This was to have a better educational experience to help children make rational decisions about drug use. The media program was to be assigned the information role of helping students evaluate the negative and positive effects of drugs.

The umbilical cord that tied media program to school and community was the planning involvement of all elements. Were this to occur more often, community understanding and support for school media programs would undoubtedly increase. With this kind of planning and preparation the media program hit the ground running when it began operating from its renovated facility.

The facility occupies a former auditorium and a library-classroom. The renovation of auditorium space into instructional space is a growing trend, and one to which school media professionals should be alert. A high ceiling presented design problems, but an acoustically treated false ceiling was installed. A balcony-mezzanine area was also built and here are located a conference room and study area. Tucked beneath the balcony are three more conference rooms. An open railing around the balcony area is used to display paintings and other art work created by the children.

The 4,000-square-foot media center is organized to relate to instructional functions or special interests. One area combines fiction, picture books, and periodicals. Another includes all print and nonprint materials, equipment, and three-dimensional objects that relate to science. Social studies and language arts areas are organized similarly.

Other special purpose areas include: an art factory, an area with equipment and materials for constructing masks, collages, paintings, macrame, weaving and puppets; a production area with a duplicating machine, paper cutter, dry mount press, and other instructional equipment, which students use as needed. A special feature here is a carpenter's table and scraps of wood to use for special projects. A complete photography darkroom for student use is also incorporated into the media center.

Media program involvement in curriculum development and instruction is evident everyday. Each Friday, at the noon hour, a visiting artist program brings to the school such events as a painter, an opera singer, a rock band, and a demonstration of Renaissance musical instruments. Spinning, making natural dyes, and Chinese writing have all been part of this program.

Thursday afternoons bring enrichment programs operated at different times for primary and intermediate grades. For the primary grades choices include: arts and crafts, colonial skills, community garden, drama, needlepoint, and photography. Intermediate grades have these same alternatives as well as office skills, film making, animal dissection, and yearbook production.

Faculty and students are involved with the evaluation and selection of materials. The district program gives strong support by ordering materials and cataloging them when they are received. In its own program evaluation the school staff has emphasized the importance of professional staffing to develop a complete instructional program. Most of the needs identified in the needs assessment survey by the Saratoga Community are being met successfully by the media program.

Individualized instruction, through the use of media, is found throughout the building. It is not unusual to find children working on multicultural learning activity packets; small groups working on instructional units taught by teachers or media center staff; children using a variety of production equipment and materials to fulfill instructional goals; or teachers planning together.

The Community Garden Project created in response to helping people understand their interdependence with nature helps children understand the ecological balances necessary to sustain and enrich life. Growing vegetables and flowers in a natural way, weaving cloth from the wool of animals, and making clay from indigenous materials emphasize this process.

The drug education need has been least successfully met. Attitudes, of teachers, family, and peer group, appear to be more significant in forming the responses of young children to drug use than pure information. Nonetheless, this component continues and the willingness of the school and the media program to recognize the need for reevaluation and changes is in itself a healthy sign.

Program Objectives
1. To integrate a media program into an instructional program and provide for curriculum development.
2. To provide for an individualized learning program for children by using media.
3. To use a media program to develop understanding and appreciation of the variety of other cultures and lifestyles that exist.
4. To use media materials and programs to lead to a fuller recognition of man's interdependence with nature.
5. To use a media program to provide information so that students may evaluate the negative and positive aspects of drugs.

Some Suggestions
1. Add additional professional to increase further the instructional impact of media program.
2. Reassess drug education program to provide for more involvement at the junior high school level.
3. Increase nonprint budget area to provide for stronger local support of program.
4. Plan more information exchange between this school and junior high programs so that the learning programs of the two will be better coordinated.

CALIFORNIA

HUNTINGTON BEACH PUBLIC LIBRARY
Huntington Beach, California

Staff
 Professional: 2
 Support: 8

Budget (1975-1976)
 Print: $22,000
 Nonprint: 2,000

Target Population: 35,000 children, ages 3-12
(850 teachers)

The question that remains to be answered for the Huntington Beach Public Library media program for children and young adults is whether facility and location can combine to sustain an excellent media program.

The library is a beautiful building, featuring a children's section that is carefully designed for them; it and the building are a visual delight. The design of the facility reflects the very openness of the program, for it stimulates children to explore and to discover on their own initiative. Curiosity is not constrained by high walls, inhibiting stacks, or other physical barriers, but is led from one thing to another naturally by the physical design itself.

An innovative facility opened in 1975, the library is excellent in design concept. The outside walls are mostly of glass, with the public service areas on the perimeter of the building. Technical Services are housed in a ground level area, and Reference Services are located on the first floor main entrance level. A feeling of Californian openness characterizes the building; stacks placed in the center of rooms add to the feeling of spaciousness and various ceiling heights for different areas sustain this illusion. Many small reading areas for all ages are comfortable and beautifully decorated.

Design is important to the program, and perhaps more than in most situations location too must be considered in evaluating program potential. As in most of California, dependence on the automobile is a way of life. Reflecting this, the Huntington Beach Public Library is located at a major crossroads, but almost nothing is located within easy walking distance. A park separates the building from nearby homes. Shops, which generally tend to attract people to an area are not close enough to provide walk-in traffic. One public school is within walking distance, but if you plan to use the resources of the Huntington Beach Public Library in most cases you are going to get there by automobile. This means that many of the children who use the library must come with a parent. In such a setting outreach is not easy.

While this can be an inhibiting factor in planning and implementing programs, it can be also a challenge to the creativity and energy of a staff. Specifically it requires maintenance of a high level of awareness by the public about programs available to it. It means involving people in a variety of ways to spread the word about what the public library program is doing for children. Most important of all it means very careful planning for the use of media to attract and involve children, making the program as compelling as possible to participants once they are in the library.

How is the library program at Huntington Beach doing this? Staff members note two major policies upon which they build: (1) all media items are available to all children regardless of age; (2) media in every format, with the exception of Super 8 sound cartridges, may be used either in the children's resource center, or at home, though parents must check out the accompanying hardware for home use. This liberal policy allows toys, games, records, cassettes, and other media to be borrowed for a period of one week. Thus children who use the Huntington Beach Public Library are constantly made aware that there are more facets to library service than book checkout and reference services.

This philosophy of service for children is of critical importance in a situation where the public library program for children must serve both as backstop and leader for the public schools. None of the elementary schools in Huntington Beach has professional media personnel on its staff. The response of the public library, in this situation, may be either to ignore the demand upon its material and staff resources or to try to fill the vacuum. At Huntington Beach a serious commitment has been made to play an effective role in bringing children to information through good media use, if possible. There is great willingness on the part of the staff to go into the schools for story hour programs, book talks or other programs. The fact that there are few requests for such service by most Huntington Beach teachers underscores the fact that it takes a school media professional working within the building to create demand, in the first place. It is essential to keep constantly before the professional staff the potential for service and instructional leadership of a school media program. Without this kind of consistent, day-to-day staff development and the direct involvement of teachers the instructional aspects of a school media program can be only minimal or nonexistent.

The public library must reach out beyond its facility to establish contact with the children it will serve. At Huntington Beach the children are brought to the library, regularly and in large numbers. The weakness of this is evident. The visit may, or may not, relate to the need of the child at that time. It is a special rather than an everyday occurrence, precluding immediate access to media, and thus to information needed. Learning, unfortunately, does not schedule itself around a weekly visit to a library or media center.

The other primary source of users for the public library program is the children brought by parents or other adults. Since a good deal of the use of this media program will depend upon the understanding of its importance by parents, a supreme effort must be made to insure that they understand what the purpose of the media program for children is.

One method of accomplishing this is continuous communication through a variety of programs and activities. There is a newsletter, *High Tide*, published each month. For example, one issue carried facts about reference services, announced a book and art sale, gave some figures on the rate of book processing, and featured an article on an appreciation luncheon given for volunteers. In themselves, these are hardly the kind of news items that make people storm the doors of their local public library demanding service. That isn't the point. The important element is steady and consistent communication that stresses always the involvement of the community in the affairs of the public library.

A free film program, operating from 7 to 9 P.M., is another example of the use of a media program to draw people into a public library program. Such films as *Dr. Strangelove, Grand Hotel,* and *Moby Dick* are of high interest. The combination of parents viewing these films and of children using the resource center is a drawing card. The point is the reinforcement of shared program participation. Such visits establish early habits for good future library users; it is likely too that parents who use library facilities are modelling and fostering good attitudes in their children. Just as negative life patterns show a tendency to be emulated, so do positive, constructive ones.

The children's resource center backs up the adult newsletter with its own publication, the *Gospel Swamp Gazette,* which proclaims, "we put it all together." Contributions to the newsletter by the children who participate in resource room programs, include bits of doggerel, snippets of history, a touch of astrology, an announcement of birthdays of the month—a fairly traditional format for this kind of communication.

The apportioning of the budget to purchase materials for the children's resource room is an important element in considering the worth of this program. Those who manage the program anticipate in the future putting as much as forty percent of the budget into nonprint media. This would include realia, rock collections, microscopes, and other varieties of instructional media. Clearly the long range goal of the development of a diversified media collection is a high priority. It is one that will require constant and consistent attention, for Huntington Beach, like many other library systems, faces severe budget restrictions just now. The will, though, is present and evident. The staff believes in serving children in a variety of exemplary ways. There is a focus to the program—and that focus is kids: not just entertaining them, but a concentrated effort to combine traditional modes such as story hours, play activities, and films with the more innovative aspects of media used to instruct children in ways that involve them directly in their own learning.

Huntington Beach is trying to fill an information gap for the children of its community by developing a unified program of media service for children. Its future is still in the process of being formed, but its approach and intent give it a validity that should sustain it.

Program Objectives
1. To provide an integrated media program for children within a public library.
2. To supplement, or provide for, media service to children in schools not having these services.
3. To create a liberal checkout program that encourages children to use a wide variety of media both at home and in a library setting.
4. To provide an unrestricted setting whereby children may develop their own ideas and concepts by using a variety of media.
5. To design a facility specifically planned to incorporate materials and equipment to stimulate learning through nonprint use.

Some Suggestions
1. Establish clearer budget priorities for apportioning between print and nonprint buying.
2. Planning more closely with school programs in an effort to relate public library media program to school instructional program.
3. Have children more involved in production of their own media.
4. Provide more programming opportunities to bring adults and children into the library at the same time.

ADAMS COUNTY SCHOOL DISTRICT NO. 12
Northglenn, Colorado

Staff
Professional: 1
Support: 3
Volunteer: 8

Budget (1975-1976)
Unified: $30,000
HEW: 10,000
(contributed to fund project)

Target Population: 1,800 children, ages 7-12

The last decade brought impressive growth in the number of school media programs in the United States. And rapid growth situations generally create some problems. For media programs, one problem has been the tendency to assume too many commitments to improve instruction and to use instructional technology and a host of other media-related activities that thrust media programs into the mainstream of the educational "action." Too often, these and other commitments have dissipated and diminished media program impact, in an attempt to satisfy too many people in too many ways.

The mid-point of the 1970s finds many school media programs undergoing a period of intense reassessment of goals and objectives. In some cases this has led to a change in focus as media programs tie into existing or newly developed programs that provide an already well-developed instructional media component. This process has the good effect of providing ready-made goals that allow the media program to make a maximum impact. As long as school media programs remain as badly understaffed as most of them are, they will not be able to deliver the strong instructional leadership role planned for them within the school. Preplanned programs that require a strong media support component allow the media specialist working alone or with limited support staff to make better contributions to the school instructional program.

One such program that requires the media program to assume a direct instructional support role is the School

Health Curriculum Project. Developed by the Community Program Division of the National Clearinghouse for Smoking and Health, a bureau of the Public Health Service of the Department of Health, Education & Welfare, the project demands much of a media program but provides the direction and focus, plus the teacher support, that permits success.

School District #,12, Adams County Colorado, has a contract with the Bureau of Health Education as a regional training center. The media specialist working with the district attests to its exciting potential, stating that teachers participating in the project cannot accomplish their teaching objectives through the traditional chalk-talk teaching. The School Health Curriculum Project requires extensive use of books, films, filmstrips, tapes, records, transparencies, realia, and slides. The entire program is designed to provide special instructional experiences for children that will result in good health habits, attitudes, and techniques for good care for their bodies.

Direct student involvement is emphasized heavily and includes such activities as: dissection and study of lungs, heart, and brain; blood typing; and study of exercise and nutrition. The project contains units on the digestive system, lung and respiratory system, heart and circulatory system, and brain and nervous system. These are given respectively at the fourth, fifth, sixth and seventh grades. A new third grade unit on the senses/eyes was added in 1976.

The program requires extensive use of nonprint media. These materials are preselected at the national level, and all school districts participating must use them. Worksheets and activities that go with the units are geared to these preselected materials and must also be used in the program. Some negative factors in this approach must be considered. Preplanned and prepackaged programs do not always fit themselves neatly into an educational media program. Unquestionably, too, this approach can place constraints on a creative and innovative media professional. And relating prepackaged media units to specific ongoing building level teaching programs can also cause problems. Opportunities for creative and innovative techniques are available, if approved by project coordinators, and these techniques may be shared.

However, media specialists who have discussed this program with visitors feel that any lack of flexibility is more than compensated for by the many kinds of media with which students must work and the encouragement of media research it demands. A positive program multiplier effect is that it encourages other teachers to try a similar approach in their teaching.

The teacher-training component of the program provides a model of thorough staff development that most media programs could only hope for. Each unit requires about sixty hours of intensive training by teams of teachers and administrators before it may be used with children. These teams usually have two classroom teachers, a principal, and one or two curriculum support people (such as a media specialist). Team training parallels closely the actual classroom experience. Follow-up sessions are arranged about nine months after the initial training, and when teams return to their home districts they must provide staff development activities for other staff involved in the project.

Another exemplary aspect of the Health Curriculum Project is that it involves children directly in making decisions about how they will learn, how they will relate to their environment, and how they will use their bodies. Special emphasis is given to motivating students. Small group and individual activities are reinforced by creative combinations of educational techniques and resource materials. Student attitudes necessary for success in the Health Curriculum Project require information sharing and helping each other succeed, two factors that all media programs try to promote. Community involvement is kept high through parent and community health personnel participation.

The interrelationship of health education to other parts of the curriculum is stressed. This interdisciplinary approach seeks to promote a new awareness of health as it relates to the ability of individuals to comprehend and deal with a total environment. Social studies, language arts—even the creative arts—have a role to play.

Each unit is composed of five basic phases: awareness, appreciation, structure and function, disease and disorders, and prevention. These phases are handled within a basic ten- to eighteen-week unit. A special emphasis of the lung and respiratory unit is on smoking prevention. The emphasis though is not on the evils of smoking, a tactic to which young people, as a result of peer pressure, are remarkably impervious. Through lung dissection and other visual experiences children are provided the kind of information they need for motivation to make decisions for themselves about how they will use their bodies. As in any good media-based program, the emphasis is on providing good information, then allowing learners to assess data and make their own conclusions.

Local districts must be committed to providing adequate funding to support the project; this amounts to a start-up cost of about $12,000. This is a program that falls within the mandates of Title IV C of the Elementary and Secondary Education Act of 1975 and funding could be obtained under the provisions of this Act, if the program is accepted as new and innovative.

The program, used in more than 200 other districts around the nation, has produced some clear and measurable results. Among these are: an increased ability by student participants to pursue a course of independent learning; increased use of media materials that require the teacher to function as a facilitator of learning not a teller of facts; and community outreach and education that has heightened parent sensitivity and awareness about such things as nutrition, exercise, and disease prevention.

The School Health Curriculum Project is one way for media programs to relate directly to classroom instructional programs. The successful integration of preplanned media teaching programs reduces professional frustration and lessens the nearly insurmountable task of being all things to all people. The structure provided by programs such as this provide excellent opportunities to strengthen media programs if they are used wisely. For, while the highly structured course content can be a restraining force on those who may not wish to use preselected materials, it can provide the impetus for many more to try media, perhaps for the first time. And the attempt to make health education an exciting curriculum study supported by excellent use of media programs has important implications for education.

Program Objectives
1. To use a media learning center concept to instruct children in health education facts.
2. To use a media program approach to incorporate media and reference skills within content area teaching.
3. To help teachers develop new instructional strategies for better teaching of children.
4. To incorporate health education as an interdisciplinary form of learning relating to other content and curriculum areas.
5. To promote through discovery method and self-directed learning behavioral change in students concern for overall health including smoking, alcohol use and drug abuse.

Some Suggestions
1. Continue to extend learning center media approach into some related subject area fields.
2. Develop some spin-off units, using locally produced materials, that could provide some local emphasis to unit.
3. Involve the public library as a community education agency more directly in the program.

STOTT ELEMENTARY SCHOOL
Arvada, Colorado

Staff
Professional: 1
Support: 2 (part-time)
Volunteer: 10

Budget (1975-1976)
Print: $7,800
Nonprint: 5,500
ESEA Title II
Special Purpose Grants:
1973-1974: $19,500
1975-1976: 12,000

Target Population: 480 children, ages 7-12

Generally, the needs of children for information, enrichment activities, and learning programs during school vacation periods have been met by the public library. Summer and vacation programs for children are a key component of most public library programs. But increasing numbers of schools also offer remedial or developmental summer school programs. Sometimes these programs use the services of a media professional and provide a full range of media programming, but not always.

It is inconsistent to provide full media programs during the school year and not to make them part of a summer instructional pattern. If summer school is a viable educational experience then it too requires a media program. Often, summer school media programs consist of study halls supervised by paraprofessionals. Frequently, materials may not be checked out but must be used within the media center. A commitment to a school media program as a year-round resource, available to students and teachers nearly all the time is a significant break-through. The year-round school program instituted by the Jefferson County Public Schools in Colorado incorporates such a media program and presents for consideration a number of important procedures and ideas.

Year-round schools appeared particularly attractive in the late 1960s and the early part of this decade. They promised increased use of expensive buildings; more efficient and economical use of staff time; and more flexible use of staff time, leading to increased productivity. Recent analysis of these theories has lead to questions about their soundness and declining enrollments have caused further major shifts in thinking about building use on a year-round basis.

The main reason the Jefferson County Schools turned to the year-round school was to find a better way to broaden curriculum offerings for children without sacrificing the basic instructional elements that are the core of any elementary school program. In recent years, many schools have added growing numbers of enrichment courses to their curricula. The intent was to make education more open, humane, and responsive to the diverse needs of children. Many of these changes have helped schools become more realistic in their teaching programs, preparing children to cope more effectively with a rapidly changing world.

While this intent is commendable, perhaps even necessary, the mushrooming course offerings caused problems. Courses were added and nothing was dropped. The problem was time: time in a school day to meet the commitment any school must make to help children gain basic skills, and to accommodate both a basic instructional program and a viable enrichment program.

The Jefferson County Schools instituted the year-round school for the purpose of broadening curriculum offerings without sacrificing other parts of the school day or year. Sixteen schools participate in the program which is called a Bonus Learning Program.

The Bonus Learning Program makes heavy use of media and aims at flexibility by providing students with the opportunity for either acceleration or remediation. It offers the option of organizing instruction to meet individual needs and interests of children within the school. Bonus Learning gives children and teachers the opportunity to participate in learning activities for periods of time beyond the usual school year. It is a learning program developed entirely to meet student needs.

Among the courses offered during the Bonus Learning Period are ecology, haiku, pottery, model building, and natural foods. These enrichment courses mix comfortably with reading readiness for Kindergarten children, Reading improvement for all grades (1-6); math readiness and math improvement and spelling and language improvement. Also offered are basic carpentry, city government, banking, and nutrition.

Such flexibility, responsiveness, and sensitivity to instructional needs mandates a strong school media program. At Stott School, the media center is a completely open access program; open throughout the day, all year round. Not only do children and teachers come to the center but the program goes out into the building. One method by which this is accomplished is classroom learning centers. Maintained by aides and volunteers, the learning centers relate to reading, science, math, ecology or whatever is highlighted at that time. Materials include both print and nonprint items and the small equipment needed for using nonprint materials, such as filmstrip previewers and cassettes. Learning areas are also set up within the media center so the media program is constantly before both children and teachers.

Part of the funding that provided the Bonus Learning Program came from a Special Purpose Grant under ESEA Title II. Some $12,000 was used for materials to support the program. An earlier ESEA Title II Grant of $20,000 was used to set up the Stott program as a model elementary media program for the State of Colorado, and so the Bonus Learning Program built upon an already strong materials collection.

The media specialist and the principal of Stott agree that the Bonus Learning Program has had numerous benefits for the school's media program. Among these are: (1) the use of the interest centers to provide a media program throughout the building; (2) the improved ability to meet effectively the needs of individual students; (3) provision for better groupings of students to make learning more efficient; (4) increased parent involvement; and (5) increased year-round student use of media center materials and programs. The increase in circulation of media materials has been astronomical: up some five hundred percent in the three years since the first special purpose grants were received. The nearest public library branch is located far away from Stott, so the media program provides a necessary supplement to these services too.

One particular problem is noted in connection with the Bonus Learning Program: acquiring enough materials to support the wide-ranging offerings is not easy, particularly when the courses are being given at every grade level of the school. The more lead time to prepare the materials needed in the courses the more effective will be the media center's ability to follow through.

Planning and scheduling of staff time must be considered carefully in this program. Vacation and work schedules must be rearranged to support it year-round. This is, however, a matter of scheduling and with good organization is not an insurmountable problem.

As an effort to show the way a school can affect a total community education program, the Stott media program has much to recommend it. Initial teacher and student response to the program that uses vacation time for bonus learning has been enthusiastic and it presents significant opportunities for media program development.

Program Objectives
1. To provide learning enrichment, remediation, and acceleration programs during school vacation periods.
2. To provide access to school media center resources on a year-round basis.
3. To accentuate the community education potential of a school media program.
4. To integrate a media program more effectively into the total curriculum of a school.
5. To extend a media program physically throughout a school by using media interest areas.

Some Suggestions
1. Set up a more formal process to involve students and teachers in selection of materials.
2. Establish evaluative criteria to see if students involved in remediation programs are exhibiting improvement.
3. Provide additional professional support to extend the program.
4. Try to establish complete media units (both print and nonprint materials) to accompany Bonus Learning Units.
5. Perhaps establish some production components as part of the Bonus Learning Programs.

BRIDGEPORT PUBLIC LIBRARY
Bridgeport, Connecticut

Staff
Professional: 1
Support: 1

Budget
Not applicable

Target Population: 40 to 50 children, ages 15-18

Parts of a program are never really tested until they work together and the sum of the parts exerts the force or drive to create an expected outcome. The media program surveyed at the Bridgeport Public Library is a print program presented in a format guaranteed to delight the most traditional teacher of English literature, but laid in an educational setting totally nontraditional in style and method—result, a unique educational program. Schizophrenic? Not if you understand how it happened.

For many years, the Young Adult Department of the Bridgeport Public Library has exhibited a concern for the intellectual, social, and psychological needs of the students involved with its programs. Educated in an urban setting these young adults confront every problem known to this environment.

An early result of this concern was a program called "Round Table." Round Table involved young people in creating library programs. This is different from having youth representatives serve on advisory councils primarily to rubber stamp programs put together by adults. Initial program topics reflected issues and concerns of the early 1970s—"Vietnam, Why?" a program of films and speakers, began the series. A program on drug addiction and rehabilitation followed, then a rock concert. A fashion show was held at a nearby shopping mall, and a karate demonstration and program about ghosts, witches, and demons took place in the library. These were programs designed to attract into the library people not usually found there. It would be satisfying to say that the

Round Table sustained itself to become a regular activity of the library. Not so, it died! It died because the enthusiasm and good intentions of a young adult librarian and a few kids were not enough to keep it going. Then too, there wasn't enough participation from the schools, some of which felt that Round Table was not a good idea. The Round Table died because not enough of those it hoped to involve, got involved. Good intentions could not translate to commitment, and by 1974 Round Table disappeared from the Bridgeport Public Library.

However, the idea that public library programs had a responsibility to reach out and involve young adults in nontraditional formats and unique programs endured in the attitude of the library. Enter, then, the Park City (Bridgeport is known as the Park City) Alternate High School Program. Alternate high school education can no longer be termed an innovative educational idea. Schools without walls, community access schools, even schools on wheels are but some of the alternate schooling patterns now in use. While format may vary, all alternate education programs have much in common. Perhaps the main commonality is the attempt to continue the learning of young people who, for a number of reasons, cannot cope with traditional school education. For some, this means drop-out prevention, for others intense involvement with advanced scientific projects of high intellectual discipline. The structure and operation of the school is geared to these students who, for whatever reasons, need alternatives.

The Park City alternate education program gives students the option of leaving their original high school in the junior year. Primary resources for the program are area colleges, local community institutions, and qualified individuals (from the community) who wish to participate as teachers.

Unique to the program is the selection process: every participant (forty-five in all) is selected by a lottery. Students who want to get into the program apply and are screened by school officials and alternate school students. This group reinforcement and sharing are an important element of the program. Attitudes and purpose are built into the program if you come to it deficient in these attributes.

While a significant number of participants do go on to some

post high school education, the lottery system guarantees that the program is not elitist. And this is insured further by a healthy exposure to the world of work as a learning alternative. The variety of work experiences ranges from work in a law office or with a probate judge, to work in the Mayor's office, a hospital, the City Zoo, or a garage. These work experiences are actually a course and students are evaluated with a pass/fail grade.

All students must take an English, social studies, or math sequence, but alternatives to these courses may be found outside the school. The Young Adult Program of the Bridgeport Library is providing one of these alternative English courses.

The involvement of the public library in this program shows some lessons were learned from the Round Table experience. One is, that while it is difficult to sustain library-originated programs for young adults without a heavy commitment of professional and support staff time and resources, it is possible to "piggy back" on programs established by others, not as a "free rider" but as an effective program component, making a solid contribution. The library program reflects too the common sense of offering to do what you know best.

The library staff knew best how to bring young people and books together and this is what brought teaching to the library. A course in popular literature is offered once a week for a two-hour period taught by a librarian. One other staff person assists in teaching the course. It's a traditional course, print oriented, using only an occasional 16 mm film to enrich instruction. The purpose of the course is to have young adults read and talk about popular literature and best selling books.

At first, best sellers meant such books as *Helter-Skelter* and *Alive*. But, the library staff found to its surprise and satisfaction that *Les Miserables,* the *Glass House,* and *Aaron's Rod* are read avidly by some students.

Students in the eight-week course must read at least four books, selected by themselves. One book is read in common by all students. For the present cycle this is George Orwell's *Animal Farm*. Grading, either pass or fail, is compulsory.

Examinations are given and oral class participation is expected. Yes, it's traditional but do not overlook the most important fact that were it not for this course being offered by this library as a part of this alternate school program, some of these students would probably not be in school. Discussions about books being read take place right in the young adult room of the library. Participants sit in a comfortable circle and important ideas, writing styles, and author motivations are discussed casually but carefully; everyone shares and enters in.

A visit brought the opportunity to talk with students who spoke of the popularity of the course. Three of the five now enrolled in it are repeaters. While there are youngsters with motivational reading problems in the class, youngsters with serious reading impairment could not participate in the course. The course is for the student who can read but doesn't. Each can freely select what he reads though selections must be approved.

Attendance, given the loose structure of the alternate program, has been a problem for a few, but it is not considered significant. Students in the course said they liked most the alternative presented by the course. They spoke too of the instructor's (librarian's) concern for teaching and her wish that youngsters learn to appreciate good literature. Changed attitudes about libraries and a heightened knowledge of library resources were noted too. Traditional material and non-traditional method place a public library program into a teaching program in a significant opportunity for young adults.

Program Objectives
1. To provide students, bored with school or unable to adjust to its routines, an alternate form of education.

2. To involve the young adult program of a public library in an alternate education program.
3. To provide a format for introducing students to contemporary and classic literature.
4. To develop student responsibility for self-direction in study and learning.
5. To help students improve the skills of reading, oral and written expression.

Some Suggestions
1. Provide more activities rather than just reading and talking.
2. Relate the course more specifically to creative writing course.
3. Consider the possibility of adding additional courses in writing to compliment the present course.
4. Use some other media, particularly audio cassettes of author or critic, to extend scope of course.
5. Attempt more specific follow-through on students who have finished the program to see if they are still using the public library.

CENTRAL MIDDLE SCHOOL
Newark, Delaware

Staff
 Professional: 1
 Support: 1 full-time; 2 part-time
 Volunteer: 3

Budget (1975-1976)
 Print: $3,600
 Nonprint: 2,500
 Special grants
 (materials): 2,500

Target Population: 826 children, ages 11-13

A visitor to the Central Middle School media program came away saying, "I was impressed—it is refreshing to see a program that succeeds in doing what others only try to do, or talk about." Gimmicks, here, are few; emphasis goes instead to a balanced blending of theories and applied educational practice. Understanding how children learn, and what makes them want to learn more, is one media program goal. This commitment is buttressed by a seemingly high degree of expectation by teachers that the children will do or accomplish more than the average. This high expectation level translates to programs and activities that involve students actively and directly in their own learning.

Interest in learning by children can be increased through higher expectation. Not, of course unreasonable expectations, that try to drive children to unattainable superimposed limits, but expectation that is reinforced through increased motivation and involvement. This means an environment that allows children to have their learning needs satisfied, and includes rewards and discipline, concentration, and understanding. While these words describe, they do not define the media program role in this school; careful attention to learning theories and concern about children provide only a one-dimensional view of the program.

A key component of most successful school media programs is a media specialist who is a skilled teacher and likes to teach children and works with teachers as a team member. The head of the media program at Central was Newark

Teacher of the Year in 1974-75. Recognition of a media specialist as an outstanding teacher doesn't happen often—or often enough. This reflects a special problem for many media programs; their failure to identify with teaching. The media specialist in this school regards teaching as her main responsibility. Supervisors and a support staff encourage her to concentrate on it while she shares and supervises other professional duties.

In the Central Middle School media program, terms like learning center, resource center, and media center reinforce each other with a clarity lacking in most programs. This results from the emphasis on the use of media as a teaching resource for instructional improvement.

The media program has established learning goals and identified the objectives that facilitate their achievement. Systematic evaluation of accomplishment and failure is included too. One goal of the media program is to have students demonstrate growth in the ability to learn independently. For this goal to be fulfilled, the student must demonstrate proficiency in academic skills while using reference materials to complete different subject areas assignments. Reading skills are necessary to use reference books, the card catalog, scan for interpretation, and select appropriate materials. Viewing skills are required to operate equipment and extract information from nonprint resources. Listening skills relate in similar fashion to viewing skills. Writing skills are used to write reports, take notes, and answer questions in writing. And production skills are used to operate cameras, make transparencies, charts, pictures, slides, and filmstrips. The listing of these media skill expectations helps to structure a media program that is systematic and rational in its goals. The media program thus makes a contribution to the process of improving instruction.

Other objectives are incorporated into the program. A specific media program educational objective is that students become proficient in social relationships while using resource materials. This objective requires students to plan projects, research them, and carry them out with others. Individual responsibility is increased through group participation and is an important process element.

Another goal of the media program states that students will continue their education and learning independently, depending on self-motivation and their own interest and ability. A program goal is that children use media program resources and facilities without being assigned to do so by a teacher. Activities that support this objective include: exploring for information; reading current magazines and newspapers to be informed; reading, viewing, and listening critically; and discussing current issues with peers.

Another goal is that students willingly and enthusiastically support the media program. Good citizenship is an objective in achievement of this goal. Good citizenship in the media program means using materials carefully, sharing them with others, suggesting ways to improve the program, and helping others in appropriate ways.

The media program is committed to a series of objectives to support these and other goals. Some of these are: (1) to provide a variety of media at appropriate levels that meet the needs of various curriculum areas; (2) to maintain a flexible schedule that permits optimum use of the facility and its resources; (3) to encourage students, teachers, and parents to help with selection of materials; (4) to help with reading guidance and encourage reading for pleasure; (5) to involve the media specialist in curriculum design and to meet with teaching teams whenever possible; and (6) to be certain that Resource Center activities are based on generally accepted principles of learning.

The evaluation of how well these goals are being met is an ongoing process. Together teachers and the media specialist design learning activities and apply criterion-referenced tests to them. Evaluation of student performance is done mainly by teachers with input from the media specialist. Interviews and surveys have been used to assess students use of the program; other records tell who uses the center, for what purpose and how often.

Precise attention to details, management, and organization carries over into the media teaching program. A Service-Careers-Vocations Unit, taught as part of a career education program, is a good example. The unit goal requires students to do projects about service occupations. Media center materials are used and relate to retrieving and using information as a library skill. The use of a career-education project to reinforce library skills adds a dimension of instructional leadership. Materials used in the unit include: encyclopedias, indexes, the card catalog, books on careers, and the *Abridged Readers Guide to Periodical Literature*. Nonprint materials and equipment are used as well at special learning stations emphasizing particular topics.

Library-skills teaching done this way becomes less a game of "find the hidden fact," for it has specific instructional purpose. And the important element is not retrieving facts but using them with purpose.

The success of the Central Middle School media program stems from its ability to use media as a learning resource, and this has been achieved primarily through the management, organizational, and teaching abilities of a media specialist who is a skilled teacher.

Program Objectives
1. To accentuate the role of the media specialist as a teacher.
2. To integrate the teaching of library skills into curriculum content.
3. To establish specified goals for a media program, educational objectives by which these goals may be obtained, and some evaluation of the process.
4. To cooperate with the reading program of a school to help improve reading.
5. To increase individualized instruction through use of nonprint media.

Some Suggestions
1. Analyze print collection carefully to make certain it has a range of appeal to less able or less motivated students.

2. Add more nonprint items to collection to provide greater depth and adaptability.
3. Ascertain that some learning activities are prepared for the less able or less motivated student.
4. Increase student production of learning materials to relate to instructional units.
5. Provide more equipment to implement more comprehensive nonprint program component.

J. C. MITCHELL ELEMENTARY SCHOOL
Boca Raton, Florida

Staff
Professional: 1
Support: 2
Volunteer: 78

Budget (1975-1976)
Print: $1,700
Nonprint: 5,803

Target Population: 950 children, ages 5-12

The J. C. Mitchell *Community* School is an eighteen-year-old complex of rambling one story buildings and portable classrooms housing nearly a thousand children (of this number, nearly 200 are enrolled in a program for exceptional children). When these children leave, other community groups use the school for educational and recreational programs. J. C. Mitchell calls itself a community school, and it does serve as a community information and recreation resource from 7:00 in the morning until 10:30 at night. Such attention to the needs of a total community by a school is unusual and adds an important dimension for media program services.

The exceptional-child program is for trainable and educable mentally retarded, and learning disabled students. Program focus for the retarded and learning disabled, but gifted, is on "mainstreaming" these youngsters into the school program so that their emotional, social, and physical growth will help them to cope effectively with a world that will demand of them some competitive abilities, despite their physical or mental limitations. The media program provides regular services to special education classes including story hours, use of remedial materials, books, and other appropriate materials. It is a program that must be planned carefully with teachers and implemented on a highly individualized basis.

"Individualized learning," "self-motivation" "competency based learning"; these and many other catchall phrases, standing for everything and sometimes meaning nothing, may be used to describe the J. C. Mitchell educational and media program. They do have meaning here, for every effort is made to see that they are fully melded into the educational program, making it hard to tell where the one leaves off and the other begins. This program provides a level of support by personnel and materials for an effective instructional program, as well as the direct leadership that stimulates and channels a teacher's desire to innovate, grow, and be more creative. The media specialist serves as chairperson of the school budget committee and is looked to for leadership and instructional program development beyond the bounds of the media center. J. C. Mitchell has then all the elements and assets to promote an exceptional educational media program. Resources, equipment, clearly focused program goals, an understanding of how children learn, and an ability to act effectively on these understandings—these attributes, combined with an excellent application of media to improve teaching, produce a program of excellence.

One specific program, the teaching of library skills, deserves particular attention. Skills, skills, skills! Anyone who has managed to find his way through the public school system has been confronted by library-skills time. The "This is good for you, you'll use it all your life" kind of library-skills teaching has usually been built upon incorrect learning suppositions (or notions) of teachers and librarians. These assumed that as children passed sequentially from grade to grade they were ready to acquire new skills appropriate to that grade. First grade gets care and handling of books and good citizenship; grade two gets shelving of easy books and how to check out books; grade three gets beginning dictionary and card catalog skills. So it goes until by grade six the child has mastered just about everything needed to cope with learning demands by using almanacs, atlases, dictionaries, card catalogs, and whatever else is necessary to retrieve and use information. It sounds logical and looks good, on paper. Logic, though, is only a systematic way of going at problem solving, it doesn't guarantee correct results. This has generally been the story of library skills as taught in American schools; systematized "right" steps leading to "wrong" results.

At J. C. Mitchell, the first thing the skills-teaching program does is to recognize some basic facts about how children learn. Development of skills has many common elements whether we are talking about learning to swim, building a shelf, punching a computer program, or assimilating a library technique. For one, they are only mastered or learned as they are needed; skills presented may be absorbed, even stored, but the pay-off of the skills comes only from use. Reward, too, is always related to mastering skills. Satisfaction for a task accomplished must be present. It may be a trophy won, or inner satisfaction; whatever, the reward must be present or the skill probably will not be learned and used. Skills too must be applied to specific learning situations and reinforced with systematic, sustained use to be mastered.

Many media programs attempt to teach skills on an individualized or small group basis. This arrangement often reflects the fact that many schools no longer schedule full classes into media centers. While this has the fine effect of freeing the media center for maximum teacher-student use, it can cause other problems. One such problem is that with decreased scheduling of classes to media centers there is a lack of regular sustained contact with children by the media specialist. Instruction in skills for many children becomes haphazard, a process of grabbing children as they appear in the media center showing signs of not knowing what they are about. Ways must be found then to systematize child contact to improve skills instruction. In any unscheduled program, skills instruction must depend upon classroom teachers to create the impetus through their teaching that requires the use of a wide variety of library-media related retrieval and reference skills. At J. C. Mitchell, a systematic process accomplishes this goal, and it seems to be paying off throughout the entire instructional program of the school.

Most successful open media centers have adopted and adapted elements of open classroom approaches to learning. This is evident in the J. C. Mitchell program, for the library-media skills program is built around the theory that learning by children comes best by engaging their interest, i.e., fostering self-direction and understanding their needs. It reflects the needs of children to find, retrieve, and use information effectively. Typical skills "learning stations" set up in the media center involve parts of a book; alphabetization of words; the differences between fiction and nonfiction books; the shelf arrangement of books; call numbers; interpreting the card catalog; and using dictionaries, indexes, and atlases.

The program operates in a straightforward, simple manner. It is, in fact, a management system made effective by excellent coordination and good communication between media center and classroom. The skills program is designed to be "entered" by children at any grade level depending upon their need for information and it is adaptable to the needs of the kindergarten child as well as the exceptional child.

As class activities determine that a child needs to know a skill, the child goes to the appropriate media center skill learning station. Most often, it is a classroom assignment that brings the child to the skills station. Activities geared to reinforcing a particular skill may be related entirely to a print sequence or they may involve a listening or viewing. Whatever is appropriate, is used.

When the child feels the skill has been mastered, he takes a short test and is checked by the media specialist. Mastery of skill brings a check mark by the appropriate learning station number on a card containing the child's name. A child who does not demonstrate mastery of the skill after two attempts is directed to a personal work session with the media specialist.

Early in the school year orientation sessions for all students introduce the use of the skills station approach. The learning stations range from the easiest kind—how to check out a book and good library citizenship—to the most complex: use of atlases or indexes. Always, the skills relate to what the child needs to know. And the key element remains the teacher who is constantly alerted and informed about the skills-teaching program through careful involvement. Analysis of the skills a child has or has not gained may be made easily by the teacher who checks the child's individual skill card.

It is the transfer from learning skills to actually using them that must be considered the major success factor of this program. Since, too, the mastery of skills is essentially a process of repetition, every effort is made to provide some "fun" as a learning stimulant. A puzzle booklet called *Media Skills Centers Games and Activities* is available and used often. It provides suggestions of activities that are fun, but also directly involve the child in learning. Other materials for the program are inexpensive and easy-to-obtain such as colored poster paper, magic markers, and book pockets, used for various games or activities.

The Mitchell approach to teaching media skills offers a self-paced, individualized, and independent means for students to master skills and relates directly to the instructional program of the school. Its attempt to cope effectively with the challenges of an open media program and to meet the needs of children for basic skills relevant to any age or time gives it an exemplary dimension.

Program Objectives
1. To provide an individualized, self-paced, independent method of teaching library skills.
2. To relate the mastery of library skills to classroom instruction.
3. To provide a management system for operating a media center program.
4. To incorporate a media program component (skills) into the regular classroom experience.
5. To attempt to meet individual student needs through an open media program.

Some Suggestions
1. Develop a school originated criterion referenced test to test effectiveness of program as it relates to the program of the school.

2. Provide for a more systematic coordination of reporting of skills program between media center and classroom.
3. Have some sort of student evaluation of the program developed.
4. Consider use of video tape for some of the introductory skills lessons.
5. Add professional staff person to provide additional and needed program support.

ORLANDO PUBLIC LIBRARY
Orlando, Florida

Staff
Professional: 6
Support: 3

Budget (1975-1976)
Print: $10,000
Nonprint: 6,000

Target Population: 17,000—teachers, parents

It is not possible to list all the ways to develop program formats that involve children specifically in deciding things about their own learning.

Sometimes, though, someone takes a new look at traditional library programs for children and tries something really different. The results, if they come together the right way, can be stimulating, even innovative. For even if there are probably no new ways of doing things, there are some exciting ways to rearrange traditional services and programs to achieve new results.

A program of the Orlando Public Library called "Sharing Literature with Children," substantiates this. It is based upon the Right to Read Program, a project devoted to trying to raise the literacy of all Americans to an eighth-grade level by the 1980s. Right to Read has been responsible for the development of a number of significant local programs such as Orlando's, as it has endeavored to relate library programs to its national goal of functional literacy for all Americans. Implied too in these efforts is the expectation that involvement in this literacy project will create large numbers of new library users.

In assessing its program needs the Orlando Public Library found, for one thing, a total potential child user population of about 85,000 ranging in age from just beyond infancy to twelve years. The problem: reaching the unreached of this number when the primary users of public library programs are children who are already active readers. As is often true, a solution was found in common sense, understanding of realities, and the ability to relate a new program to ongoing programs of proven worth.

Common sense, substantiated by research, tells us that if children see adults reading and enjoying literature, they are more likely to copy this behavior model themselves. And it is reality, also well supported by research, that the more a young child is involved with books and reading, the more likely he is to increase vocabulary, improve language development, and appreciate the importance of reading to the fulfillment of life goals. Finally, it is sound judgment to accept the fact that a professional staff of four has little hope of personally reaching a potential target group of 85,000 children.

Thus, the decision was made for these four professional librarians to serve as teachers. They would train and work through other adults and a variety of other agencies who worked with children. Identifying these agencies and the appropriate contact personnel required a systematic, wide-ranging, and inclusive effort. Private school, and continuing education students, 4-H Club leaders, Scouting leaders, hospital staffs, playground directors, and retired persons were but some of the groups that could be used to implement the goals of the local Right to Read effort. The grafting of this literacy effort onto these agencies is the heart of the Orlando Sharing Literature with Children program.

Premises of the program were: (1) that children who are read to at an early age will more likely become readers; (2) that early exposure to good literature improves understanding and perception for children; and (3) that many adults should be involved in these programs. These premises related to a series of immediate, intermediate, and long-range objectives. Immediate objectives were identification of specific agencies to establish communication with the adults to be involved. Since many of these persons do not normally use library services, specific outreach contacts would have to be planned.

While these contacts were established, workshop programs were developed to instruct participants in how to tell stories, read picture books, use flannel boards, make puppets, plan story hours, and utilize nonprint materials to enrich reading programs for children. To ensure effective workshop follow-through, a large collection of nonprint items was purchased, items to be used with children by those who had completed the workshops. A kit containing samples of simple puppets, handmade flannel board materials, picture books, and some nonprint items was also prepared.

Participants also received a detailed manual after completing the workshop. This manual, *Sharing Literature with Children,* is a complete handbook that among other things provides information about storytelling, using picture books with children, and using the flannel board (including a section with cut-out figures to use on the flannel board.) A section on puppets advises how to use puppets to tell stories, provides sample scripts, gives stories suitable for puppet shows, and tells how to make a variety of puppets. A final section on nonprint items that relate especially to literature is a bibliographic listing of 16mm and 8mm film and filmstrips.

The manual provides security and support for workshop participants who will go back to their agencies and do these programs. This reinforcement helps make it more certain that successful program follow-up will take place.

The workshops themselves are the other essential for the program. When a site and date have been selected, a professional staff person presents a workshop tailored to meet the needs of the particular participants. Depending upon several factors including background, experience and preparation of the participants, a workshop may last from forty-five minutes to three hours. Numbers of participants may range from 2 or 3 to 120.

A three-hour workshop has the following activities: (1) storytelling, including how to choose, learn, and tell a story—demonstrations of storytelling are given and usually a film about storytelling is included for reinforcement; (2) storytelling with props, including reading picture books; (3) use of the flannel board, and (4) puppetry.

Audiovisual equipment is displayed and used. Using the overhead projector with transparencies of story characters and story lines is demonstrated; using the overhead to "draw-a-story" is demonstrated too. The opaque projector, a fabulous attention-getter for children because of its ability to project enlarged pictures of favorite characters, is also used. In these workshops, many nonprint materials are demonstrated through use with appropriate pieces of equipment.

Some 17,000 adults have participated in the training workshops, yet the library staff is still requested to produce between five and ten workshops each week. An institutional library card is provided for those agencies participating in the workshop, and this entitles agency members to check out collections of print and nonprint materials and equipment to use with their own programs. Long-term loan of paperbacks can be arranged for agencies that do not have ready access to books.

Examples abound of successes by local workshop participants. A group of high school students enrolled in a day-care aide training program took a workshop. The entire class later re-examined the sample puppets and constructed their own puppets to be used in shows for children in the day-care center. In a school, a sixth-grade language arts class began storytelling for kindergarten and first grade classes after a workshop experience. This activity provided the older children with an opportunity to develop written and oral language skills, and younger children benefitted from hearing good literature. The possibilities of adapting workshops to the needs of many participants is nearly limitless. Goals and objectives are always expressed clearly to participants who are expected to involve themselves fully in the workshops.

The workshop activities, the manual, *Sharing Literature with Children,* and the in-service preparation for the library staff always lead back to the overall project goal to "ensure that every child hears stories told, is read to, sees puppet shows, views story films and encounters literature in any of many formats, by encouraging all adults who work with children on a regular basis to share literature with them." The program initiators believed that adults could be effectively trained and motivated to share literary experiences with children on a day-to-day basis, and they have been proven right.

An initial LSCA grant of $16,000 was used to purchase materials and equipment for the project as well as cover the expenses of workshops and printing the manual. Local funds now support the program. The professional staff involved with the program has increased from four to six and they are hard put to maintain the program, for they have routine library duties in addition to the workshop leadership. An attitude of flexibility and a willingness to assume responsibilities as needed make it possible for the staff to perform the tasks associated with the program.

In October, 1975, a publication called *A Study of the Effectiveness of Orlando Public Library's "Sharing Literature with Children" Program,* was released. Authorized by the Orlando Public Library and prepared by a group from the Florida Technological University, the study concluded that "The Orlando Public Library's 'Sharing Literature with Children' program has most effectively met and will continue to meet its ambitious goal of stimulating thousands of young children's interests in a love for story activities." It is a model program in all respects, representing all that is best in good use of funding money, careful planning, follow-through, and evaluating results.

Program Objectives
1. To identify agencies through which the public library could work in its effort to involve adults in the Right to Read effort.
2. To ensure that children are exposed to hearing stories, seeing puppet shows, and viewing nonprint materials in an effort to encounter literature in many formats.
3. To provide a library program to teach and motivate adults to use children's literature well with children.
4. To use print and nonprint materials and activities in combination or separately to reinforce appreciation of good literature in children.

5. To develop in-service library staff training to insure the ability to conduct successful workshops for others.

Some Suggestions
1. Provide specific tie-in to home situations for reading evaluation follow up.
2. Create closer cooperation between school media programs and the program to assure in-school follow up.
3. Use video tape workshop sessions so that workshops do not always require a professional.

AZALEA MIDDLE SCHOOL
St. Petersburg, Florida

Staff
Professional: 1
Support: 7
Volunteer: 3

Budget (1975-1976)
Print: $1,700
Nonprint: 1,200
Special Grant: 3,700

Target Population: 975 children, ages 11-14

An enthusiastic parent who is also a staff writer for the St. Petersburg *Independent* related that she honestly believed that the institution of schooling is going to—or has—changed. It seems that her 12-year-old and chief school hater comes home turned on by what he is learning at the Azalea Middle School.

A problem with most of the great philosophical movements of American education has been their frequent inability to translate theory into educational practice except under laboratory conditions which can be both unreal and misleading. At Azalea, the philosophy of involving children directly in some pretty basic decisions about their own lives and their own learning, is a reality and the theory that this is sound educational practice has not been disproved or discredited.

Azalea does try to be a family unit. It recognizes that no school can ever replace a parent or a family. But, it recognizes, too, that the comfort and protection of the family unit can be incorporated into a school program. Teachers at Azalea Middle School work together and are given time to plan together. They are encouraged to look at their students as persons and to have their teaching reflect this. These middle school grade students experience a philosophy based on cooperation and teamwork by teachers, a unique type of scheduling, and a variety of curricular offerings.

Probably the greatest enemy of a child's learning is boredom. Educators have failed generally to understand or react properly to this fact, for the opposite of boredom is not necessarily amusement, diversion, or merriment. Boredom, in the form most often experienced in public schools, is alienation of children from a learning environment which they recognize as being mindless, pointless, or invalid. There is a certain adult discomfort involved in accepting that children, from a very early age, do make those judgments and act upon them accordingly. But they do.

The theory behind the practice of education at Azalea Middle School is that behavior can be modified through an enriched curriculum, use of professional and support staff to create a learning environment that is humane and responsive to the needs of children, and a school that adapts to the intellectual and social needs of children without becoming either a three-ring circus or a Las Vegas casino.

Often behavior-modification has a negative connotation to it: rats in mazes receiving electric shocks to prod them into acceptable response patterns, outright torture or coercion to force a modified behavior, or other unpleasant things. But education and upbringing themselves are a form of behavior modification. Schools, teachers, and parents, from time unremembered, have practiced behavior modification on children. Threats, outright force, bribery, appeals to better-nature, promises of swift retaliation: these and a million other ways, both subtle and direct, have been tried on children to get them to respond in a way determined by adults to be acceptable, or whatever the going adjective of the time has been.

Azalea Middle School, in St. Petersburg, Florida, has a clear and distinct philosophy aimed at *positive* behavior modification of those children delivered into its care. This involves a lot of love and care and concern about children. But, it also involves helping children to meet the demands of life in realistic ways. The programs reinforce the belief that the best discipline is self-discipline; that there is enormous satisfaction in mastering the basic skills that allow one to stretch creative learning to its limits; and that while the individual is a unique and singular entity, that person must also learn when it is appropriate—necessary—to merge into a group.

States the proud parent-reporter, "I have been given scientific information on why one leaves open the door of the stove when broiling, on VD, and on film making. He remembers his lunch money, his notebook, and even has less difficulty finding where he put his shoes when he comes home in order to put them on again to go to school on time."

Is all of this possible? Apparently so, if you judge from the Azalea Middle School program. At Azalea, the children, their teachers, and their parents are making it together, and an effective media program is making a successful contribution to this.

The media program is considered by many to be the nucleus of the strong behavior formation program at the school. Unusual resources, unique operations and novel activities are its hallmarks. Unusual resources—how about a bumper pool table and a regulation billiard table? Novel activities—how about a Friday sit-in? Admission, by ticket only. The tickets are given out by teachers participating in the behavior modification program and entitle the bearer to such varied activities as film viewing, bicentennial program celebrations, scrimshaw demonstrations, and puppet shows. To get the ticket, you must prove you can produce academically and socially in the classroom. Azalea teachers feel this activity, one of many at the media center, refinforces positive behavior in their classes.

Another factor essential to the success of the Azalea media program is the able and effective way its staff interacts with the other members of the building staff. The art department works with the media center staff to help students in their media productions. The reading program reaches out to find better ways to help children unlock whatever it is that turns them into readers. Always the emphasis is on positive reward for success, no matter how limited, as opposed to punishment for failure. Reflected too is that behavior-modification does not rest on one method alone but represents an array of techniques.

The entire school becomes involved in the process of support by praise. Success certificates are displayed prominently throughout the building for one and all to see and savor. To the child who mastered a difficult rhythm on the flute, praise and public notice; to the best archery marksman, recognition and the responsibility of being first; to the best manipulator of math modules, a suitable public acknowledgement. Praise, pride, and support are evident everywhere.

Azalea is coping effectively with one of the inherent problems of this "recognition approach" to creating positive behavior: that someone, or a certain group, is always going to finish last and be known as losers, the also-rans. The proper response to this concern is to create a learning environment that is so supportive of children's efforts to do their own best—rather than somebody else's—that they do not start their work afraid of failure. Fear of failure should never be allowed to deter children from pursuit of the human need to be recognized for doing *something* right, or good.

The pattern must be to establish a curriculum and learning environment that is broad enough to ensure a necessary measure of success to all. Teachers and the media specialist at Azalea Middle School, working nearly always in teams, have time and imagination to plan how most effectively to "track" their subjects. The professional staff decide together how much of the daily three-hour academic period of the school should be devoted to each learning activity. Time is flexible within this three-hour period and may vary from day-to-day. Working with the academic subject teachers are the media specialist, reading specialist, and others who will make important contributions to the success of the program.

Special interest courses run for periods of six weeks and include such offerings as: Fun with Math, agriculture, sewing, language arts, and science. Considerably in advance of most schools, Azalea has recognized the changed concept of the American family. Children are taught to understand and accept such patterns as the two-career family, the growing indistinction of the mother and father roles in the home, and that a marriage is, after all, two people who have chosen to live together who, to stay together, will need all the help, understanding, and support from each other they can muster.

Obviously no media program could sustain with a minimal staff the kind of leadership and support role expected of it in this school. There is a media specialist with a support staff of seven; two paraprofessionals, whose primary responsibility is to help the children within the media center; one library clerk, to help with cataloging and to perform other clerical tasks; one audiovisual aide, concerned primarily with equipment distribution, maintenance, and training student media assistants in the use of the various types of equipment; and three resource room instructional aides whose responsibility is to do both remedial and enrichment work with small groups of children. In this sense, they help the media center function as a true extension of the instructional program operating in every classroom.

The Azalea media program may very well be pointing the way to the future in terms of staffing media programs. For, rather than relating professional staff positions to the number of children, as the present guidelines do, Azalea has reoriented its focus to deal with what an entire staff is to do with children. At this time both educational and economic factors militate against the additions of large numbers of professional staff. As professionals we may debate the negative effects of this forever with little hope for change. Rather, let's face reality, which is that the professional will be asked to accomplish educational innovation, curriculum development, and instructional leadership, with little or no additional *professional* support. It is to support staff that our attention should go.

It is the support staff that, to a large extent, is responsible for the Azalea media program success. Some 975 students and their teachers are being effectively involved in a building-wide media program led by a single professional. Granted, too, that though this support staff is extraordinarily large by anyone's standards, they have been tied in nearly every case directly to the instructional program and therein lies their value and the reason for their jobs.

As a program that leads, helps, and sustains a whole building instructional program, the Azalea media program exhibits excellence in all areas.

Program Objectives
1. To improve children's performance in school by participating in positive behavior modification program.
2. To involve media center professional and support staff directly in the institutional life of the school.
3. To increase direct student participation and involvement in the media program.
4. To involve the media center program in a human relations program.
5. To help the student learn, through an excellent media program, the purpose of his own learning.

Some Suggestions
1. Establish a testing strategy that could indicate specifically the contribution of various media components of individual learning.
2. Show through budget format the cost of varieties of unique media used to support this program.
3. Articulate with senior high school programs to indicate the strengths, and limitations, if any, of the Azalea program so that the high schools may be better prepared to deal with the kind of learning pattern that children have established.
4. Involve more community volunteers in media program.

ASTORIA PARK ELEMENTARY SCHOOL
Tallahassee, Florida

Staff
Professional: 1
Support: 1

Budget 1975-1976)
Print: $1,774
Nonprint: 2,056

Target Population: 750 children, ages 5-12 (K-5)

This book places special emphasis on the fact that schools that commit themselves to an open concept child-centered learning program need not sacrifice basic educational skills. Architecturally and philosophically, Astoria Park elementary school is such an open concept school. The philosophy of the school expresses a respect for the worth and dignity of the individual child and says, "Every child is unique, and his own sense of worth is his greatest asset." Architecture supports these convictions, for the school is arranged to encourage maximum freedom of movement by children and teachers. Physically open arrangements encourage team teaching and other interdisciplinary teaching methods as the instructional staff seeks the best ways to meet individual student needs. Every teacher—and the media specialist is a teacher at this school—is expected to "Help the child develop his potential, to meet the challenges of an ever-changing world and to be a contributing member of his group."

While these may be annoying words to those who have "had it" with education as a socialization process, the Astoria Park media program shows that there need be no confrontation between those who believe in basics and those who support an open education. Not that these issues are ever so simply drawn or as neatly divided as the two groups would have others believe.

The media program is both sensible and sensitive, encouraging instructional innovation and providing strong learning support within the school. Commonsense ideas, efficient methods of operation and clear purpose to achieve are balanced with a humaneness and concern for the individual child providing an exceptional media program.

Recently, media programs and professionals have been committed to an awesome array of goals and objectives that relate mainly to instructional support. National guidelines premise a program that helps develop curriculum, encourages educational innovation, teaches teachers how to be more creative by using media, and demonstrates the use of educational technology to improve instruction and learning. An inherent problem with so many responsibilities is establishing program priorities and following them through.

The Astoria Park media program delivers what it promises because it has not promised everything to everyone. The program sets clear priorities, and shows an efficient way of operating to meet these priorities. Two elements, structure to achieve stated goals and creativity to promote spontaneous involvement by children and teachers, provide the program framework.

The media program aims to show even the youngest children that a media center is a special and important thing. The puppet show, a standard public library program, is used in Astoria Park to introduce kindergardeners to the program and demonstrate the role of a media specialist. Sometimes this activity takes place in a classroom area, reinforcing the idea that a media program goes out from a media center and that media specialist is a teacher. The puppet show and storytelling experience continue for students in grades one through three, promoting understanding of the media program and encouraging language development activities while stimulating an appreciation for literature. Indeed, a special priority at Astoria is to convey to children an appreciation for literature. It is a program highlight and children at the earliest age are brought in close, continuing contact with books, through a variety of media and programs.

Thoughtful attention to a media skills instruction is evident as well. Probably no other process consumes the attention of the school media specialist more than how best to teach skills. Too often when we "teach" library skills we overlook a basic tenet, which is that skills are the result of learning patterns that must be repeated often, consistently, and with a purpose. The vacuum theory of a whole class "learning" the card catalog through two or three group exposure sessions in the media center is properly rejected by anyone with any knowledge of how children learn. Theoretically, this is replaced by the efforts of subject-area teachers to provide learning experiences that require use of media center skills such as use of the card catalog, reference books, or magazine indexes for the successful completion of work. There is still, however, an operational tendency to let the teaching of media retrieval skills fall between the cracks.

At Astoria, a sequential media skills program is used to help teachers become more effective and capable in their instructional role. A top priority of the media program is to work with teachers in assuring appropriate skill uses.

It's not the search for new skills that should occupy the attention of media specialists but rather how better to accomplish some traditional skills teaching. Really it is doing better what we already know how to do. Teachers and children must understand exactly how they relate to the skills program and what they must do to make it a success.

Some skills programs look like management charts created by systems-oriented educational technologists. Inputs, variables, outcomes, reinforcement modes, and a host of other jargonese illustrated by bold arrows, dotted lines, and boxed data cause teachers to recoil in confusion, frustration, and annoyance. The purpose of skills instruction should not be to obscure, to make understandable and useable. In Astoria Park, this is done by a simple page and a half ditto called a "Scope and Sequence Chart." Since media skills are classroom activities, every teacher has a chart, understands what it is, and uses it. The exemplary aspect of this part of the Astoria program is not a new skills teaching program, but the effective way their teaching is blended into the ongoing instructional program.

Studio production of media, for skill reinforcement and instructional support, is also a priority program. Astoria students create their own video program called WKID. Produced, directed, and filmed by fifth-grade students, under the supervision of the media specialist, it provides a "channel" for those who wish to present news, plays, reports, or other instructional activities to the school. Before a program is prepared it must be written out and approved by the media specialist, to the benefit and reinforcement of language arts skills such as organizing reports, stressing main ideas, and writing paragraphs. Student-produced video tapes are shown to classes in the media center. Specials, on such topics as drugs, Watergate, or Florida, are produced and used as well. These video programs reinforce that teachers, media specialists, and children working together can relate valid learning experiences to special educational programs.

A photography workshop is offered for an hour-and-a-quarter Mondays through Thursdays some twelve times during the year. Students learn the use of the 35mm camera and other aspects of taking and printing photographs. This has provided an important media production component for the program as well as utilizing the unique instructional capabilities of a media specialist.

A cinematography course alternates with these photography workshops. Stressing the skills needed for story boarding, script writing, and planning various kinds of 8mm films, it is another enrichment program with effective instructional sequences. In these workshops students from third through fifth grade work with different animation techniques such as cut-out figures and clay, as well as live-action techniques. Fifth graders created a film documentary about Florida government. Both the WKID and an 8mm animated ecology film created in the cinematography course have won state awards. The ecology film also placed second in the National Student Media Festival (AECT 1976).

"The Essential Ingredient" is a 16mm film created for the Florida State Department of Education. This film shows the significant contributions media programs make to quality education and includes the Astoria program. Creativity tied to specified educational outcomes makes this media program a significant educational program.

Program Goals
1. To establish sequential library skills program that relates directly to and integrates itself into the instructional program.
2. To use video production format to reinforce language arts skills.
3. To use photography workshops to help students use the 35 mm camera as an instructional and recreational tool.
4. To use cinematography workshop experience to reinforce language arts, art, and social science skills.
5. To establish teaching role of the media specialist.

Some Suggestions
1. Add professional staff person to permit strengthening of teaching role of media specialist.
2. Obtain more local support money to underwrite photography and cinematography workshops.
3. Establish a specific skills testing program to better judge effectiveness of skills program.
4. Provide more equipment and space for increased local production program.

GEORGIA

SPRING STREET SCHOOL
Atlanta, Georgia

Staff
Professional: 1
Volunteer: 3-5 + 1 high school independent study student

Budget (1975-1976)
Combined Print and Nonprint: $812

Target Population: 250 students, ages 5-12 (20 in special program)

Project Seek, Explore, and Discover (SED), has about it an aura of the might have been. A lesson, rooted in the harsh facts of the mid-seventies, is that even well-managed, educationally sound programs have only a limited and finite ability to deal with overwhelming economic and social realities. Some fine programs get run over and closed down because of the disaster situation of city budgets combined with the declining school enrollments. These conditions, which now confront many school districts in this country, can have a devastating effect on media programs. Project SED provides valuable lessons because it lived through these experiences and still survives.

Much of our professional attention about the use of media with children has gone to improving the learning of less able children. Recently substantial money to help the less able child has been allocated due to a high priority at national, state, and local levels. Undoubtedly this is overdue, if one agrees that the proper role of the public schools is to educate *all* the public; thus special education programs have found their way increasingly into the public schools and are showing an "explosive" growth pattern.

We have sometimes overlooked the creative and instructional value of media programs for the brighter, more able student. True, the brightest and best can proceed on their own, but special education does not mean attention only to one end of the scale; Project SED, a media program for the gifted, demonstrates a unique special education program. Project Seek, Explore, and Discover was the inspiration of a media specialist who was able to translate an interest in individualized instruction, a perception of how to apply media to learning, and an ability to get a disparate group of teachers, administrators, and children to work together, into a program.

The Spring Street School where it began, is an unusual school. It is small (250 pupils), yet representative by its racial and economic mix of the total population of Atlanta. A library program, begun in the 1960s, became a media program with flexibility and high student involvement built into it from the start. Media skills are taught as needed. Individualized instruction is a high priority, and serious and purposeful attempts to generate an enthusiasm for reading are exhibited by book fairs, student writing projects, and an annual Spring Street Book Parade. Throughout the school the effort to develop individualized learning motivation and activity for children under the aegis of an effective media program is evident. It's the kind of program that should exist when sufficient resources and personnel are available.

In 1973, though, the media program made a significant change in course when the school was selected as a pilot school for an Elementary Curriculum Revision Program. This program brought together for program planning the principal, the media specialist, a teacher from each instructional level, and some special area consultants. The concept of this cooperative team planning for an educationally innovative program is outstanding in any setting. That it was sponsored by the media program makes it particularly noteworthy. As this team reviewed the needs of the school, programs for the intellectually gifted children were considered. There was no special education teacher in this building so an individualized, independent study program for these children was devised to operate within the media program. The media specialist would coordinate it. Using the media specialist as a special teacher adds a vital dimension frequently lacking in school media programs. Of course, a media specialist is not and cannot be a subject area teacher, but to find those special or unique teaching programs in which the media specialist can serve as teacher or learning coordinator should be a top priority for all media programs.

The name Seek, Explore, and Discover was chosen by the children themselves. Criteria for student participation included: performance on standard achievement tests, class achievement, and observed ability to work well independently. The initial group contained twelve fifth graders and sixteen sixth and seventh graders. Following a school grade level and grouping change in its second year, the program changed to one group of twenty fourth and fifth graders.

While the media specialist continued to serve as the primary teacher, the principal, the art, music, and speech teachers, and the classroom teachers met periodically with her to assess and evaluate the program. SED occupied three one-hour time periods a week; these limited time periods demanded careful preplanning by this teaching team.

A refreshing, though perhaps naive, hope was that these children would serve as change-agents within the school. This group, with its potential for creativity and leadership, could serve to stimulate and to energize an entire school community.

Little overt structure was provided for the children. Their mission, to seek, explore, and discover, was reflected in the name they appropriated. Emphasis was placed on problem solving, inductive reasoning, and a shared attempt to establish learning goals and the objectives by which these goals would be met. Questioning, and free flow of the process of learning how to learn, were the heart of the program. The media program was the facilitator of this process, something for which media programs are especially qualified.

Underlying the process, though, was attention to skills instruction, specifically retrieving, organizing, and reporting data to support instructional objectives. Student participants organized their study through developing a hypothesis, drafting objectives, completing the study, and identifying findings. Good intellectual discipline provided, in this instance, the opportunity for greater creative exploration to increase learning.

The course required a final report which had to be both a written and visual presentation. A typical study concerned America's wildlife and natural resources. All the resources of the media program were used to investigate, develop, and complete the project. Teams were organized and each team took responsibility for the preparation of one portion or subtopic. Community resources were employed by using speakers and field trips. Eventually, a taped guide was prepared for visitors who came to an exhibit prepared as part of the program. The use of traditional print reference tools (encyclopedias, atlases, special handbooks, and indexes) developed one important research aspect while a variety of nonprint media were used for reference and information. The SED program rejects the limiting notion that media programs must be contained within the media center.

Much of the success of Project SED rested upon the force, persistence, and ability of one individual to "drive" it. Unfortunately, when due to budget limitations and declining enrollments the Spring Street School lost its full-time media specialist, it lost an important part of the program.

A teacher now directs the program with some support from the media center. A current project of the SED group at the school is the preparation of a filmstrip on the three branches of the federal government. The project involves intensive research into the mountain of facts available about this topic, sketching and painting of pictures, the preparation of posters, and a good deal of photography. While one half of the group does these activities the other half prepares a script for the tape that accompanies the filmstrip.

In the school to which the media specialist was transferred, the program under a new name, Learning, Exploring, Accomplishing, Discovering (LEAD), lives and makes its special contribution. A recent research topic was "Our Heritage and Horizons '76." It sought to explore important firsts and significant contributions that blacks have made to art, government, entertainment, literature, and science.

Activities included: interviewing, reading, observing, viewing of nonprint media, and other appropriate activities. These activities reinforce both individual and group work to achieve program objectives. The effective components of the program compel the interaction of children and media-information resources (including people) and activities to reinforce individualized learning. Student participants were asked, as part of the course requirement, to analyze how well the learning objectives they established were fulfilled, then to draw and substantiate conclusions to support their evaluations. Again, intellectual discipline here supports rather than restrains important learning. Student participants and their teachers were asked to complete written evaluations of the programs. Their recommendations, and those of others, have been used to make changes in the program.

A visitor to the programs observed that for projects such as SED and LEAD facilities, finances, and collections of materials are less important than the personnel to spark them. The extraordinary ability of the media specialist to be an outstanding teacher of children is the heart of the success of this program.

Program Objectives
1. To offer a media program to intellectually gifted and highly motivated students.
2. To provide an inquiry-oriented process experience to involve children in directing their own learning.
3. To emphasize the nature of the media center, the school, and the community as a learning laboratory.
4. To involve the media specialist as a member of the teaching team.
5. To provide for joint planning among a number of professionals to best use a media program for the education of gifted children.

Some Suggestions
1. Seek to involve more community volunteers in the program to extend its potential into the community.

2. Provide a more specific evaluative mode for program to follow-through on its change process impact within the school.
3. Provide more specific links to special education (gifted) program so they could possibly become more involved.
4. Create learning activity packets from the program that could be used directly in classroom instruction.
5. Clarify relationship of the programs to the total educational programs of the building: specifically, what contribution they are to make back to classes.

As this book went to press Spring Street School was closed. However, Project LEAD continues at the Carter G. Woodson School.

GEORGIA

PEACHTREE ELEMENTARY SCHOOL
Norcross, Georgia

Staff
Professional: 1
Support: 1
Volunteer: 10

Budget (1975-1976)
Print: $4,000
Nonprint: 2,200
PTA: 500
Other (book fairs, etc.): 800

Target Population: 800 children, ages 5-12

Media centers and schools should be designed and built to live in and work in rather than just be looked at. But it is possible to combine beauty and design symmetry with functional utility and workability. Designed to facilitate operation of an open-education program, Peachtree Elementary School illustrates such compatability and has been recognized by the 1975 National Architectural Convention for both excellence and utility in design. The media center is open to class areas on three sides and this assures a steady flow of students. A visitor spoke of the comfortable atmosphere in the media center, one that is inviting to use yet controlled in purpose.

The school media program was planned around an open education program and it supports and leads teachers and students in this program. This requires clear perceptions about what the media program can accomplish for children, teachers, and the school community.

This open media program invites the fullest possible utilization of the media center and its resources. The top priority of the media specialist, support staff, and volunteers is to get the fullest possible use of materials, equipment and instructional media services. To accomplish this, the needs of the teacher and the student must be quickly perceived and met. Then, too, almost continuous review of program goals and objectives must be undertaken, for the openness of the school's program mandates a media component able to respond in many different ways to meet a constantly changing range of needs and expectations by those using it.

Discovery and development of the child's natural curiosity to learn are the focus of the media program. This is self-discovery based upon careful discipline that relates individual rights to responsibilities. While students occupy themselves with learning how to learn, clear expectations and specified outcomes are proposed and required of them.

The Peachtree educational media program has taken the *idea* of making the media center program the instructional hub of the school and translated this into separate component parts. Within the media center are located learning stations and interest areas. These learning stations may be thematic, built, for example, around a topic like the Bicentennial. They include equipment necessary to listen to or look at the media used for the lesson.

These learning stations may also relate to specific content areas, such as math tutoring. The media center has an electronic calculator that allows children to practice a variety of enrichment or remedial mathematical activities. Self-correcting and self-pacing, the program helps the child move from one problem to the next if correct answers are provided. Wrong answers require repetition until the correct answer is given. Here new technology is related to basic computational math, providing media program innovation within a framework of structured sequenced learning experiences.

One media center learning station is for media center skills. It contains a variety of activity cards, and is used by students to incorporate media skills in their learning. The activities are prescribed by either a teacher or the media specialist, or they may be used for enrichment or remediation by individual students. Other typical media center activities include use of a recessed pit area for puppet plays and stories; print-oriented research; a reading program using comics from the comics corner; and periodical use.

The flexibility and adaptability of this program to a number of uses are another key to its excellence. An ability to relate to needs and concerns of children, building administration, teaching staff, and support staff, is crucial. Total educational needs as defined and refined must be translated into media program leadership.

This media program recognizes that no media specialist working alone can achieve these broad program goals. Team concepts of planning and implementing program must be developed within the building for a media program to succeed, and the media specialist must act as a catalyst for change and for managing innovation within the building.

At Peachtree the opportunity to assume this media program role came when the media specialist recognized the potential presented by a series of staff-development programs to help teachers understand and use open education concepts. This ability to recognize opportunities and "ride" on them to advance a media program is an important factor in success, underestimated and underused by many media professionals. Working with teachers to define such terms as individualization, interdisciplinary teaching, and open education can help teachers understand how to use media programs in new ways and with improved instructional purpose.

As it passed through this transitional stage, the media program did not scuttle everything to embrace a new and untested program. Within the open media program, it is possible for classes to come to the media center for reading, storytelling, or other activities. If there is *purpose* for the activity and known results to be obtained, needs can be met this way. The heaviest use of the media center, though, comes from children working as individuals or in small groups using the center as their personal or instructional needs require. A media program objective is to enable teachers to help children to ask right questions as they seek to know and to understand, two processes which are after all quite different.

As the Peachtree media program is examined, one returns always to the basic structure that supports it. The program demonstrates that demands for accountability and creating measurable objectives can be accommodated within media programs. For example, media program objectives for the 1975-76 school year included special focus on introducing third graders to beginning dictionaries, encyclopedias, and the card catalog. Each activity was based upon relating skills to be learned to instructional purpose and future needs. Skill teaching must relate always to agreed upon outcomes by teachers and the media specialist. Results thus far substantiate that individualized and small group skills teaching, reinforced by a systematic and coordinated effort between teacher and media center program, have increased student retention and use of media skills.

While the program openness and instructional involvement displayed by the Peachtree media program may be found in other schools, it is the ability found here to encompass and manage change that best bespeaks its exemplary character, and earned it a citation as one of the three most creative school media programs in Georgia.

Program Objectives
1. To provide an open access media center program for students and teachers.
2. To use interest centers and learning areas in the media center to reinforce specific teaching strategies.
3. To incorporate an objectives approach to teaching media skills.
4. To provide for teacher and media professional planning to develop special programs.
5. To utilize open space design concept to create open media programs.

Some Suggestions
1. Increase nonprint budget to provide better collection balance.
2. Provide for more student-teacher production of learning materials.
3. Extend learning-interest areas to include science.
4. Develop media skills objectives sequence at grades four and five.

5. Establish a more valid criterion-referenced test to demonstrate special relevance of media skills program.

LILIHA COMMUNITY LIBRARY
Honolulu, Hawaii

Staff
 Professional: 2
 Support: 2 (part-time)
 Volunteer: 1
 Instructor: 3 VISTA Action

Budget (1975-1976)
 Print: $ 1,318
 Nonprint: 1,714
 LSCA Title I: 20,000

Target Population: 4000 children, ages 7-15

The Hawaiian verb form to cooperate is "kokua." A willingness, in fact an eagerness to "kokua" with a community got the Liliha community library After School Project started.

The Liliha branch is situated in an area of Honolulu that serves many children living in lower and moderate income housing. Typical of such urban areas it is densely populated and lacks sufficient recreational areas. It reflects, too, the Hawaiian racial polygot with its population of black-Americans, Chinese, Filipinos, Japanese, Koreans, Hawaiians, and caucasians. These children share generally a lack of opportunity for family-planned or family-initiated activities, and few community recreational activities are available to them. Many of them have reading deficiencies or other skill-related educational problems.

Strange as it may sound, the program and the kids just got together. Focus, objectives, and goals followed and were developed as the project was defined and refined. This is not usually the best way to organize a program but it worked here. Because the public schools got out early on Wednesdays and by mid-afternoon on other days, many children began to gather around the public library; there wasn't any other place to go and it was a convenient place to wait for parents. Trying to get these children to read was well-nigh impossible; many of them had turned off reading already. Mostly the children wanted to draw or do other creative activities.

From this fragile beginning, really an attempt to cope with a troublesome situation, developed the After School Project. Before devising any project, the library talked to other community agencies (mainly schools and churches) to be sure they would not duplicate available services. With some 4,000 children in the area, and severely limited recreational or educational resources available, there was little danger of duplication. Cooperation with city, state and federal agencies in planning and coordinating activities was built into the project from the start.

Applying for LSCA Title I monies mandated establishing specific program goals and objectives. The Project would serve the needs of nonreading children, ages six to fourteen, in a selected poverty area by providing: (1) afternoon, after-school programs and activities based on programs in art, music, science, model making and other interests; and (2) a clearing house of information about tutors in reading and learning skills.

Combining children's interests in creativity with applied educational techniques established other program objectives. The main purpose was to provide imaginative, educationally valid programs for children. It was hoped that the programs would motivate children to use and enjoy library materials.

Community resource staff persons used in the program include: an ACTION Volunteer who helps the children's librarian determine children's interests and assists in planning activities, arranging field trips, and making periodic project evaluations; a graduate student aide who performs clerical tasks, freeing the professional to work directly with the children; and an additional aide who orders materials and maintains necessary records. These persons are all paid from the federal LSCA grant.

Of the $20,000 LSCA Grant, salaries used just over $8,000 while materials (mostly nonprint) used $5,000. Equipment costs were about $4,000. The remaining $3,000 was used to pay music, art, and crafts teachers. These contract workers were paid on an hourly basis, and they taught courses in art, ceramics, guitar, and ukulele.

The courses display an adaptability that is both creative and imaginative as they try new ideas and new ways.

Included in the After Schools Activity program are ten weeks of ukulele lessons for beginners; an eight-week art course, including Easter egg decorating, creating art with wood, trash, and "found" objects, and picture making on fabric and paper. A ten-week guitar course for beginners is also given. To enroll in these courses children must be in fourth grade. Generally, ten or twelve children are enrolled in the music course while the art courses enroll twenty. These courses are repeated twice, and more than 150 children at a time are involved in this part of the After School Program.

Activities and programs take place in the children's room of the library and a meeting room adjacent to it. Some physical alterations were made, including a special outlet for the ceramic kiln that was purchased for the program. The activity room has no sink, a must with arts and crafts programs, but in the Hawaiian tradition of accommodation the sink in the janitor's closet makes do.

Paperback racks, picture files, wet (electrified) carrels, and equipment such as cassette players, super 8 loop projectors, filmstrip viewers, record players, and headsets comprise most of the equipment inventory. A large salt water aquarium and its inhabitants from the sea are a popular item of realia.

Programs are scheduled on a daily basis and several are available on Saturdays too. Careful attention goes to individualizing and personalizing of the programs for children. One exciting example: after reading the play and listening to the music, "My Fair Lady," an eleven-year-old decided he would produce it. He did, twice, successfully to standing room only audiences.

Ceramics, drawing, and painting and paper sculpture are the primary art offerings. An acting course specializes in puppetry and play production. A science program is built around the aquarium and this leads to the ocean and the study of ocean life. Of course, storytelling and film viewing programs are available and used heavily.

The Liliha After School Project is also making strong bonds within the community. "My Fair Lady" was videotaped and, after editing, shown on local public access TV. The Graduate School of Library Studies at the University of Hawaii used the project as a field seminar opportunity for its students for telling stories, helping children use nonprint media, and teaching equipment use. A creative writing class was started by a community volunteer who became involved in the program; while a high school club volunteered to help children with reading on a one-to-one basis. Lack of training or supervision skills necessary to work closely with children limited the success of this particular program.

A visitor to the project stated that examples of excellence abound. Chief among these is that so much of the program planning comes from the children themselves. The responsibility to create one's own program and successfully follow it through is an important learning concept. Other exemplary aspects are flexibility and adaptability; the integration of print and nonprint materials and equipment into a unified program; an instructional staff with close ties to the community; the freedom given children to pursue their creative interests; and the ability of the program to attract many children who otherwise would have no contact with a public library.

One failure to meet objectives is the lack of success in setting up a reading tutorial program. As noted, initial efforts to use student volunteers failed. This could have worked out well, for several successful reading tutorial programs rely entirely upon student volunteers. The essential element, though, is *training* to prepare the volunteer to teach successfully. Good intentions are not enough, for tutoring is a very demanding form of teaching. An effective tutor training program and good continuing supervision is required for this program component to be successful.

There have been beneficial spin-offs. Adults have begun to use art prints, film loops, and film strips. Other libraries have investigated the program with an eye toward adapting it. A measurable increase in book circulation that relates to project activities is also noted. Disruptive behavior, one of the primary reasons the program began, is simply not a matter of concern now. Indeed, when kids have a day off from school and spend the entire time at the nearest library, that library must be doing a whole list of things right!

Program Objectives
1. To provide organized library programs for nonreading children from low income families.
2. To attempt, through organized library programs, behavior modification from antisocial to cooperative.
3. To use print and nonprint items to provide for learning support programs.
4. To involve community resource persons as teachers.
5. To establish a tutorial referral service for those needing remedial help.

Some Suggestions
1. Rethink tutorial program. Attempt to attract adults into the program and provide them with proper training.
2. Establish more effective communication with schools from which the children came to get tutoring program in operation.
3. Use nonprint media in a more specific instructional way as a program tie-in.
4. Extend program into summer if funding and staff can be found.
5. Provide program offerings for children under grade four level.

ILLINOIS

RIVERSIDE-BROOKFIELD HIGH SCHOOL
Riverside, Illinois

Staff
Professional: 4 (includes 2 classroom teachers)
Support: 4

Budget (1975-1976)
Print: $ 9,700
Nonprint: 10,300

Target Population: 100 children, ages 15-18
(2,000 in school)

Some quotes from *Media Programs District and School,* the 1975 guidelines for school media programs, developed jointly by the American Association of School Librarians and the Association for Educational Communications and Technology, provide an appropriate introduction to the media program at the Riverside-Brookfield High School.

According to the guidelines, media programs should be capable of "Utilizing instructional sequences of tested effectiveness to reach personal and program objectives." The media professional, says the guidelines, should "Participate in curriculum development and implementation and recommend media applications to accomplish specific instructional purposes." Further, the media professional should "Help students develop good study habits and techniques, acquire independence in learning, and gain skill in critical thinking." Related to this is a responsibility to help students develop competencies in listening, viewing, reading, and other communication skills, attitudes, and appreciations. Finally, asserts the 1975 document, the media professional should function to "Assist users in the techniques of finding, using, abstracting, translating, synthesizing, and evaluating information."

This role for the professional media specialist has not found universal acceptance with school media professionals. Many fear that these bold assertions of instructional leadership, educational innovation, and curriculum development may overwhelm media programs and specialists not prepared to cope with them.

Superficially, at least, these assumptions are true. Too often, the attempt to apply the guidelines to specific building-level instructional situations leads media professionals to make the incorrect assumption that they alone must implement successfully these instructional and support functions. The guidelines were never intended to be so interpreted.

It is certain that an individual media specialist, even with the resources of the richest media collection and the most capable support staff, is programmed for failure in any attempt to go it alone. The message of the guidelines, quite generally misunderstood, is that the media professional's greatest contribution may lie in being a catalyst for all the resources—human, material and equipment—and helping to put these together into combinations that will ensure the kind of instructional innovation and exemplary program leadership expected within the modern school.

The media program at Riverside-Brookfield demonstrates this approach, for this is a program with every resource structured to promote instructional goals. Specific focus is found in the pilot project called "Seminar-centered U.S. History: a Media Laboratory Approach". The media laboratory approach is a student-centered, or inquiry approach, to the study of American History. To understand this media lab approach a brief course description is helpful.

Quoting from the course introduction, "Seven major concepts form the basis of this course.... These include mobility, politics, dissent, business and labor, war, diplomacy, and nativism." Because the course stresses an inquiry approach, the learning emphasis is on finding the whys and the hows. The student is compelled to do independent research, reading, and viewing and to work in small discussion groups to meet successfully the course demands. Students are advised that the "focal point of the program is their performance in the seminar," and that preparation for seminars is done best in the learning lab, a part of the media center. Here the student does the required reading, views film strips and movies, or listens to the tapes and records that form the core of the course.

From this description, there is nothing extraordinarily different about the Riverside-Brookfield program. Many American high schools have inquiry method courses and many have learning labs filled with excellent materials, expensive equipment, and, too often, mindless students being entertained or sedated by their use. It is the capacity of the media program to provide outstanding support to achieve learning goals that gives dimension to this program.

A great deal of structure and guidance is provided for the student participating in the learning. The intent is to require students to make a number of right choices from the many alternatives presented to them. The learning lab is a place for concentrated study and the acquisition of information necessary to prepare for the seminar situation where ideas are exchanged, theories substantiated (or disapproved), and free exchange of opinion supported by facts is expected. Self-discipline, individual responsibility, group responsibility, the limitations of freedom—these and many other things combine to provide the structure for this learning lab situation. Students are expected to tolerate large amounts of self-direction, but they are not left to flounder and falter, for structure is provided to help make appropriate decisions. Learning packets, rather than text books, are used for the course. A learning packet contains paperbacks, periodicals, handouts, bibliographies, reprints, and a complete listing of nonprint resources available to support the objectives of the particular lesson. Direct suggestion, specific guidance, and constant evaluation lead the student to the most useful learning resources. Many inquiry programs make the location, retrieval, and assimilation of information a cat-and-mouse game, with the media professional playing cat and the student a hapless mouse; this is not so here. The emphasis is on an orderly and sequential presentation of information which the student masters and uses according to immediate needs and long-term goals. It is only through use of the relevant print and nonprint media resources that a student may meet, successfully, the course demands.

For the school media professional this represents not just the opening of the gates of paradise but an invitation to enter in. For the program results of the cooperative team work involving a media professional, teachers, support staff, and volunteers can come close to perfection.

Staffing is a key element in the success of this instructional media program. Much of the need for the large staff results from the extensive facilities used to house the program, which include a media center, various offices, a reading room, a reference room, a work room, and two small sound-proof conference rooms. Joining this are remodeled areas housing a listening-viewing area; across the hall is a media production room. These areas are used by the entire school as well as the media-laboratory program. It is a lot of program space, and because of the structure within the program operates it must be staffed properly.

Within the listening-viewing area there are still other facilities including a twenty-seat mini-theatre, a projection booth, study carrels, a work counter, and a small conference area for individual or small group viewing, listening, or planning. A wireless headset operation provides a taped walking tour of this area and acquaints all students with the services available and the proper use of the room. This wireless system is also used for all audio-programs in the mini-theatre—16mm film, sound slide programs, and sound filmstrip programs.

The media lab has a small studio for video taping. Some TV studio equipment is available and a portapak unit may be used by all students under the direction of an AV associate (a subprofessional position), who aids in producing a wide variety of media. Most of these requests fall within the more traditional activities of making transparencies, slides, posters, pictures, and laminating.

Excellent student use of these facilities and their materials is not left to chance. Successful outcomes are planned for carefully, they do not just happen, and the successful expected outcome for this course can be traced back directly to the leadership and support of the media program.

Another focus of this highly individualized course is the requirement that each student produce three special projects. "Doing" the media presents the only way to achieve success.

The projects may be in the form of Super 8 movies, tapes, live performances, multimedia kits, games, or models. The media staff works closely with students taking the course. Using media formats, producing and matching media to the message and writing project proposals, are priorities. And the staff participates in evaluation too, having an equal voice with teachers in evaluating the work of student participants. Visitors to the program report that some very intricate games, involving complex strategies and compound outcomes, have been developed. The games must work, though, and students are asked to defend their workability.

Students know exactly what is expected of them and keep a looseleaf notebook in which are listed all the nonprint materials the student has used to prepare for seminars and projects. This form of self-evaluation is underscored by the requirement that the participant record in this notebook the following information: How was the lab hour used? What kinds of materials were used? What ideas, concepts, or sample of factual materials were gained during the lab hour? Finally, the student is required to prepare and answer questions in writing regarding content or attitudes expressed in the material used. This latter procedure makes the student frame questions, and consider responses, that may be developed in the seminar component.

A heavy emphasis on the grade as the end product of successful completion of the course is evident. It is clear though that this grade represents not the bestowal of teacher approval upon the student, but is honestly sought, and worked toward by the student.

It is evident, too, that the heavy intellectual demands and personal self-control factors are requirements not all students can meet. An ability to read reasonably well and work well independently are essential. Student applicants are screened and appropriate ones invited to participate. Most students who wish to enroll in the program are allowed, however, since it is the school's belief that all should have an opportunity to try. While the program may have a touch of elitism, it stands as an example of how media programs can help provide an instructional pattern that is both valid and valuable for the more able student, a group often overlooked in this era of compensatory, "catch-up" education.

From the start the media program and the inquiry history program have complemented each other. Getting it all together, is a realistic characterization for the media program at Riverside-Brookfield. Enthusiastic staff, excellent learning materials, imaginative programming, and a structured mediated approach to learning make this program well deserving of emulation.

Program Objectives
1. To improve use of nonprint materials by students in a media laboratory approach.
2. To facilitate teaching of an inquiry approach to American History through use of a mediated program.
3. To involve students in self-evaluation of their work, rather than being entirely evaluated by teachers.
4. To involve the media program directly in design and planning of curriculum and instruction.
5. To help students use a number of production techniques and a variety of media to achieve predetermined course goals.

Some Suggestions
1. Extend the history-oriented program approach to such fields as science, home economics, and language arts.
2. Consider adapting the program approach to students less able to compete at the level demanded but still able to learn by individually directed effort.
3. Increase student participation in the creation of learning packets so that their views and learning experience may be passed on to others.
4. Attempt to involve teachers of other disciplines in the team approach to increase their effectiveness.

5. Explore the possibility of more structured experience outside the school in relation to business or industry.

INDIANAPOLIS-MARION COUNTY PUBLIC LIBRARY
Indianapolis, Indiana

Staff
Professional: 2
Support: 2½

Budget
Not applicable

Target Population: 75-100 children, ages 6-12

In the adult world, psychiatrists discern Sunday as a day of increased anxiety; people worry over what lies ahead for Monday—the week. For children it is the moment of truth about homework assignments undone and now looming large, insistent and unfinished. Sunday! Some think, that like New Year's Eve and birthdays after 35, it's a vastly overrated experience. Maybe yes, maybe no. Like everything else it depends on what you make of it.

For some people, Sundays have come to mean regular visits to the library. The library is the Indianapolis-Marion County Public Library and the program that brings in the families is called the "Sunday Kaleidoscope." On a Sunday when a Kaleidoscope program is operating, inner-city church groups, parents with preschool children, and unaccompanied school-age children are likely to show up. Operating from the months of October to April, Sunday Kaleidoscope for children, which began in 1974, offers a complete media program experience for children and the community.

A kaleidoscope, in case you have forgotten from your own childhood, is an eye-catching device that changes pattern, shape, and color in an infinite variety of ways as it is rotated by hand. The programs at Indianapolis-Marion County are not intended to be that quick changing, but the media experience is varied and entertaining. A major purpose, after all, is to attract *family groups* into the downtown central library. This emphasis on family use of the public library, when there are such serious dislocations in family living styles, is noteworthy. Bringing the family unit together in an outreach program is a sound idea.

Since no other branches of the library are open on Sunday, the Kaleidoscope program commands a high priority in system planning. A typical Sunday program may use books, slides, sing-alongs, and, of course, the ubiquitous puppet show. Film presentations are frequently offered too.

A sampling of program themes for the past year includes the following: "Mirror, Mirror on the Wall," built around stories by the Brothers Grimm and using books, slides, recordings, puppets, and a flannel board. The following month the theme was "We'll be Comin' Round the Mountain." For this program, a guest, with banjo, augmented the recordings and books that were used for this program of Appalachian stories, songs, and folklore.

Other programs have been: "Mother Goose Rides Again," featuring modern and traditional versions of the rhymes of Mother Goose and the tales of Charles Perrault; "Tomfoolery to Boogle the Mind," promised "trickery and foolery with words to include riddles, tongue twisters and stories!" These offerings, cleverly mounted and presented with imagination and without affectation never fail to please children and their parents.

Anyone wanting to adapt these programs should be able to think of several locally oriented themes. These could involve "home-grown" performers, authors, or other creative personalities. Tie-in's to historical events and famous personalities are other obvious candidates for programs. Children's artists, musicians that appeal, and craftsmen are other possibilities.

The staff involved in preparing the Sunday Kaleidoscope programs has other responsibilities within the overall program of service to children. Planning and conducting the Sunday program uses part of the time of two professionals and two-and-one-half time clerical employees. Support staff work at developing props, constructing puppets, doing photography, and creating other necessary items for use in the program. It does take time to prepare and produce this kind of high quality program. While no specific analysis is available for the exact time required, a figure close to eighty-hours-per-Sunday show for all staff is a reasonable estimate. This is time that must be found within the framework of other responsibilities and includes the total hours of everyone working on the Sunday program.

The heavy demands of preparation for some of the Sunday programs are balanced by varying the programs to have one special presentation and one that uses 16mm film. The film programs have included such titles as *Little Women*, *The Adventures of Tom Sawyer*, *Misty*, and *Brighty of the Grand Canyon*. The latter two films are excellent versions of the ever-popular horse stories by Newberry Award winner, Marguerite Henry. To organize the film program takes less time; previewing and administrative time for booking and renting being the primary time demands. These could be absorbed within any library with a film library or access to a film cooperative.

Staff members from other branches of the library occasionally participate in the programs. And sometimes the Sunday programs go to other branches, but time and fiscal constraints prohibit this happening often. Most of the programs are held in the auditorium of the central library adjacent to the children's room and juvenile service area. The auditorium has a clear advantage in that it allows for flexible arrangements of furniture, has adequate electrical outlets for media presentations, and permits good listening and viewing from anywhere in the room.

All books used with the Sunday Kaleidoscope programs are available at the central library and may be checked out after the program. While no exact records are kept for this program, the boost in ciruculation of materials after a Sunday program clearly is substantial. An unanticipated, but welcome, outgrowth of the Sunday programs is the exposure of adult materials to those adults accompanying children. In fact, the temptation to create some specific programs for adults is but one exciting multiplier possibility from the program for children. Preschool and senior citizen programs represent other potential. Children and adults are hungry for enrichment programs and information. This hunger, tied to a day in the week when it may be satisfied easily, is the reason a program such as the Kaleidoscope shows the way to new patterns of library service for communities.

Of course, there are problems. The Kaleidoscope program was devised to relate specifically to children age six to twelve. Preschool children often do not have the attention span or the conceptual abilities to relate to the Kaleidoscope offerings. Through errors in judgment or failure to understand program purpose, parents sometimes "push" their children into programs beyond their capabilities. For this kind of program it must be established that children younger than school age have to be with a parent.

While not exactly a problem, it is symptomatic that large numbers of the children attending the Sunday Kaleidoscope do not live in the immediate area. Rather, they are transported to the library from outlying areas. Inner-city resident participation in outreach programs will never be guaranteed by proximity of location. The use of Sunday afternoons for entertainment and learning appeals instinctively to the values of the middle class. Nevertheless, clients in the central city can be sold on the values and recruited actively into the programs.

For staff, a positive aspect of the program is that some administrators, who often just don't get the chance, have an opportunity to work directly with children. Even though it is a time-consuming activity, the reward of doing what one was trained to do and finding great satisfaction in this are important staff development factors. Cooperation and satisfaction of administration, staff, and community are reinforced and make an impact in other program areas.

The Kaleidoscope program shows that a community can be brought to an increased understanding, appreciation and enjoyment of the services and programs of a public library through media. It is the spontaneity of the Sunday Kaleidoscope, a spontaneity that results only from the most careful kind of planning and preparation, that provides the focus and impact of this program.

Sunday can be a great day! Especially if you are a child and you find yourselves in Indianapolis.

Program Objectives
1. To provide an enrichment program for school age children in an urban area.
2. To encourage family use of a central library facility.
3. To increase use of an important public facility on a day (Sunday) when it is not traditionally available.
4. To involve library administrative staff in program implementation and direct contact with children.
5. To stimulate children's enjoyment and learning, by using a variety of media.

Some Suggestions
1. Increase use of video tape and cable TV access to extend program.
2. Extend the programs to include other age groups: pre-school, and senior citizen groups are good possibilities.
3. Develop greater community participation through more use of individual performers and other volunteers.
4. Move programs to other branches or locations in an effort to outreach into more areas.
5. Increase inner-city participation through use of public transport or volunteer transport service.

TOPEKA WEST HIGH SCHOOL
Topeka, Kansas

Staff:
- Professional: 2
- Support: 3
- Volunteer: 20 parents
- 54 students

Budget (1975-1976)
- Print: $ 6,000
- Nonprint: 6,000
- ESEA Title III Demonstration Grant: 19,000
- Federal Career Education Grant: 8,000
- Mini-Grant Bicentennial: 2,500

Target Population: 1,500 children, ages 15-18

An aggressive search for nonlocal funding and imaginative use of these funds is usually a good indicator of commitment and competence. The Topeka West High School Media Program has demonstrated this ability to search out, find, and use money wisely. However, this is only one of several successful dimensions of this media program. A visitor remarked that no matter how many times one returns here, new programs and projects are always going on. Over half of the student body of Topeka West High School use the resources of the media program each day and uncounted others feel its impact within classrooms. Teacher and student involvement in the media program is extraordinary; this is matched by a high level of parent volunteer support as well.

Adjectives like warm, alive, appealing, and attractive come quickly and appropriately to mind when describing the program and the facility which houses it. To this add a staff that declares that "caring about kids" is the most important program goal—easy to say, but here, the staff means it! Their enthusiasm translates to an unusual commitment to provide the materials and services that are the heart of an excellent media program.

An excellent media program means more than keeping abreast of curriculum change, or knowing the most recent technological innovations. It means that the professional media staff must constantly read about, listen to, and look and search for information of interest and value to young people. How young people think and feel about life and living must be a primary focus to determine media program goals. This interest in young people and their needs is like the rudder for a ship, and without it materials, equipment, and personnel are peripheral. Like an ecologically balanced environment, a media program environment must also be carefully balanced. It must be capable of nurturing good human growth in learning and thinking and finding out.

Housed in a separate building, in a campus-like setting, the Topeka West High School Media Center gives easy access from three adjacent classroom buildings. A ground level floor contains a reading area, career education center, preview room, and a reference-classroom area. A small conference room, production center, processing room, and office are also lodged on this level. The lower provides an additional classroom and periodical storage area. Facility alone cannot implement program which is our concern but it does influence it!

A career education program operates from the media center; its purpose is more than to provide information on work or career choices, even though materials and information about these are available and used heavily. Here the media program involves guidance counselors directly with the program, for each of the five counselors spends one full day in the media center each week. They are used as a human resource, providing information, suggestions, and help for young people trying to make important decisions about their lives. Counselors report that this arrangement allows them to see and talk with more students than if they remained in their offices. And they can work directly with students to make the best possible use of the career education materials.

A priority for the professional staff is to work in the media center classroom or other teaching areas, for this is a staff whose members think of themselves as teaching professionals. Their teaching activities range from the standard reference units for student users, such as introduction to the media center, to actually teaching consumer education or Canadian history. The media center staff does not observe or react passively in a "service only" role; it assumes an important teaching responsibility within the school.

The many parent volunteers have a training course and are then supervised by other volunteers. Like all volunteers, they fill in wherever they are needed most. Often, they work with students to schedule and deliver equipment and media materials to classrooms. Volunteers, though, do have a special responsibility for maintaining a community resource file. This releases them from some of the drudge work of running the media center and increases their feeling of program participation. Their many community contacts offer an excellent opportunity to put together an important media program component. Seminars using local residents as resources are incorporated into the program. The active volunteer role supports the belief that it is possible to involve community volunteers in high school programs, providing they are given some important and satisfying jobs to perform.

While they work directly with students as teachers, the media staff also performs a teaching function with professional staff. Traditional are in-service workshops showing teachers how to use equipment and materials or how to produce films and videotapes. Not so traditional are small group instructional programs. Here, teachers work with resources and decide, with the media specialists, how to get the most instructional impact from the media collection.

Phenomenal is the appropriate word to describe the outreach capacity of the media program. Projects now on-going involve students with the Kansas Historical Society, the Topeka Public Library, special libraries, community business and civic clubs, youth centers, the State Department of Education, and a state college. Resources for learning are found far beyond the walls of the media center or the school and incorporated within the program.

The Bicentennial provided one specific program example in the development of an oral history project. To relate media programs to specific historic events provides an outstanding opportunity, and an oral history program is most satisfactory. Students can record interviews with important local personalities, the reminiscences of senior citizens, or conversations with political leaders. This reinforces the use of an entire community as a resource, allows students to participate in the making of history, and makes them producers of material for the media center.

An example of the determination of this media program's leadership to involve students in productive and useful school-wide programs is the publication *Passport*. A collection of book reviews written and published by students of contemporary literature, *Passport* serves many purposes. It allows students to express themselves about the kinds of books they are reading and what they think of them. And they do express themselves. A recent issue of *Passport* contained reviews ranging from *Sex Isn't that Simple* to *Duey's Tale*. Not all reviews are of high literary quality, but they are honest and useful to other students. *Passport* is big, well over 100 pages, and a bestseller too; for one recent issue sold over 3,400 copies.

Another important part of the media program involves its close relationship with participants in student teaching programs of nearby colleges. Future media specialists and future teachers work into the media program. Workshops are conducted in the media center and they add to an understanding of how media programs should be used. The increased teacher awareness that results from these programs is both valuable and long lasting. If the habit of using media program resources is made part of a teacher's training from the earliest moment, significant steps ahead have been taken.

The Topeka West media program changes and renews itself constantly. It is a natural process for the program to extend itself into new and different instructional areas. Remaining constant, however, is the central purpose of the program; to teach young adults how best to develop their own uniqueness and the best ways to fulfill their roles in life.

Program Objectives
1. To integrate a career education program, using materials and counselors into a media center program.
2. To provide through the publication, *Passport*, an opportunity for students to review books that interest them.
3. To involve teachers directly in the selection of media materials.
4. To incorporate the human resources of the community into the media program.
5. To reinforce the role of media specialist as teacher through cooperative program planning.

Some Suggestions
1. Increase local support for program to lessen dependence on federal and gift money.
2. Add additional professional to strengthen program teaching capacity.
3. Consider including some creative writing sections in *Passport*.
4. Involve students more specifically in evaluation and selection of nonprint materials for the program.

NEW ORLEANS PUBLIC LIBRARY
New Orleans, Louisiana

Staff
Professional: 1 (served as director)
Support: 0

Budget
Not applicable

"Your Child and Books," a seminar program sponsored by the New Orleans Public Library had a brief, relatively uneventful life but it contained several important concepts and activities recommending its consideration by libraries as they explore alternative methods to increase outreach, children's reading and adult participation programming.

While the special program focus was children and reading, the method chosen by the library to reach the child was through the parent. This kind of planning reinforces a concern of this book; namely, that programs that increase the capability of the parent as teacher should receive high priority in library program planning. A parent, carefully attuned and sensitized to the learning needs and expectations of a child can be expected to make significant and lasting contributions to developing good habits and attitudes about how to learn. Parents will use their increased knowledge about and expectations for learning by their children to expand the entire home learning environment.

All programs must rely upon the ability of professional and support staff to fulfill established program goals. An insufficient staff committed to a multitude of programs involving children with reading and increased use of library services will realize only frustration and futility with its inability to *deliver* programs that satisfy expectations. How then to overcome the shortages, common to nearly all public libraries, of enough professional and support staff?

Libraries developing parent-centered programs should consider that these programs offer the potential to maximize professional staff contributions, through more energetic, determined attempts to involve parents directly in library programs. "Involvement" means the parent assumes the dimension of becoming a learner, passing on improved attitudes, understandings, and expectations to children. Parenting—if you will! How to do this, and do it well is becoming an important program element for public libraries. Programs that upgrade the ability of the parent to understand and teach the basic reading skills are especially important. This extension then of a library professional and support staff that is always limited in its capacity to stretch resources (human and material) is a wise accommodation to reality.

With this in mind, the New Orleans Public Library developed its seminar program for parents. As with many other programs described in this book, its intent was not a directly child-centered program. Its focus was the parent who would learn how to become more knowledgeable about and helpful to developing reading activities.

The programs aimed at practical, specific information that would help parents become more effective home teachers. Concepts and methods relating to reading development were emphasized; specific activities and suggestions were given to help parents be more effectively involved with their childrens' reading.

For maximum community involvement each program was repeated twice. They were built around the following topics: (1) Growth, Development and Language acquisition; (2) The Acquisition of Literacy; (3) Mind alive: Books for the youngest; (4) World alive: Books for the upper elementary reader; (5) The Sounds of Childhood; (6) Children's Books and Minorities: Introduction; (7) Non-sexist Books; (8) Books about blacks; (9) Information Books.

A further special intent of the seminars was to provide outreach into the black community. It was planned that from the initial eight-week program experience would come other spin-off programs to explore other relevant and useful community-related topics.

Of particular interest was the decision to involve experts in children's literature, child development, and reading from various colleges and universities and community agencies and organizations in the New Orleans area. The effort to involve universities and schools in cooperative programs with the public library is sensible and imaginative. All have much to gain from the experience of working together to present worthwhile community outreach programs. Several staff members from the library participated as well, either introducing the speaker or actually presenting a program.

Another innovative technique used in the seminar was video taping of the sessions. It was expected that the video tapes could be reused several times and in many locations to extend the impact of the programs by reaching a greater audience. Then too, the video tapes would be used in staff development. Librarians who had not been involved specifically in preparing or presenting the seminars would still be able to learn from them by using the video tapes.

The easy portability of the video taping format; the convenience with which tapes may be stored and reused; and the unique capacity of the video tape to replicate exactly an excellent instructional lesson recommends its use to all libraries. As video tape machines become easier to operate and move about, their use to extend library programs should grow. Particularly in the area of staff development, video tape programs present extraordinary opportunities for libraries to upgrade their staff capabilities.

Everything possible was done to maximize program participation. Baby-sitting services were offered and sessions were scheduled during the day. Further, elementary schools were notified of the programs and requested to lend their endorsement and support. They did this willingly, and a newsletter prepared by the Superintendent of Schools supported and publicized the program.

Program locations for the sessions were moved about so that seminar repeats were always scheduled for different branches, guaranteeing wide geographic access and public contact. The use of the video tape maximized program accessibility further since the tapes could be shown in still more locations.

Careful attention to details, arrangements, program topics, speakers, and site locations was evident. Purpose, planning, and follow-through were impeccable, representing the highest level of effort for community outreach programs. Certainly, if these preparations were the measurements by which the programs are to be evaluated, this program was a success. Yet, as success is measured in program continuation, by degree of community participation or the merging of program goals with those of other programs, it did not achieve its purpose.

Attention to specific "how to" questions about reading and children were reflected in the seminar topics. The information books seminar, for example, included a discussion of encyclopedias and how to choose an appropriate one. Other seminars dealt with specific books, their selection, and their use with children, and these seminars also had a direct and timely relevance for parents concerned about their child's reading and intellectual development.

A problem may have been that the seminar offerings were too advanced for the intended audience. And participation was another problem, for the reason that most of its intended audience had to work and could find no time to attend the seminars. While the use of video tapes can maximize and make more flexible the program potential, they too must work around certain "realities" of contemporary city life. One reality is that most people do not willingly venture forth at night. Some alternatives to cope with this are possible. Among these might be showing the tapes, or holding some seminars in community action or local social centers in late afternoon hours. To integrate these programs into strong ongoing community programs would ensure greater visibility, exposure and perhaps success.

The New Orleans Library makes strenuous efforts to increase its program impact for children by using a wide variety of media and participatory programs. The idea and concept of the "Your Child and Books" seminar for parents remains a valid idea for library programming and is an approach to library service for children, through parents, that represents a significant break-through. It is a thoughtful combination of human and technological resources to provide a useful and badly needed service while demonstrating the potential for innovative programming to be considered carefully by other libraries.

Program Objectives
1. To improve parent understanding and attitudes about reading development for their children.
2. To develop a community outreach program to involve parents in library programs.
3. To use video tape format to extend programs for community use.
4. To develop library program of community service by using professional staff members of local colleges and universities.
5. To provide a program to increase general parent understandings of childhood needs and expectations.

Some Suggestions
1. Vary site locations to improve attendance.
2. Attempt to offer some programs as part of actual school program offerings for parents.
3. Place highest emphasis on creating practical "How-to-do" or on accomplishing specific reading activities with children.
4. Use tapes more extensively for staff development activities.
5. Relate reading seminars to other child-care or rearing activities, i.e., preventive health or nutrition.
6. Train a core group of neighborhood mothers to create interest, bring friends to the sessions, and offer follow-up assistance.

WATERVILLE HIGH SCHOOL
Waterville, Maine

Staff
Professional: 3
Support: 5

Budget (1975-1976)
Print and nonprint: $11,000

Target Population: 1,300 students, ages 12-18

For the last decade many media professionals have heard that there is something big going on in Waterville, Maine. Some heard about a super facility crammed with a huge array of media and equipment, the result of a whopping ESEA (Title III) grant. Some heard about the programs, programs that were making a big instructional impact because of the excellent use of these materials. Some heard about the staff of eight—three professionals and five support—to serve 1,300 children and 75 teachers. Waterville was doing then what *Media Programs: District and School* would recommend to others nearly a decade later.

From the start, the media program got involved with helping children want to learn and helping teachers want to improve their professional abilities. School media specialists like to talk about media and instruction and information programs; at Waterville they like to just do it, and without the jargon, please!

The American Association of School Librarians' *School Library Manpower Project, American Libraries; The Maine Teacher,* the *National Association of Secondary School Principals Bulletin,* and *School Media Quarterly* have all recognized the excellence of the instructional media program at Waterville and told something about it. It's a bit like those occasional Derbys where there is such a superior horse in the race that he easily distances the field. It's exciting, but it takes the edge off to be too good all the time. If we were just judging winners, the Waterville entry could have retired to a last hurrah, long ago.

Not so. Excitement, motion, improvement, and new growth continue to pervade this media program, and success represents only the challenge to reach out and do still more. The most outreach-conscious public library media program would applaud a school program that makes its materials available to community groups and private schools, that works closely with adult education programs, and that relates directly to the local communications media. Waterville High School also works at seeing to it that hospital patients have access to the resources of the school media center, and provides phonographs and records and a film program for summer playground programs and other community-oriented outreach programs.

The concept of community outreach is almost nonexistent in the planning and management of most school media programs. The materials and personnel of the school media program serve what amounts to a narrow, exclusive, and self-contained clientele. Some school programs like Waterville's are showing that outreach and concern with the quality of community life are a legitimate concern of school media programs, and, that school media programs can support, without supplanting, other public information programs. This is stated as goal number one of the *Waterville High School Media Center Philosophy and Goals*. "To provide equal access to the resources of the media center for all members of this school community, and, whenever practical, to other schools and the community at large."

A renovation and reallocation of space in one wing of the high school in 1966 turned an entire wing into a media center and got this program started. Money from an ESEA Title III Grant, phased over three years financed the project. Approximate grant amounts were: first year grant, $100,000; second year, $60,000; the third year, $50,000. The purpose: "To establish a model media program for Maine." Beginning in the same year, and continuing for a total of three years, an amount of $25,000 from ESEA Title II monies was used to purchase print and nonprint materials for the program. In itself, this was not necessarily a unique project, for in the lush days of the sixties lots of federal money, under a wide array of titles, was available and used by many schools. At Waterville, though, the money got used the right way. One proof is that the community through its own local taxes now supports this program begun with federal money. Of course, the level of funding is not that of the initial program, but an acquisition budget of about $11,000 a year (excluding supplies and equipment) is capable of adding to and extending the large materials base. Most important, the personnel to staff the program are all still there, again paid for with the local tax dollar. In these times, that is success.

The 8,000 square feet of facilities available are important to the program at Waterville. A circulation room, a reference room (used by classes and for quiet study), a video viewing room, a preview room, a dark room, a graphics room, office, and workrooms provide the variety and flexibility of space necessary to sustain the potent kinds of instructional media program goals established here.

The renovation of space to establish proper school media program facilities should be considered carefully, for in this period of declining school enrollments increasing amounts of space are going to become available for program use. Here is a target of opportunity for school media programs! Here too, the Waterville Program was well in advance of events, for it acted upon the concept of renovation of existing space to create adequate quarters for exemplary program.

An outstanding component of the media program was recognized and expressed by a visitor to the school who said, "I have not seen a media program which is involved to the same degree in education as defined as a lifetime pursuit." This book returns again and again to this theme, that education and learning cannot—must not—be considered the exclusive province of the schools, the public library, or special libraries. Free access to information wherever and whenever it is needed is neither a horizontal or vertical monopoly. Service, from the earliest months of life until its end, must be the preoccupation of all information programs. The Waterville school media program understands and accepts this mandate.

For students this means a media program that is preoccupied with its role as a specific educational force within the school. This educational role, in a program such as that at Waterville, is comprehensive and leaves little to chance. It is possible, for instance, for a student attending the high school to receive academic credit through instructional sequences prepared by the media center program and supervised by its staff. Such programs are both remedial and enrichment in nature and reinforce the instructional role of media. Other courses tie their academic course credit structure into the media program. For example, students may receive credit in an English course for planned reading, completed during the summer. The media staff and the teachers plan and administer this program together, thus reinforcing a cooperative and shared approach to teaching.

Individualized instruction modules, so important in helping each child seek and find a level of proper attainment, are an integral feature of the Waterville media program. Students receive individual instruction in an impressive range of skill-related production activities. These include photography, recording, and graphics. The potential of student as teacher is recognized too, a fine example being a senior student who is a member of the team that teaches photography.

The program recognizes that the education of teachers and teachers-in-the-making is a responsibility too important to be left exclusively in the hands of the teacher preparation institution. Student teachers, preparing at such nearby places as Colby College and the University of Maine at Farmington, may receive academic credit for a course given at the high school media center. This course includes such elements as the preview and evaluation of instructional materials and the development of learning packages that relate to instructional design. The implications of media programs being directly and specifically involved in the process which prepares the future classroom teacher are profound. This idea of preparing a teacher to be a wise selector of media with an increased perception of how best to apply media to learning is light years ahead of what exists, generally, anywhere else.

This dedication to reaching out, to involving and to change appears again and again in the Waterville media program. A century of tomorrows would not be enough to think upon the programmatic, personal, and persistent attempts to bring school administrators and media specialists together to plan for the kind of instructional leadership that is built into a program like this. Generally these attempts have failed and conditions remain pretty much as they have always been. Librarians, well, they stamp books, supervise the study hall overflow, and collect fines on the overdues!

The Waterville experience provided the guiding force for the New England regional planning efforts that brought media professionals and principals together to develop the most effective ways the two groups could work together to promote the kinds of educational changes both wanted. It is this continuous, unceasing effort to move into areas beyond a building, a locality, or even a state that makes the leadership of a media program like Waterville essential. Some will dare, some will do, and the truly exemplary program will always make an impact beyond its narrow geographic boundaries without undermining its credibility at home.

Constant attention to local needs, while asserting a broadly based leadership role, is built into this media program. A media center open from 7:30 A.M. to 10:15 P.M., Monday through Thursday and from 7:30 A.M. to 6:30 P.M. on Friday is a clear example of commitment. Always evident, too, is the attempt to tie resources and personnel into the planning and program of others. For instance, the extended evening hours are made possible through a tie-in to a vocational technical institute and an adult education program. Everyone gets service and satisfaction.

The enriched back-up of instructional media available as a community resource serves to extend the program in a multitude of ways; 16mm and Super 8 films, audio and video tapes, games, models, framed prints, posters, filmstrips, and kits are used in many excellent ways to make a community impact.

The second paragraph of the *Waterville High School Media Center Philosophy and Goals* states that, "All students should learn how to learn, and libraries and media center should be a part of the *continuing education* of an individual's entire life."

The precision of this when applied, via the media program format at Waterville High School, is clearly evident throughout the school.

Access to materials and resources of information and learning by everyone; integrating media into the curriculum; the provision of reading, viewing and listening guidance for the community; the provision of instruction in the best use of materials and equipment; the provision of a specialized staff concerned with and sympathetic to the needs of the learner and the teacher; the concern with the promotion of literacy in all the media; and the cooperative planning for learning activities using media resources are but some of the priorities of the Waterville media program. Here, the future has been seen, accepted, and made one with the present.

Program Objectives
1. To provide easy and equal access to all materials and resources of a media program by a school community, a local community, and a regional community.
2. To provide, through a media program, a wide variety of learning possibilities to suit individual and group needs.
3. To promote "mediacy as literacy" helping persons use with success media in differing formats.
4. To demonstrate the large infusions of federal project monies may be grafted successfully into local programs and continued after the cessation of this funding.
5. To integrate a media program directly into an instructional program.

Some Suggestions
1. Enlarge area for local production of graphic materials so that this program may be made available to more persons.
2. Increase local funding for materials so that both print and nonprint materials collection may be kept up to date.

3. Extend program of direct teaching of student teachers in training to enlarge impact of this program.
4. Extend summer activities beyond the realm of recreation to more specific instructional ones.
5. Extend career opportunity program that helps train media aides to work in other schools.

MIDDLETOWN HIGH SCHOOL
Middletown, Maryland

Staff
Professional: 2
Support: 2

Budget
State Funded: $2,500

Target Population: 1,200 children, ages 12-18

How does the consumer, confronted by the perplexing array of forces that shape decisions about buying, selling, or saving find reliable information to make good choices? We know that useful consumer education is a process of learning to see alternatives and to make right choices; rationality, foreknowledge of consequences, persuasion techniques, and other factors enter into this process too.

An important concept of this book is that while the media can manipulate or control in sinister ways, they contain equally the potential to inform and alert persons about how to make good decisions. If the media can hoodwink the consumer, they may serve equally well to inform and educate him. Clarification of alternatives, rather than imposition of choices, is the heart of sound consumer education programs and the media are critical to this process.

Attitudes and aspirations have a great deal to do with how decisions are made and advertising, that reflector and creator of the society's wish fulfillment, is probably the most important factor to understand. Advertising has created such terms and realities as "planned obsolescence," "bad preferences," and "throw-away goods"; each of these implies mass manipulation and persuasion by forces more sophisticated than the average consumer.

Terms that formerly defined our economic system—"free market," "free enterprise," and "capitalism"—have a much reduced validity as we become increasingly a society of consumption rather than production. This is reflected too in our transition from a work-ethic oriented culture, rooted firmly in agriculture and industrial production, to a services-received culture, dominated by automation and consumption of goods.

With these thoughts in mind, in 1974 the Maryland State Department of Education prepared a report titled "A Plan to Integrate Consumer Concepts into the Public Schools of Maryland." The proposal was to develop, over a five-year period, an action plan for consumer education for school children in Maryland. The plan proposed to instruct young people about good consumer education with an interdisciplinary approach, integrating it into existing curricula of the public schools. A strong media component would be required to accomplish this purpose.

One of the media formats chosen was television. A number of formats were possible, but the video cassette had the greatest teaching potential because of the ease with which it could be used by students and teachers, the high quality of production that it could insure, and its portability.

Program focus—the enlightened consumer! Program objectives: (1) to improve the consumer's ability to evaluate, purchase and use goods and services; (2) to help the consumer develop sound decision-making processes based on his values and goals; (3) to help the consumer become aware of and use reliable sources of consumer education; and (4) to help consumers understand their rights and responsibilities.

A series title, "Consumer Survival Kit," was selected and eleven program-theme cassettes were developed around this title. These included: (1) Advertising; (2) Auto Repair; (3) Clothing; (4) Cosmetics; (5) Credit; (6) Family Budgeting; (7) Food Buying; (8) Mail Order; (9) Sales; (10) New Cars and Used Cars; and (11) Over-the-Counter Drug Sales.

High production quality was assured, since the series was produced professionally by the Maryland Center for Public Broadcasting, then distributed in cooperation with the Maryland State Department of Education's Division of Vocational-Technical Education and Instructional Television. The process of planning this program as a cooperative effort at this level helped provide educational integrity and excellence to the Consumer Survival Kit. And when state education departments and local education agencies jointly plan and implement programs, there is increased probability that the learning of children will be benefitted directly.

Education of the teacher was crucial to proper program implementation, for unknowing teachers are unlikely to produce informed consumers. The resources to accomplish this staff development—materials and instructors—are not available to most school systems. Therefore, the information, directions, goals, and objectives for the program must be made as failure proof as possible. Accordingly, the Consumer Survival Kit contains, in addition to the cassette telelessons, a packet containing follow-up reprints of pertinent magazine articles, a program summary, bibliography, and a teacher supplement.

The teacher program supplement provides the directions. First, an overview, intended for use as a general discussion guide for the specific topic. The overview for the advertising sequence, for example, explains how to differentiate between the tricks of the trade and the truth. Lesson objectives call for recognition of common advertising techniques, evaluation of the accuracy of advertisements, and identification of regulations governing advertisements.

Second, a synopsis gives the teacher a brief summary of program content. A guide called "Previewing of Activities" contains questions designed to provoke class discussion. In the "New Car" lesson, for example, a discussion statement says that "New Car warranties guarantee the consumer a vehicle that will perform normal automotive service." Such statements are designed to get students involved in a discussion about the telelesson which follows.

Third, a teacher guide provides a series of subject-oriented activities to carry over the lesson into separate but related subject fields. The Over-the-Counter Drugs guide suggests that an English class might examine information given on an aspirin bottle, then rewrite the information in the clearest possible terms. An industrial arts class might explore the kinds of the over-the-counter drugs that affect reflexes. This activity would help determine if and when these drugs should be taken if driving or operating dangerous equipment. For a science class there are suggestions about experiments to help determine the effectiveness of antiseptics.

The purpose of these activities is to weave the concepts of good consumer education into the fabric of on-going courses providing additional dimension and strength to the entire program. It is good sense to integrate the teaching of wise consumerism into on-going programs, for informed consumer decisions are rarely made in a vacuum. They involve many interrelated factors.

A fourth component of the teacher supplement contains suggestions for general class activities. For instance, a general activity suggested for the Used Car Lesson suggests that the class examine and discuss used car warranties. Fifth, a bibliography list attached to the Supplement is provided. Selected from the holdings of a large public library and solely a book listing, it seems curiously irrelevant to this program which is otherwise so skillfully mounted.

The Middletown High School Media Center houses the Consumer Survival Kit program. Money to fund the consumer education program came from a special federal grant, channeled through the state agency. This money provided the eleven professionally prepared telelessons, two video tape players, and a television monitor. The major component contribution for the media center is the staff time required to operate and supervise the program.

The video tapes are arranged alphabetically in cabinets easily accessible for students and teachers. Individual students use the tapes in the media center, and they are requested to fill out an evaluation form after using a tape. Questions about grade level, purpose for using the program, and usefulness or applicability are asked. This provides an unsophisticated but useful evaluation.

A teacher survey-evaluation asks the number of students who saw the telelesson and how the teacher used the supplement materials. Other questions probe the usefulness of the teacher manual and the informational value and instructional relevance of the program.

Exemplary program elements displayed include: the integration of a media program into the existing curriculum and instructional program; use of video format to instruction children and teachers in the art and skill of consumer survivalship; the excellent cooperation between state and local education agencies. The program is easily adaptable into any institution providing the video capacity and equipment are available. The commitment of resources and personnel for staff development and instruction would have to be considered as well.

Program Objectives
1. To use a video format to present eleven separate consumer education programs designed to help individuals become informed, conscientious, and skillful buyers of goods and services.
2. To use a media format to integrate a consumer education program into the on-going school curriculum.
3. To plan, implement, and evaluate interdisciplinary programs for consumer education.
4. To coordinate a consumer information program using federal funding through a State Department of Education to a local district.
5. To provide staff development programs in teaching consumer concepts for teachers using this media program.

Some Suggestions
1. Produce programs in other formats for greater use possibility. Consider especially 16mm film.
2. Consider targeting programs, in revised format to an earlier grade level, possibly intermediate grades.
3. Develop more community awareness of the program for better carry-over into homes.
4. Provide general activities that give more direct contact between students and the business practices they are studying.
5. Enlarge program offerings to such areas as installment buying, financing education, and taxation.

FITCHBURG YOUTH LIBRARY
Fitchburg, Massachusetts

Staff
Professional: 2
Support: 4

Budget (1975-1976)
Equipment: $15,000
Materials: 7,000
(LSCA Grant)

Target Population: 12-15 children at one time. Over 250 children have been involved, ages 7-12

In this age of anxiety and haste it is reassuring to discover that something of proven excellence can be started, maintained, and even expanded for a period of twenty-five years. In 1950 the Fitchburg Youth Library was "built with the pennies of the children of Fitchburg." Of course, even before these times of double digit inflation, it took more than the pennies of children to build a library, but certainly it was this kind of inspiration and motivation, coupled with a tremendous effort by children themselves which brought the project to fruition. That same attitude, spirit, and determination continues to infuse the Fitchburg youth program with a contagious dynamism.

A rich and exciting array of media are available at Fitchburg. Knitting and crocheting lessons take place in the learning center; a bicentennial patchwork quilt, the patches illustrated and sewn together by the children, is displayed; a huge puppet stage; a patio for parties and outdoor story hours; framed paintings for loan; bins of records for browsing and use; and a collection of manipulatives of various shapes and sizes are but some of the immediate reminders that this is a program for fun *and* learning.

The audiovisual licensing program, initiated in 1973, is an attempt to deal with a built-in inhibition toward use for many media programs: lack of the skills and attitudes necessary to operate and maintain properly the equipment necessary to the program. There is a vague, and quite incorrect, notion around that today's children are endowed with an innate ability to know how to operate any piece of equipment they find. The corollary, equally wrong, is that most adults over thirty are reduced to simple helplessness when faced with such tasks as threading a video tape player or a 16mm projector. The hardware and the software do go together; obvious, yes, but often overlooked in planning effective media programs.

As with all effective programs, the AV licensing program is not so much a separate entity but is an integral part of an entire program of media services for children. The program deals with two specific goals: (1) to encourage children to explore new types of learning materials; and (2) to instruct children in the proper use, care, and maintenance of equipment.

Facilities are important to a program such as the AV licensing. They need not be elaborate or even specifically designed for the purpose of using listening or viewing equipment, but the better the facility and its resources the better will be the quality of the program. At Fitchburg, a number of carrels with the proper electrical outlets are available to serve the machines used in the program. Carrels, by the way, are not essential, for any table or flat surface will do; it's access to electric power that is essential.

The AV licensing program usually is scheduled for an early evening or a Saturday morning. A typical training session may involve about ten children. These children must be grade three and up, since they must be able to read and follow simple directions for the operation of equipment. The end product of the training is for the child to pass a test in the running of some ten pieces of media equipment, whereupon he becomes licensed to use the equipment in the library learning center, or with parental permission, to borrow it (usually on an overnight basis) for home or school use.

The kinds of equipment used in the licensing program include: the opaque projector, the record player, a Kodak Carousel projector, the filmstrip projector, the 8mm projector, the cassette player recorder, and other small and portable equipment. Because of its size and the fact that it is used mostly for adult and regional library programs, the 16mm projector is not included.

An instruction packet provides easy, step-by-step directions for the child to master equipment operation. The instructions for the cassette player provide some fourteen separate steps to the completion of the licensing process. One convenient way of providing greater assistance to children as they master operation of the equipment is to use color coding on various buttons, switches, or plugs. This procedure makes for easier references and clearer directions. On some pieces of equipment when the buttons are large enough, the library uses numbers, but a colored dot system seems most usable. Since the dots tend to fall off, they can be protected with a clear nail polish.

The training to operate any piece of equipment consists of understanding the procedure step-by-step, and then practice in operation. As the licensing process is completed for each piece of equipment a notch is punched beside its name on the license.

This license contains the name and address of each child and it is the responsibility of the child to care for his license. It may be left at the library or kept by the child. Either way, when the child wants to borrow a piece of equipment for home use, the license is presented at the circulation desk and the equipment is given out. If a child loses a license, every test must be retaken. As with any licensing system, there is an expiration date and the license to operate the equipment must be renewed, through retesting, when the expiration date arrives.

Parents are involved in the program. First, they must give permission for participation in the program. Some bring their children and remain during the instruction period, others drop in before or after a session to monitor progress. Since equipment is usually more costly than most print or nonprint items available in the library, the parents must assume some special responsibility in the form of a letter. The letter by which parents grant their consent is short and to the point. It states that before anyone borrows equipment from the Fitchburg Learning Center, the staff will test the borrower's ability to operate the equipment and the license issued is the check on this.

Since the start of the program some 300 licenses have been issued, backed with about 150 permission letters from parents. The initial term of the license is for three years which means that a renewal process will soon have to be instituted.

It appears that the public library AV licensing program has served as a stimulant for better school media programs. This is not a usual situation and doubtless contains food for thought about the value of simple, grass roots level networking or information access programs. Regional groups of public library and school media programs could and should cooperate in a manner that permits the assets of one program to be used wisely by the other. This cooperation means looking at the resources available in each domain, talking about the possibility of sharing them, and providing the opportunities whereby children may have the easiest possible access to these resources.

Adults, too, may have access to and borrow freely the equipment available at the learning center. Though adults don't have to have a license, they receive careful instructions when they borrow the equipment.

The production of materials is not tied directly to the AV licensing program. The community, (children and adults) is encouraged to use equipment in a number of ways. The Fitchburg Learning Center lends 35mm cameras and some photography workshops have been held. The production center has such equipment as a spirit duplicator, a Thermofax machine, a copy stand, a Kodak Visual Maker, and a dry mount and laminating press. These are, of course, pretty standard items of equipment, but not very many public libraries make them available for use by patrons. Their use is definitely stimulated by the AV licensing program. Their availability reflects the consistent determination of the staff to create an environment in which nonprint materials and equipment are as extensively available and used as possible. Most of this equipment was made available through an LSCA grant from the Massachusetts Bureau of Library Extension.

This production component of the program, matched with the AV licensing program, recognizes the public's need to obtain information and to learn from a variety of media. The public library at Fitchburg knows that to serve the total learning needs of its community it must provide a range of new learning materials. Related to this is the library's recognition of the need to provide instruction and guidance in how to use these materials in productive ways.

The staff time devoted to overseeing the AV licensing operation is minimal once the program is developed and put into operation. Only two staff members are involved at any one time, but any of the staff can help out if necessary. Since the time of a licensing workshop is scheduled in advance, the one or two staff persons working that session will always be well prepared. If more children appear than can be handled effectively in one session, they schedule a second session.

One success factor of the program is the involvement of the chilren in planning the program. Children actually wrote the first directions for the step-by-step mastering of operation of the equipment. They were thrilled when their efforts proved acceptable and were prepared in multiple copies to help instruct other children. It is noteworthy, too, that the written directions often provide a stimulus rather than a handicap to the poorer reader. Why? It seems that often the poorer reader will turn to a companion for help in puzzling it out. The reward factor for mastering operation of a piece of equipment with its related prestige and status attainment are important to the child. Since, in the end, the only way to get there successfully is via the step-by-step follow-the-directions route, it gets done. Adults are always available to help decipher directions, but they don't just "do for" children. They encourage and direct and assist, but they expect the children to seek, find, and accomplish on their own.

The AV licensing program has also succeeded in bringing into a library program youngsters not reached before. These are youngsters who are attracted by and able to use nonprint materials, fascinated by the equipment and its use.

There are other good results. The close involvement of children in the program design; the publicity that springs from this enthusiastic group of children telling others about the programs of the library; the carry over to adults of good equipment usage (written instructions accompany every piece of equipment loaned); the application of reading skills to following directions to reach desired results; and the intrinsic value of a program where every child succeeds.

Though expediency created the AV licensing program, it has developed a true set of values and successes on its own. These values support a broader program aim of service to a total community in the nonprint area and lead the way toward a greater community awareness of the potential of media.

Program Objectives
1. To encourage children to master the operation of various items of AV equipment.
2. To streamline instruction in use of equipment so that staff time may be saved.
3. To teach children the importance of reading, following directions carefully, and respect for the property of others.
4. To increase community understanding of the importance of nonprint media.
5. To involve children who are not readers or have not been previous users in library programs.

Some Suggestions
1. Expand workshops to include operation of video tape recorder, 35mm and 8mm camera, and other production equipment.
2. Specifically include adults, particularly senior citizens, in a similar program so they will be stimulated to borrow equipment and use nonprint media.
3. Allow outstanding children to work with less able children within the program.
4. Establish workshops or in-service opportunities for teachers in public schools to do the same step-by-step operation procedure.

5. Stimulate production of media by children to go with the equipment being mastered. This would include, e.g., film, slides, and tapes. The two activities could be mutually reinforcing.

NEW BEDFORD HIGH SCHOOL
New Bedford, Massachusetts

Staff
Professional: 3
 Media coordinator
 Librarian
 TV instructor
 Support: 2
Subject Area
 Specialists: 7

Budget (1975-1976)
Print: $12,000
Nonprint: 12,000

Target Population: 4,000 children, ages 15-18

Early in the school year it's traditional in many schools that the library "bulletin" be sent to the staff. Nearly always, it welcomes everyone back, lists a page or more of new acquisitions, then gets on to the heart of the matter: the rules and regulations governing library use. As a communications link, it's a disaster! And it is a depressingly widespread start-up to the year in many schools.

At New Bedford High School, the teacher orientation bulletins reflect positive service attitudes and sell a refreshingly different program. Some samples: from the Business/Foreign Language Resources Center, the announcement that six new typewriters are available for student use. Available, too, an individualized short-hand belt with tapes, workbooks, and self-testing capability to instruct in shorthand. The Social Studies Resource Center announces a number of rental films on historical topics, ready for use. The English Resource Center urges teachers to preview materials on speed reading, English Literature, and dictionary skills. The Science Resource Center issues a two-page update for the nonprint catalog provided to each teacher so that they may plan better for good use of nonprint media in their teaching. The Math Center bulletin explains an individualized math program that helps students weak in basic mathematics skills. It asks teachers to help recruit students who are able and willing to tutor other students in the math center. A teachers guide to a commercial television show comes from the Social Studies Resource Center. It suggests activities before viewing the show, gives a synopsis of it, and recommends teaching activities that relate to the show. So it goes; cliche expressions—"heart of curriculum," or "hub of school"—used so often to describe imaginary media programs, assume true dimension at this school.

Here, facility is important to program operation. Clearly, the subject centers are the key to the success of the media program. The argument about separate resource centers diluting or weakening school media programs is irrelevant here, for the resource centers are the core of the program and strengthen its educational impact. Physically, imagine a wheel, and the lay-out of the facility is clear. The hub is the media center itself, and four of the five resource centers are the spokes from the hub. Directly above the media center is the Science Resource Center. This unity of program and facility continues into the adjacent television studio and production area.

New Bedford High School is an urban inner-city school. A visitor to it spoke of its "traditional" nature. There is no open campus, no unstructured day for students, and few individualized learning alternatives. There are plenty of study periods scheduled and students must go to them. At New Bedford, this program seems neither limiting or stultifying, for an extraordinarily creative and energetic media program prospers.

What are the reasons? Foremost is the utilization of professional teachers as part of the media program staff. The teachers who direct the resource centers are subject area teachers not, by certification, media specialists. Their job responsibilities demand the competencies of a media specialist. Using media and equipment in a number of ways, they work directly with teachers and students. Their purpose is instructional, for they work with materials and programs as media professionals with subject area teaching specialization. These professionals are assigned full time to the media center. The media coordinator and the librarian work with these subject area specialists to help them develop the skills they lack in media. The librarian, who reports to the media coordinator, is the key person in making policy and establishing media program direction. It is an innovative concept—teacher as media specialist.

The certified media professionals are three; a media coordinator, a librarian, and a television instructor. The total *professional* staff of the program is ten. The certified media specialists by competencies and job expectations are teachers, and the teachers, by competencies and job expectations are media specialists; this is the mix that joins the hub and spokes together into a smoothly turning wheel. Their combined enthusiasm, eagerness, and abilities make for the communication and planning that move the program ahead.

The media program has stated a philosophy defining its purpose within the school. Speaking in terms of the complexities of society and rapid sociological and ideological changes accelerated by advanced technology, the program pledges itself to the goal of developing each student's ability to think and behave rationally in his environment. Media used to rationalize environment is a broad and ephemeral concept. How does the media program seek to implement its goal?

The New Bedford media program states its objectives clearly and is specific in its methods of implementing them. Among these objectives are: (1) to provide a learning environment that meets the needs of students; (2) to serve as a consultant, for teachers and students, in the selection, evaluation, preparation, and use of print and nonprint media and equipment; (3) to work with teachers and administration in designing and programming instructional media for classroom use. There are other objectives, but these provide the framework within which the media program does its job.

There is an impressive involvement of students throughout the program. Nationally, there is a growing trend to involve students in media programs as workers and learners. This kind of program is available at New Bedford High School and students may receive half a unit of credit for work-related programs in the media center. As many as 300 students a year do this.

The heavy flow of students into the resource centers could present management problems. Design helps prevent this, for the centers are small, suited to a maximum of about forty persons and each center has developed its own personality. All are attractive, have comfortable and functional furniture, and provide an atmosphere that is friendly and orderly. Their comfortable intimacy permits informality with special focus on subject area concerns. Each center is loop wired with a multichannel program format to increase its instructional capacity. Nonprint materials are displayed openly for easy access from the desk area. Equipment, also checked out at the desk, is amply available.

An American preoccupation with enshrining educational change in concrete is evident in many school media centers built in the last decade. Too often they represent the sad results of literal interpretations of design standards expressed in square feet. Many have been prettied up with carpets, planters, super graphics, and other attention-getting (or diverting) devices. These mask ineffectively the trouble with many media centers; they are just too big! They are warehouses, perhaps elegant warehouses, but warehouses they are. You cannot put together in large spaces some two or three hundred young persons without inviting management problems! Everyone needs to feel secure, comfortable, and uncrowded in his environment. Security promotes the ability to be self-directed and responsible, the essence of excellence in learning. The New Bedford media center concept has, through design, provided the environmental conditions that invite media program success. They permit the operation of a program that is friendly, concerned, aware of and attentive to the needs of the individual. That some 4,000 students use the facilities and resource of these centers in a six-day cycle, without creating chaos, is all that needs saying.

No media program is ever implemented successfully by a media staff without good teaching strengths or winning personalities. These fundamental components must be supported by a carefully planned program for staff development. One Thursday a month, school time is provided for staff development programs. Some deal with the nuts and bolts of equipment operation, but others concern innovative uses of equipment and media to improve teaching. Using the video tape recorder for self-evaluation is one such program.

Courses in television are offered as part of the media program, and many student media volunteers work in the TV studio. Classrooms are connected to the studio via a closed circuit system. Heavy use of the TV studio is made by teachers to increase the variety and quality of communication experiences for their students.

A visitor to the media program identified some of its success ingredients. They include (1) the talents, contributions, and catalytic force of the media center staff and the subject area specialists working together to provide a total, curriculum integrated media program; and (2) the systematic attention given by the staff development programs director to communicating the media program to staff, students, community, and administration.

So we have effective administration, thorough planning, unique staff utilization patterns, and program/facility unity—all the results of careful attention to and thoughtful analysis of what a media program is. The ability to establish priorities for the media program and operate it in terms of these priorities is clear too. In these ways the New Bedford High School Media Program shows exemplary methods of sound program leadership.

Program Objectives
1. To integrate a media program into the total curriculum of a high school.
2. To assist professional staff in planning and programming the use of media in classrooms with small groups and for individuals.
3. To relate a media program specifically to the needs of students and staff.

4. To use professionals trained in subject areas as part of a media program.
5. To use subject area resource centers to individualize and make more effective a media program.

Some Suggestions
1. Emphasize more heavily student production (other than television) of materials for their own learning needs.
2. Emphasize more teacher production of learning materials specifically useful to their own teaching needs.
3. Involve more departments in the use of the television studio.
4. Offer credit courses for students in effective use of media (reference and research) as well as work credit.
5. Involve some community volunteers in the program, possibly through television component.

A. PHILIP RANDOLPH BRANCH
Jackson County Library
Jackson, Michigan

Staff
Professional: 1
Support: 3
Volunteer: varies

Budget (1975-1976)
LSCA Grant: $15,000
YWCA Trust Grant: 3,600
(for materials and equipment)

Target Population: 318 children, ages 3-14

A visitor to the A. Philip Randolph branch library remarked that if it were in a suburban location there would be little of significance to tell about. The children's program features film shows, storytelling, reading clubs and appropriate holiday celebrations; all standard programming from any good public library children's room. It is not just that the program is good that makes it outstanding, but the uniqueness of its circumstances that provides its exemplary dimensions.

Its most innovative aspect is the concentrated effort it makes to develop close ties to the community it serves. Predominantly black and inner-city, this is a population that traditionally does not use public library services. Today many outreach programs seek to serve socially and culturally isolated minority groups by involving them in library programs. But while many programs publicize the level of community involvement they achieve, too often this is a superficial exercise of telling community advisors about plans and programs the library staff has already decided upon.

From the start, the A. Philip Randolph branch library built public involvement and participation directly into its program. In fact, the program could not have begun without strong local community support. This came initially from the Randolph Institute, a national nonprofit, service agency which works with black communities to develop improvement and self-help projects. Staff members from the Jackson County Public Library System planned carefully with the Randolph Institute staff how best to start up the program.

The Jackson Randolph Center, a community institute, provided a location, utilities, and necessary maintenance. Materials, equipment, and start-up staff came from the county library system. The site selected was formerly home to a black activist group, and was situated hard by the railroad tracks. Initially, the branch site was named Kangaroo Tracks; the Kangaroo being the mascot symbol of the county library and the railroad track location obvious. Later the Board of Trustees of the Jackson County Library Board voted to rename it the A. Philip Randolph Branch, after the membership of the A. Philip Randolph Institute requested this.

Dedicated efforts by some of the library professional staff had much to do with bringing the program to this location. These staff people involved not just the Randolph Institute but the Community Action Agency and the YWCA. The latter, for example, contributed over $3,500 from a trust fund to purchase materials used in the program. This excellent combination of community service agencies and library staff provided clear focus and specific program goals that got it off to a strong start.

The infusion of $15,000 in LSCA Title I funds permitted a significant increase in services and programs. In fact, these funds provided the major part of the 1976 program's operating budget. They were used to pay the salary of a community librarian, for print and nonprint materials, and for some additional furniture and equipment. A concern about the program is its ability to attract necessary local support to continue when LSCA funds terminate. The people involved in the program appear to view this more as a challenge than a threat and accordingly face the future with optimism and high expectations.

Staffing patterns in this kind of outreach program presented unusual challenges and opportunities. The professional in charge of the program has many other duties, for she is the only professional librarian for children and young adult services in the county system. While enthusiasm, commitment, and dedication to see that program goals are met can carry a program far, they cannot replace proper staff. This is reality!

At the Randolph branch this reality brought into the program a library trainee. Called an assistant branch librarian, she supervises the facility, helps children find materials, tell stories, shows films, and does other programs. The assistant branch librarian is aided by an administrative assistant who works for the library about five hours a week and has special responsibility for budget control. The professional's responsibility then is to plan and administer the program; on-site personnel carry it out.

It is no longer extraordinary for public library programs to find their personnel within the community they serve. It is nonetheless a strength of this program to incorporate as staff an individual from the community, who takes pride in the program and enjoys and takes seriously her job responsibility. The assistant branch librarian, a community member, serves as liaison to the A. Philip Randolph Institute and attends their chapter meetings.

For the professional, programming like this requires an ability to cope well with such matters as coordination among sponsoring agencies, recruiting and training volunteers, supervising staff and planning programs. The professional spends about ten hours a week on these matters, and a requirement is good organization and the ability to delegate responsibility with security.

While service to the black community was a main outreach program goal, service to children is its immediate focus. Within the library, colorful carpet squares, record jackets, and bulletin board displays perk up the area and make it an attractive and inviting place to be. An unusual creative art addition to the building are the white walls of the main room which are covered with children's drawings and graffiti. Initially, the idea of having children use the wall to express themselves artistically was a come-on to attract them into the program. But it proved so successful and attractive that it has remained, adding color and interest to the room. Given an unattractive old building with cramped quarters, wonders have been worked. Furniture is functional and leans heavily to steel, including the shelving.

The heaviest use of the program comes after school hours. It is encouraging to note that activities other than selecting and checking out books, hearing stories, or watching filmstrips have found their way into the program. For instance, a site visitor noted four youngsters studying arithmetic and spelling. The branch is an oasis of calmness and stability which helps make it a good study area for children who often do not have such conditions available in the home environment. Study help was not a primary goal of the program, it just "happened," but it is possible the program will move even more into this area. Outreach to community day care centers has been incorporated into the program and these centers regularly bring children for story hours and other programs.

Equipment is readily available to children and it is used primarily to watch filmstrips and to listen to cassettes or records. Part of the regular program includes 16mm film showings.

Storyhours, film showings, a reading club, and book circulation are the main program offerings. It is a priority to make programs like this available to children when they need them and are most able to use them. Accordingly, the program operates on Monday, Thursday, and Friday 9-11:30 A.M. and 2-5:30 P.M. Wednesday; service hours are 2-8 P.M., and on Saturday the branch is open from 10 A.M. until 4 P.M. This maximizes staff contact with children and allows for more relevant program development. The library tries to vary its hours to meet community needs.

Every attempt is made to involve children in reading, and books received the highest priority for materials purchased for the program. Heavy emphasis in these books is on contemporary, easy-to-read biographies of sports and entertainment figures. The small room allows the staff to work personally with many of the children who use the branch in helping them select appropriate and interesting books. Story hours, film showings, and other program activities relate always to promoting and increasing reading interest.

The branch keeps records on the kinds of programs and

activities that go on as well as the number of children that attend them or participate. And the staff records information about materials that are especially useful; how children were involved in programs and if specific programs were a success. Additional evaluative records define kinds of materials used and any publicity that resulted. These are helpful, though unsophisticated, measurement criteria for program evaluation.

It is too early to judge the ultimate, long range success of the Randolph Branch program for children, but it is very much alive and well and contributing to the community. Plans now call for the addition of an adult reading room which will add an important dimension to its role within the community. There is reason for optimism about this program for the strong initial multiagency sponsorship built into the program has translated to a solid base of community support. Many individuals and groups have put time, money, talent, and energy into the project and the psychology of defeat is not part of this program.

The program is exemplary as a model of what can be accomplished when several committed librarians see a need for service, take initiative, pursue a variety of resources for support, and give extra time to get it started. A little money and a lot of determination have carried this a long way.

Program Objectives
1. To provide an outreach program for children in a predominantly black community.
2. To involve community agencies and self-help organizations in the process of planning the program.
3. To establish a library program that would be part of the community.
4. To provide library services for young children to encourage and sustain their interest in reading.

5. To utilize paraprofessional and support staff to operate a library program under the direction of the professional.

Some Suggestions
1. Introduce adult programs to add an important dimension of their involvement in the program.
2. Continue to expand programs wtih day care centers to involve them more fully in the program.
3. Be certain of good communication with school programs to insure coordination wherever possible.
4. Try to increase more volunteer participation in program.
5. Try more specific evaluation of reading programs to see if children are reading more.

BUCHANAN ELEMENTARY SCHOOL
Livonia, Michigan

Staff
   Professional: 1
   Support: 2
   Volunteer: 40

Unified Budget (1975-1976)
$1,040
ESEA Title I: 500

Target Population: 600 children, ages 5-12

The media program at the Buchanan Elementary School shows that transition from traditional school library-enrichment programs to a direct instructional support role is possible without compromising the best of the school library tradition.

For years, the library program at Buchanan consisted of storytelling, book talks, reading guidance, and skills instruction. However, the faculty, the media specialist, and the principal knew there was another dimension they wanted: direct instructional support and curriculum development through the media program. A key to understanding the relative ease of this transition is the democratic style by which the school operates. Teachers are asked to contribute leadership and direction for programs. This is encouraged by a principal secure enough to have his professional staff evaluate building programs and make suggestions and recommendations about improving or changing them.

Aside from knowing what they wanted, the Buchanan staff faced a series of problems and situations shared by many schools. The areas designated for media center use were large and used randomly by teachers for many noninstructional reasons. With little program focus, confusion was often the dominant mode. Access to equipment was a problem too; it was often in the wrong place or misplaced, and this curtailed the program. A host of instructional materials, some commercial programs and others locally produced, were located around the building. Most of these materials were broadly based and unfocused for program application.

A committee examined the entire program and recommended for one thing that materials be broken down into smaller, better focused skills-related task units to help teachers teach and children learn more effectively and efficiently. Management, organization, and participation were crucial elements in this process. Faculty participation in establishing media program goals is a sound idea since teachers are the main clients of the program. The Buchanan faculty committee represents each grade level and is a school-wide committee, not a media center committee. This committee helps shape what the building media program is to be. A second thing the committee decided was that support staff was crucial to media program operation; they convinced teachers to agree to the exchange of one teaching position for two aides for the media program.

Finally, the committee designed a Prescribed Learning program. Prescribed Learning is something many schools could adopt, since it is not a new program requiring large outlays for materials or equipment. The program aims to improve instruction by getting maximum instructional use from available materials. Its adoption at this school both expanded and changed the responsibilities of the media specialist, for the direction of this program is this specialist's responsibility.

These new responsibilities have not eliminated important traditional support or enrichment programs. Special emphasis is directed at getting children in grades one through three "into reading." Reading clubs and many other enrichment activities are available to stimulate reading, and the media specialist interacts personally with many of these children every day. It is the ability of the media specialist to internalize management and organization skills and set priorities, while maintaining good human relationships, that explains much of the program's success. This is a component that must be present in any exemplary school media program and is necessary for a successful program.

The organization of materials and their coding into specific prescription skill areas are the responsibility of the media specialist. This enumerating and organizing process is essential, for eventually all these instructional materials go into a Prescribed Learning catalog. Included are developmental learning materials, kits, filmstrips, and other kinds of commercially prepared instructional materials. They are entered by subject into the catalog. Entries are broken down further by listing specific skills to be reinforced, lesson objectives, descriptive information about the program, and a teacher code that indicates suggested use.

For example, there is a language arts skill lesson on sentence structure, specifically, punctuation. The catalog gives the program title and tells the grade level for which the program should be used. It also gives direction notes describing how the program should be used with children. There are comments on the different learning rates at which children will use the lessons, information on what the student will need to do the prescribed lesson, and descriptions of skills that will be introduced or reinforced.

Each teacher has a catalog in the classroom so that the teacher knows exactly what activities the child will be doing at the media center. Teachers write prescriptions, using the code system from the catalog, and they assume the final responsibility for evaluating the learning by the child. Contact, direction, and involvement are maintained even though the child is away from the classroom. Thus the media program contributes to the instructional program, yet the teacher maintains the key position in the learning process.

The two aides used in the Learning Prescription Program are essential, indeed they are the key to the successful operation of the program. They assemble the materials necessary for the child to complete a prescription, monitor the learning activities, and check out the children before they return to the classroom. Volunteers are involved too, but the hour-to-hour operational control rests with the aides who receive their direction from the media specialist.

There are two primary learning center areas in the media center, science/math and language arts; one aide is stationed in each area. When a teacher decides what prescription is indicated, a prescription form is filled out and the child takes this to the center. The prescription slips are coded to relate to each subject area and are printed on different colored paper for orderly program maintenance. Duplicate prescription copies are sent with the child; the original is returned to the teacher and a copy is kept for the media center records. Each prescription contains a section labeled, "How did I do?" This section is used by the child for self-evaluation, or the aide may make appropriate comments.

Time and task control are maintained carefully, for each task is written from listings in the Prescribed Learning catalog. Teachers are requested to provide time estimates for the child to accomplish a prescription. The catalog helps them do this, for it provides notations of time expectations for task performances.

Follow through and evaluation are built into the program, for when the child returns to the classroom the teacher must check the prescription slip to determine if the child has accomplished the assigned task successfully. Many of the tasks require use of ditto sheets or other specific measurement devices, and the teacher reviews these with the child to evaluate success or failure and determine what steps should follow.

Management of the heavy flow of children into and out of the media center must be planned carefully. Between the months of October and May the Science/Math Learning Center experienced more than 10,000 visits by children working on a prescription basis; a similar number of visits were registered in the Language Arts Center. Clearly, this program could not be done without adequate support staff. Even now the program closes on Wednesday to allow time to catch up with the heavy volume of paperwork the program generates.

Teachers working within the program are enthusiastic and involved and use the prescription process for both remedial and enrichment purposes. They like most the options the program provides. Diagnosing learning needs of individual children allows the teacher to locate appropriate tasks for the child. The large amounts of materials available for every grade level permit an individualized learning process that significantly increases good learning experiences. The results: children are more confident of their ability to learn and willing to take more responsibility for their own learning.

A library skills instruction program is being designed for the individualized prescription learning mode. Here, too, teachers must consider the needs of individual children for skills relevant to their learning. If a lesson in the card catalog or reference books or indexes is appropriate, it is prescribed and specific direction and follow through is maintained by the teacher.

No new technology is necessary to support a program like this. The materials and equipment necessary for it are found in most schools. And it could be adapted at other levels as well, since its intent is management and organization.

An additional program strength is that the professional staff and the media specialist decide together what the job description and responsibilities of the media specialist and aides should be. This model mandates heavy faculty participation in the entire media program, giving it the kind of priority it must have to accomplish its goals.

This teacher support is a constant program strength; for if teachers are to undertake individualized instruction, they must have ready access to the media that can be used to relate to small individualized tasks. While the primary role for the media specialist in this program is direct instructional contact with teachers, rather than service to children, the end result is a media program that is involved deeply with the instruction and learning of children.

Program Objectives
1. To organize instructional materials into small units so that teachers may use in either a remedial or enrichment mode.

2. To have professional staff and media specialist together plan selection and use of materials for meeting program goals.
3. To individualize instruction of children to better meet unique learning needs.
4. To help develop necessary skills in specific subject areas.
5. To provide, via book catalog format, a complete listing of resources available in a media center and suggest for an guide their proper use.

Some Suggestions
1. Obtain more clerical support so that the program may be operated every day.
2. Sponsor more production of local materials to better support instructional programs.
3. Put Prescribed Learning catalog into a looseleaf format so that it may be updated and changed easily.
4. Increase local budget support for materials.
5. Do not place a disproportionate reliance on auditory program. Each skill should be reinforced with materials which exercise all senses.

SPRING LAKE JUNIOR-SENIOR HIGH SCHOOL
Spring Lake, Michigan

Staff
Professional: 2½
Support: 3

Budget (1975-1976)
Print: $ 4,153
Nonprint: 4,068
Local foundation grant (1964-66): 37,500
(to upgrade secondary school collection)

Target Population: 1,250 children, ages 12-18

Media Programs District and School, the present guidelines for media programs issued by the American Association of School Librarians and the Association for Educational Communications and Technology, emphasizes the necessity to relate media programs to instructional design, management by objectives, and better use of educational technology. The purpose of this is to accent the interrelationship of media programs and educational programs. Media professionals must have the competency to devise strategies that will integrate media programs into instructional programs. To accomplish this, media professionals must know and participate in curriculum development, understand the application of technology to learning, and even understand theories of learning.

For many school media programs some of the more revolutionary expectations of the guidelines are inoperable or developed only in a peripheral way. The relationship of media programs to instruction remains too often a statement of what should be rather than what is. There is need then to examine school media programs that are successfully implementing these guidelines in the hope they may be used as models.

The Spring Lake Junior-Senior High School media program is such an outstanding model. The excellent media program results from its integration into the curriculum; its ability to satisfy in a planned, systematic way the needs of students and teachers who use its instructional materials and services;

and the establishment of program goals and measurable objectives to assess the achievement of these goals. As media program goals for students were established, the competencies necessary to fulfill them were specified. Among these competencies: the ability to learn independently; the ability to locate information; and the ability to abstract, translate, synthesize, and evaluate information.

Management objectives for operating the media center, student use of the media center, and use of instructional materials have also been incorporated into program planning. They evidence a sensibility for structure and precision lacking in many media programs. This concern for precision, specific outcomes, and expectations provides the framework within which the media program relates most effectively to the instructional program.

Media skills teaching is also based on expected competencies and operates to increase the ability of individuals to locate, process, and use information to facilitate independent learning. This skills program relates to, and reinforces, overall media program goals; it is designed to authenticate and enrich learning. Classroom teachers and media professionals agree that media skills are taught as they relate to student needs and integrated into the instructional program.

Structure, to support learning growth, is stated in terms of conditions, performance, and criteria. Conditions are the kinds of research students might do while performance is the learner activity required to locate necessary information. Criteria are the assessment measurements established to evaluate how successfully this process was accomplished. For example, a sample reference skills assignment using the encyclopedia for special reference work reads: *Conditions:* given locational questions such as a series of problems or topics and a list of reference sources.—*Performance:* the learner will match the locational question with the reference source most likely to yield the answer.—*Criteria:* at least seventy percent of the students will perform this task successfully. Another sample, use of *The Readers Guide to Periodical Literature.* Condition: given a sample entry from the Reader's Guide.—*Performance:* the learner will be able to identify: (a) subject heading, (b) subheading, (c) title of article, (d) author of article, (e) descriptive information, (f) name of magazine, (g) volume of magazine, (h) pages of article, (i) date of magazine.—*Criteria:* the student should be able to identify correctly seven out of these nine items.

Aside from systematizing the teaching of library skills the program provides clearer direction and increased understandings for students. It is monitored carefully, with pre- and post-tests for student and program evaluation. The extra dimension for skills teaching is provided by the link forged between teacher and media specialist. This teaching relationship is articulated in the publication, *A Team for Better Teaching,* a locally produced guide for teaching, locating, and processing of information. It commits the media specialist and classroom teacher to work as a team constructing units and specific assignments that will increase learner competencies for individuals and groups.

The guide divides teaching activities into categories of when, what, who, goal, where, with what, and procedure. The *Readers Guide* provides a useful example. Its use is seen as a skills process to be taught and reinforced in the seventh and eighth grade. The media professional and teacher work together toward a goal of providing instruction that enables learners to recognize subject headings, article titles, descriptive information, and other necessary information to locate appropriate articles. The instructional process to accomplish this task takes place in the media center and classroom. Instructional support materials are 16mm film, slides showing the index table, check-out procedure sheets, and sample pages from *Readers Guide.*

A pre-test is used to eliminate instruction for those with sufficient skills to use the *Readers Guide.* Classroom teaching activities include use of the 16mm film and slides, followed by discussion and a classroom assignment relating these activities to using the *Readers Guide.* A post-test measures learning margins and instructional development.

Important to this process is the orderly sequence by which it is applied. Teachers must tie their teaching to specific assignments; students are not turned loose, willy-nilly, in the media center to "find out" about the reference books. Expectation, process, outcome: each is stated clearly, and responsibility for them accepted accordingly by the teacher, media specialist, and student.

These relationships once established provide additional program support for other areas. A catalog of nonprint resources of the media program is made available to each faculty member, and staff development programs relating media to improved teaching are incorporated into the media program. An excellent nonprint preview operation puts materials into the hands of teachers for evaluation and use *before* they are purchased.

The facility is important to this program, for without adequate space the heavy use by classes, small groups, and individuals is not possible. Remodeled from a cafeteria and student commons area, and incorporating an adjacent court yard, the media center has about 7,000 square feet available for student use. An additional 2,000 square feet are used for teacher conference areas, media production, workrooms, magazine storage, and offices. "Attractive," "inviting," and "spacious" come easily to mind as describing the facility. Art display panels, five feet wide, extending from floor to ceiling, are used to display student art work, adding a dramatic and pleasing tone to the room.

A full range of production activities—laminating, dry mounting, audio and video taping, and photography—are part of the media program. The production laboratory has been used by Western Michigan University for its extension courses in production and utilization of media. Significantly, over half of the Spring Lake staff enrolled in these courses to increase their competencies in this area. Team planning, careful follow through, continuous program revision and evaluation, use of media to relate instruction and learning have created a unified media program with a profound influence within the school.

The most exemplary aspect here is the continuous reassessment and refinement of the program and its resources. Frequent reassessment of its goals assures that they continue to meet the needs of students and are incorporated into the instructional mainstream. The key is sound management and clear objectives to obtain goals, and a media program that is an instructional resource for an entire building. Spring Lake demonstrates the essence of what the *Media Programs: District and School* is all about.

Program Objectives
1. To plan sequence of retrieval skills that coordinate directly with curriculum.
2. To incorporate the media center staff into the instructional staff of the school.
3. To use a variety of media to stimulate a comprehensive "processing of information" program.
4. To provide on-going staff development opportunities to increase good teacher use of media.
5. To provide a media program of student instruction based upon expected competencies.

Some Suggestions
1. Try to keep budget for print and nonprint items up to at least present levels.
2. Extend skills program to upper grades of the school.
3. Use video tape for some of the more repetitive skills lessons.
4. Try to recruit some volunteers into the program for additional clerical support.

SEA GIRT ELEMENTARY SCHOOL
Sea Girt, New Jersey

Staff
Professional: 1
Support: 1
Volunteer: 3

Budget (1975-1976)
Print: $4,300
Nonprint: 2,650

Target Population: 300 children, ages 5-12

The New Jersey School Media Association publishes a useful booklet called *Programs of Media Centers Recommended for Visiting and Observing; Innovative Provisions and Practices in School Media Centers.* Among the criteria for inclusion in it are a unified media program and the service of at least one full-time media specialist. Other, fairly standard criteria are provided about the factors governing site selection. The general notes of the booklet state that " . . . The programs (selected) are operating at an outstanding degree of effectiveness in media services."

By any standard of measurement, the Sea Girt Elementary School media program which is included in the New Jersey book is effective and has an exemplary impact far beyond the media center. Opened in September, 1970, the school, enrolling about 300 children in grades K-8 was designed and staffed to function as a nongraded school.

Team teaching, differentiated staffing, multi-age groupings, and individualized scheduling are integral parts of the school's structure. Everything possible is done to protect and nurture the essential uniqueness of the child as an individual learner. All well and good, but hardly unique. Today there are many schools like Sea Girt; they have programs similar in many ways.

One factor that gives the school program a more effective dimension is the existence and leadership of the innovative media program recognized by the New Jersey School Media Association. It is a media program that operates well, one which gives real meaning to the cliche phrase that "the media center is the learning hub of the school." Here, it's true! The curriculum, the teaching, and the different modes of learning are dependent upon the media center program and could not operate separately from it.

Much of the effectiveness of the program is traceable to a principal who knows the kind of media program he wants and needs to provide leadership and support in accomplishing the school's learning goals. If you expect a media specialist to work well with teachers, acting at one time or another as a leader, coordinator, guide, or supplier of innovative ideas to improve teaching, it helps if this person has experience as a successful classroom teacher. The media specialist at Sea Girt was, and is. If teachers are going to be led by a media specialist, better this be someone who understands exactly the meaning of the words teaching, learning, and instruction and how they are done well. And if a media program is to identify clearly with the teaching program then it is good sense to have the media specialist do some teaching and be involved in some genuine learning programs. These programs may be separate from others in the school, but they relate to the overall goals of the school.

Within this school several learning goals are stated, which provide specific program focus. For one, skills are to be built sequentially, each new set upon the foundation of those preceeding it, for continuity of learning. Teachers are encouraged—expected—to work together to maximize experiences, insights, and creative efforts. The evaluation process is continuous, relying not on norm-based tests but on individualized criterion-referenced factors.

For any school librarian, forced by recent events to adopt the role of media specialist with slender competencies to support this, here is a kind of showdown at the Last Chance Gulch. For the media specialist who expects to be a part of the instructional team, wants to participate in curriculum design, and knows how to help develop in children their innate capacity to learn, this is an extraordinary opportunity.

Many, nongraded, multigrouped, and individualized programs cause insecurities in persons who do not understand them. Fears are most often expressed in the concern that with individualized progress and openness of learning experiences, the child will not get the "basics." Response to these concerns takes a number of forms. Many of them miss completely the fact that open education programs and letting children learn in unique and individual ways does not replace, and need not exclude, attention to basic skills. In fact, the better the child learns the basics, the freer is that child to explore, discover, and learn on his own.

Of course, the most basic of the basics are the skills of reading. Years ago, the National Book Committee distributed a beautiful poster that stated a simple but powerful message, "Send me a man who reads. . . . " To the *reader*, indeed all things *are* possible!

The Sea Girt Media program, with an intuitive manner and in an explicit way, has recognized these and other truths and has acted in response. A wide variety of media and the equipment to insure their good use are available and used throughout the school's instructional program. Video taping, filmmaking, and other media production possibilities are available in abundance at Sea Girt, and they are used. Perhaps the most exemplary element of the Sea Girt program is its evident success in using the print medium without denigrating the nonprint medium. This approach aims to develop both a literary and technical competency for children and reflects the importance of good literature to their learning. This, in turn, has an important bearing on the ability of the child to develop the entire visual literacy component.

Literature that comes alive is one of the most important facets of a multifaceted media program. "The Living Literature Program," as it is called, seeks to provide children with a broad literary background and to develop critical thinking about literature, in either a print or nonprint format. Eventually, objectives of the Living Literature Program, plus others for the total media program, become part of the language arts curriculum. Another exemplary feature of this media program is that its goals and objectives have been incorporated into the curriculum of the school. It reflects the fact that the best media programs have few unique or isolated goals and objectives. Yet, no other instructional program may achieve its goals without a heavy reliance on use of the media program; thus media philosophy becomes educational reality.

At Sea Girt, the media program has adopted both a Great Books course, a survey of world literature adapted especially to the needs of the school, and the Junior Great Books Program. The former is used for students with advanced reading skills and is taught daily by the media specialist as a part of the structured reading program. The latter is used as reading enrichment for interested students from grade two through junior high school. Two-thirds of the students population is involved in these discussions, which occur once a week under the direction of two volunteers for each group. The volunteers are parents, teachers, and the media specialist, each of whom has been trained carefully by the Great Books Foundation.

We endorse no commercially marketed reading programs in this book. These evaluations and decisions must be made based only on whether or not the reading program will help accomplish a particular set of learning goals. For some, these reading lists may seem stodgy and dated. It's amazing, though, the number of youngsters who can still be turned on to *Dr. Jekyll and Mr. Hyde, The Count of Monte Cristo,* and *Robinson Crusoe.* Sometimes, it takes some inspired teaching and almost always an extraordinary amount of patience and persistence. But it can and does work.

Further words of caution. Adopting a commercial program for use in a school setting must be carefully thought out and based on the needs of the building and its children. Too many media centers and classrooms are full to bursting with unused commercially prepared programs intended to develop the love of reading in the reluctant reader, to develop library skills, or to make the apathetic child more creative.

Perhaps the best way to use a commercial package is to balance it with something locally originated. At Sea Girt the Poet-in-the Classroom Program does this. The program is sponsored jointly by the National Endowment on the Arts and Humanities, the New Jersey State Council on the Arts, and the local school district. It consists of a three- or four-day series of visits by a poet, carefully selected for professional qualifications as well as an ability to relate to children. Each day the poet returns to the same class. A workshop for the professional staff is also conducted so that the program is related closely to instructional goals.

Children still love meeting a real honest-to-goodness author. A poet discussing the creation of poetry, the uses of poetry, and the value of poetry cannot help but have a positive impact upon a school. The sponsorship of this interaction with a creator by the media center provides another strong instructional program relationship.

The efforts to make literature a living thing for children are supported by an Uninterrupted Sustained Silent Reading (USSR) program. One excellent aspect of this approach is the positive attitude reinforcement when children see adult models reading. At Sea Girt Elementary School, when USSR time comes, everyone—principal, teachers, and students read together silently at the same time. The program provides an oasis of contentment, is easy to do, and costs nothing.

The Sea Girt media program displays much that is exemplary: a staff that is involved in planning with teachers and in the teaching and learning of children; a program that supports all the learning within the school, yet is capable of providing effective independent leadership in special areas; a program that has reached out to the community to involve volunteers in productive and meaningful ways; a program that helps serve a community's need for information by supplementing a minimal public library service. Talent, commitment, dedication, purpose, and a desire to maintain excellent standards are the heart of the program.

Program Objectives
1. To integrate the media program into the total instructional program of the school.

2. To use nonprint media to promote and support visual literacy.
3. To involve community volunteers in media program operations.
4. To promote the enjoyment and appreciation of literature through a Living Literature Program.
5. To use federal, state, and local funds in imaginative combinations to promote appreciation for literature.

Some Suggestions
1. Develop specific criterion-referenced tests to show the impact of media program on total instructional program.
2. Consider having students work with other students in the Living Literature Program.
3. Consider more local production of materials (print and nonprint) to give a local focus to Living Literature Program.
4. Use video tape for the Poet-in-the-classroom program to insure retention and reuse of programs.

ESPERANZA BRANCH
Albuquerque Public Library
Albuquerque, New Mexico

Staff
Professional: 1
Support: 1
Volunteer: 10

Budget (1975-1976)
Print, Nonprint,
and Equipment: $5,000

Target Population: 40 children, ages 3-5; 20 parents

Esperanza! Spanish, for hope! Where there is no hope, there is little concern, no desire, no future. Hope is a worthy name for this branch of the Albuquerque Public Library, for it has brought this priceless commodity to the community.

Located in an area where a majority of children are bicultural, primarily Spanish-American, the library confronts daily familiar urban problems—disintegrated families, poor housing, and insufficient social services. And while a bicultural environment presents rich and challenging opportunities for learning opportunities, it presents enormous difficulties too for the young child trying to accommodate to the demands made by living and learning in both cultures. The frustration level and failure rate are both high.

For children, the effects of this environment of insufficiency are apparent at an early age. By the time they go to the public schools, many are already below their grade level in most learning skills—reading being usually the most obviously deficient. But other skills need development or reinforcement: manual dexterity, spatial relationships, verbal communication, computational, listening, and looking. These skills are essential if the child is to assimilate and learn.

The Albuquerque Public Library decided some time ago that it should play a role in child development programs, particularly for the preschool and primary school age child. The program that developed from this decision recognized that there was little value to be gained in bringing a bunch of tots together for weekly story hours or lessons in arts and crafts. If the impaired early learning abilities of these children was to be enhanced, then parents must become involved.

The middle class, with its built-in aspirations for upward mobility and material and social success, has generally recognized the importance of the parent acting as teacher to provide an educational head start. It is expected that children will be programmed for success and achievement as they move from home to preschool and school environments.

For the poor parent, personal success expectations are remote, often impossible, and these attitudes may be passed along to their offspring. But new research shows that parents of disadvantaged children have the same aspirations for a better life for their children as middle-class parents. Esperanza branch reflects an attempt to capitalize upon these attitudes and expectations.

Total child development and complete parent involvement are the educational and psychological foundations of the program. Its purpose is to help children learn by gaining and holding their interest and promoting their personal involvement in their learning. Plenty of encouragement and support prevail, reflecting an open education philosophy. The learning readiness program seeks to prepare children for entry into a formal education program by developing creativity, social participation, self-initiated activity, motor expression, reading readiness, listening skills, matching skills, language expression, and an interest in books.

This is not a community baby-sitting service, and parents are encouraged and motivated to attend with their children. It is expected that the ninety-minute period spent by the parent with the preschool child each week, directly involved in helping the child to learn, will carry back to the home.

Another premise is that use of nonprint materials will promote an interest in learning by children not attracted to print. The reaction of children and parents to programs using equipment and nonprint materials is observed closely for evaluation by the professional staff.

The State of New Mexico provided a support grant of $2,814 to be used to buy equipment including listening stations, record players, cassette player-recorders, a slide projector, a filmstrip projector, filmstrip viewers, a 16mm projector, and super 8mm projectors. Local funds provided about $2,000 to purchase materials used in the program. Preliminary workshops for the library staff were held to explain the philosophy and purpose of the program. Learning how to operate equipment was included in this training experience.

Program interest areas were identified as letter recognition and phonics, matching concept skills, perceptions of color and shapes, language expression using stories, films, finger plays, puppets, flannel board and cassettes, memory skills, listening and following instruction skills, and sharing and social activities.

Only four or five of these interest areas are used at any one instructional session which generally lasts for an hour and a half. Group activities such as role playing (to develop language, self-expression, and self-identification) finger plays, discussions, and singing are also included. Program operation emphasizes the simple and uncomplicated procedure.

Planned originally to last for eight weeks, the program was later extended to thirteen weeks. Eventually, ten weeks proved the best time span, and the program is given twice a year, in the spring and fall.

For each series of ten programs, ten parents and up to eighteen preschool children are enrolled. Program interest areas are created by setting up five separate tables, each table contains an interest area. Interest areas used in one typical program include arts and crafts, cooking (simple cooking equipment is available), Spanish phonics, and story taperecording by children. Equipment and materials used included a record player, sound filmstrip machine, puppets, cooking equipment, flannel board, alphabet practice cards, beads, and a Language Master machine. The Language Master is used to improve phonics skills.

Individualized activities are always reinforced by group activities. Individual arts and crafts activities include making figure and bookmarks with magic markers. Children write the first letters of their names or put together simple puzzles to reinforce individual phonics, lettering, and manual dexterity skills. Shared or group activities include having the group make the sounds of animals, act out stories, or listen together to a story.

Capacity enrollments and waiting lists are always present in the preschool readiness programs. Highest priority must go to obtaining parental involvement. The staff advises that a requirement is parents *must* attend the orientation session and each of the ten sessions. Keeping enrollments small makes this task easier. Some of the activities used in the program, cooking and carpentry in particular, require careful supervision.

Parent participants in the preschool program must complete a program evaluation form. The questions ask: What does the parent think of the program? What benefits has the child received from the program? What has the parent learned about ways to help the child at home? Suggestions to improve the program are also requested. Parents of school children formerly in the program are interviewed to help evaluate their child's adjustment to school and to determine in what ways the program most helped in this process. Parent participants are always asked if they know of other children eligible for the program.

Because of extensive involvement by volunteers, no extra staff was hired. The professional staff at the Esperanza recruits and trains these volunteers so that they too are committed to the goals of the program and understand the mechanics of its operation. A healthy program development is that some volunteers have become so interested in it that they return and work for successive sessions.

Although program focus is the preschooler and the parent, clearly after four years of operation the program is having an unanticipated result of bringing more people into the branch; it is another successful outreach component of the program.

Program Objectives
1. To involve parents (especially mothers) in a preschool program to better help their children cope successfully with school.
2. To provide an outreach preschool program for children of bilingual background.
3. To involve parent volunteers in an ongoing public library instructional program for preschool children.
4. To use a variety of print and nonprint media to foster the development of the logical thinking process.
5. To introduce children to library services and programs at an early age.

Some Suggestions
1. Do some follow-up evaluations with children who have entered school from the program.
2. Develop some closer links with the schools to which the children go in an effort for more continuous evaluation.
3. Attempt more volunteer participation to increase the number of times the program could be offered and the number of children it reaches.
4. Consider involving other locations (day-care centers or community centers, for example) in doing a similar program.
5. Attempt to seek additional funding (business, for example) to extend the program.

SANDIA HIGH SCHOOL
Albuquerque, New Mexico

Staff
Professional: 2
Support: 2

Budget
Not applicable

Target Population: 700 freshmen

Correction of a host of economic, social, and educational problems is currently a major preoccupation of many educators, parents, and public officials. About correction, everyone has an opinion; but few really "know" how to correct the many contemporary problems, and institutions acting alone usually cannot correct these.

As far as education is concerned, the institutional challenge focuses mainly on the learning or teaching of basic skills. School media programs need to establish a reasoned, sensible response to this challenge. This is a paramount necessity, for media programs are being challenged and held responsible for leading schools away from teaching basics—whatever "basics" are. The end result is that school media programs are required as never before to *prove* they contribute specifically to the school building instructional program. The most common "expected" contribution is from a library skills program. Since one program analysis in this book examined how an elementary school media program approached the teaching of library skills, it is appropriate to look at a high school program as well.

The skills teaching program at Sandia High School is thorough, comprehensive, and specific in its purpose. Seven hundred freshmen are instructed in the use of research materials and equipment while participating in a media program orientation unit. The intensive three-week program is conducted by classroom teachers and the media staff. Required are (1) use of references and research techniques, (2) production of visual and audio materials, and (3) a culminating classroom teaching activity combining the skills learned. These activities require use of many media information tools including the card catalog, standard reference materials, magazines, pamphlets, and nonprint media forms.

Of first importance, the program reflects good planning about what outcomes are expected before goals and objectives are developed and the program begins to operate. Good student use of media for information, to be retrieved and used as necessary or appropriate, is the basis for the program. Incorporated too is the use of media to stimulate creativity and guide learning toward reasonable and expected outcomes.

Just as there is no stereotyped media program, the Sandia skills program cannot be labeled conveniently nor followed exactly by others. There are, however, specific processes and results that should be part of the planning for any successful media skills instruction program. First, skills must not be regarded as adjuncts or add-on's to other learning; they are woven into the instructional program. Second, the program relates subject matter information needs to using skills; for the former to be satisfied, the latter must be used. Third, skills instruction is based upon student involvement, with heavy emphasis on the "doing," and minimal on the telling; it respects the truism that to hear is to forget, to see is to remember, but to do is to understand.

Classroom teachers develop work sheets which form the core of the skills course and they are mainly responsible for the skills instruction program, which generally follows a seminar format. The media staff performs a teaching capacity, serving as consultants, while presenting specific media center related activities to students.

Classes are divided into two sections for the first two weeks of the skills unit. One group works with print and nonprint materials, while the other receives instruction in operating the equipment used most often in the media program. These include 16mm projectors, 8mm projectors, 35mm filmstrip and slide projectors, overhead and opaque projectors, and tape recorders. An introduction to television equipment is included, assuring some familiarity with television cameras, recorders, and playback units.

The program is truly home grown, expressing the needs, priorities, and objectives of the building learning program. This clarifies priorities and results in programs relevant to the needs of the building. The focus always is the students and their need to get at and use well the information that will make them more able to meet the demands placed upon them. The resources used in the skills program are rearranged, changed, and applied in different combinations to promote individual learning, and students are expected to help develop in each other new interests and abilities while participating in the unit. Students work right along with the professional teaching and media staff in carrying out some of the instructional aspects of the program, including work in the production area, work with media equipment, and work in the circulation area.

Program objectives are specific, and the main goal is to bring freshmen into close contact with the varieties of resources (human, material, and equipment) which the media program makes available to them. The main strategy to achieve this objective is to make students use these resources by integrating them into the classroom instructional program. All elements of the media program lead back to and reinforce this. Another objective is to help students make a successful transition from a junior high to a senior high school by getting them to use media resources in ways that relate to their own personal instructional program. Achievement and satisfaction are used to reinforce each other.

It is expected that the skills unit will increase student responsibility in handling materials, and equipment. Since there is a great deal of student production of media, this is an important concern. And since nearly all of the resources of the media program may be taken home, common sense dictates that a high priority go to developing attitudes that are responsible and careful about use of materials and equipment outside the media center.

The print skills portion of the program blends traditional questions requiring students to consult and use such standard reference sources as almanacs, dictionaries, handbooks, and encyclopedias with activities that require production of nonprint materials; thus research is integrated into learning and production of instructional materials. Eventually students must give an audio or visual classroom presentation that represents the culmination of the three-week reference/skills unit.

One result of this unit is an increased ability by students to locate and use more useful media. Teachers, students, and media staff have verified that student research, using print and nonprint materials, is handled with greater confidence and competence. The program also helps improve communication between students and media center staff, because students know how to ask more precise questions about what they seek and need. And their knowledgability about using basic reference skills makes them more confident to try more unfamiliar resources. Teachers of junior and senior classes report that students who take the freshman skills orientation unit show continued ability to use reference materials.

There are drawbacks. While the program takes place, personnel and equipment are engaged nearly full time. But this is a tolerable price to pay if the program shows the results this one does. Intricate planning with teachers must be done, but this is another agreeable burden to bear. With so many students experiencing a program at the same time, little individual attention can go to less able students and this can be a limiting factor.

Curriculum integration, comprehensive management, clear objectives, and specific strategies to achieve them provide focus to the Freshman Skills Unit and make it a useful model for others to consider and adopt.

Program Objectives
1. To introduce freshmen students to the resources of a media center and reinforce their use through specific assignment.
2. To integrate the teaching of library skills into the curriculum of the school.

3. To incorporate the learning of reference skills, the operation of equipment, and the production of materials into a required Freshman Skills Unit.
4. To teach students how to use media more effectively in their school work.
5. To teach responsibility and good citizenship in the use of equipment, materials, and facilities.

Some Suggestions
1. Provide for greater flexibility in program content to better meet the learning needs of a variety of students.
2. Use more video tape procedures to reinforce introductory reference skills to make presentation more effective.
3. Design a student evaluation of the course for clearer input from them as to its effectiveness.
4. Relate production aspects of program more specifically to skills retrieval.
5. Try to relate the program more clearly to such things as career awareness or the world of work.

NEW MEXICO

CLOVIS-CARVER PUBLIC LIBRARY
Clovis, New Mexico

Staff
Professional: 2

Budget (1975-1976)
Approximately $700
(if commercially produced
materials are used

Target Population: In class sessions, 15-20 parents and 30 children, ages 3-5

A recurring theme of this book is that public libraries are educational institutions with a teaching role that complements and enriches that of public schools and other community institutions concerned traditionally with education.

The Parent/Child Toy Lending Library developed by the Clovis-Carver Public Library is representative of this growing educational dimension for the public library and illustrates clearly the potential for reaching and teaching the preschool child through parent involvement. The Toy Lending Library capitalizes on the theory that the parent is the most significant teacher for the child, and that the preschool child who from an early age (almost from birth) is deliberately involved in the process of discovering and learning will be able to deal more effectively with the formalized learning procedures of schooling. A core concept of the Parent/Child Toy Lending Library program is that parents should be creatively involved with their child's learning.

Educational potential for creative play can lead to such specific results as improved language skills, better understanding of forms and concepts, improved performance of problem solving tasks, and the ability to begin reading at an earlier age.

The initial idea for this program was less an idea than a reaction to a series of related events. The Auguust, 1972, issue of *Woman's Day Magazine* contained an article entitled, "Do You Know How to Play with Your Child?"—this sparked interest among a library staff seeking innovative ways to help children with reading problems. The Toy Lending Library itself is the outgrowth of research and development programs from the Far West Laboratory for Educational Research and Development, a nonprofit California organization. A government guide called *Guide to Securing and Installing the Parent Child Lending Library*, also suggested potential uses for such a program. The *Guide* describes how to make learning toys, where to seek funding sources, how to start up training classes for parents, and how to evaluate programs. County level government got involved when the interest of a county home economist was piqued by the potential for the program. Eventually, the County Extension Agency and the Clovis Carver Public Library agreed to sponsor the program jointly.

Its focus would be the parent of the preschool child. Through a systematic training process parents would learn how best to use toys and games to aid their children acquire the skills that stimulate the desire and ability to learn. While the learning activity would be play, the program goal was improved reading readiness. Skills to be stressed were those of seeing, hearing, and feeling. It is these skills that reinforce the ability to think conceptually, a process leading eventually to the development of problem solving ability.

Using the parent-child link the goals of the program became: (1) to facilitate reading readiness; (2) to foster and build a positive self-image in the child; (3) to establish an early basis of rapport and communication between parent and child; and (4) to involve a broader section of the community in the library program.

Ten years ago the idea that a program of play could improve the ability of a child to think clearly was not universally accepted. Now most reported research substantiates this theory. Understanding how children feel about themselves relates closely to the perception, understanding, and acceptance with which children will fashion their learning styles. Children must believe that their thoughts and comments will make a difference in learning and will help solve problems involving conceptual thinking. Such attitudes must be reinforced by some experience of success, for self-esteem is a critical learning component from the earliest age.

The toys used in the program are (1) sound cans, for sounds that are the same and not the same; (2) color lotto, for color matching and color naming; (4) stacking squares, for sizes that are the same and not the same; (5) wooden table blocks, for differentiation between longer and shorter sizes; (6) number puzzles, for number and observation; (7) Bead-o-craft, for pattern repetition and extension; and (8) flannel board and shape for shape-size-color discrimination.

These toys may be purchased, or made from "found" items. While making the toys is an attractive money-saving idea, it can distract attention from other important aspects of good program start-up. So, if budget monies are available (approximately $500) it is best to purchase the toys, which are available from several commercial outlets.

The course sequence of the toy lending library was planned originally for eight weeks and later reduced to five weeks. During this period the eight basic toys are introduced and the learning skills associated with each toy are developed.

During the parent classes, sound filmstrips are used to demonstrate good use of the toys as well as other understandings about the needs of the very young. Each session introduces two toys; parents see the filmstrip, do some role playing, and learn some ways to use the toys in structured play sessions with their children. A parents' manual and the toy(s) are taken home, and parent and child are expected to play together with the toy. Encouraging children to discover new ways of learning by playing with the toy is an important program expectation. At the next class session these experiences are shared to deepen understandings and appreciations.

A parent diary is used to heighten these understandings. Intended as an informal record of what happens while the parent uses toys with the child, it seeks answers to such questions as (1) Did you ask your child or children to play with the toy? (2) Does your child like to have your help? (3) How does your child like the toy? (4) What other things did you do with the toy?

Extensive record keeping is not expected; brief anecdotal responses are requested. Parental involvement in the program has led to other programs. One is the family center, where the library has put together a variety of media relating to all aspects of family living. Home education materials for preschool children are available as well as other relevant materials.

Evaluation of the parent course occurs at the end of each of the five-week sessions. Descriptive answers to such questions as "What did you learn that was useful?" and "What was the most interesting part of the experience?" are requested. Other questions concern course content, course development, and the effectiveness of training of the parent participants. Suggestions for changes that would improve the course are also solicited.

Although registration for classes is always filled, some participants fail to show up without notice. It is good planning then to have ready a list of alternate enrollees who may be quickly placed into the course. Good planning too dictates that the courses be given in the evening and mornings when participants are most able to attend. Evening courses will increase the possibility for fathers to enroll in the course.

The focus of this library program is the parent, not the child, so the parent accompanied by the child is a distracting influence. The activities connected with the child take place at home, not at the library. Extra effort too must be made to recruit into the program parents of lower socioeconomic background. Middle-class response to a program like this is assured, but racial and economic minority groups must be recruited into it.

To a visitor, a staff member expressed the belief that the improved understandings of parents about the learning of their children is a major program success. Also noted is the fact that a number of nonlibrary users have become regular users as well as strong supporters for the program.

Program Objectives
1. To present a program aimed at parents, specifically involving them in the learning of their preschool children through structured play activities.
2. To improve reading readiness of preschool children through structured play activities.
3. To help preschool children improve their self-understanding and self-image.
4. To involve parents directly in the early learning progress of their children.
5. To provide library service programs that involve more of the community.

Some Suggestions
1. Involve more volunteers (perhaps former course members) in preparing the course.
2. Consider giving the course in other locations (day-care centers, public housing programs) to involve a wider range of parents.
3. Do some video taping of activities at home to demonstrate this aspect of program.
4. Carry on more formal contact with schools the children enter to evaluate program impact.

FINGER LAKES LIBRARY SYSTEM
Ithaca, New York

Staff
Professional: 1
Support: 1

Budget (1975-1976)
$1,400

Target Population: Uncounted

Sometimes, everything seems just about perfect with a program. It has a sound purpose to generate its start-up and attracts to it the talents and energies of able and committed people. It has clear goals and specific objectives for obtaining them. It has it all together, but—as success is judged—it doesn't quite make it.

This best describes the brief life of a TV story hour for children done by the Finger Lakes Library System in New York State. It was a great idea but the program was discontinued after its initial run. The purpose of the TV story hour program was to tap into the enormous popularity of television with children in the expectation that this could promote creativity and imaginative reactions to story hours. Use of television to heighten imagination, tied to the eternal excitement of children about a story, was the program focus.

Trying to promote a love of reading in children by using television is not a new idea. Commercial and public broadcasting has for years done story hour television. Educational television programs that promote the importance of reading, introduce excellent children's literature, and support the rich impact that reading has upon the life of a child represent good use of television and are available in most areas.

It is not the usual procedure, though, to tie storytelling programs directly to the video experience, which was attempted in the Finger Lakes Program. It was planned that a television storytelling program would "Introduce children, via stories, to the folk literature of all countries and cultures as well as the best in children's books both old and new."

Another goal of the story hour program was to stimulate an interest in reading for pleasure. An ancillary expectation was that attention would be called to the services and resources of the public library and that people would be put in touch with these services.

The format of the story hour video program was simple and uncomplicated, without the juggernaut approach so often associated with video programming. The show involved one storyteller and was taped before a live audience of six to ten children, whose ages ranged from seven to ten years. The children were selected from various Ithaca public schools. The program was in all ways strictly traditional, including the lighting of the story hour candle followed by a story, or two, if time permitted.

Among the stories told were "The Elephant's Child," by Rudyard Kipling, "Aladdin and the Wonderful Lamp" from the *Arabian Nights*, "The Skull" by Ruth Manning-Sanders, and "Shrewd Todie" and "Lyzer the Miser" by Isaac Bashevis Singer.

The televised story hour program began because of the enthusiasm of one individual who wanted to do it. Contact with the local commercial television station, preparing the project proposal, selection of the stories to be told, and telling the stories rested with this one person. Others got involved only peripherally, which may be one explanation of why this excellent idea for using media with children did not catch on. While the motivation of one person can energize a program, commitment and involvement from others must support sustained program growth.

The storytelling program consisted of two thirteen-week sequences. The fifteen minute programs were taped during the day, then aired twice each week, at 7:30 and 10:30 P.M. The television channel provided all technical direction and assistance necessary. The storyteller acted as producer and hostess for the series.

Occasionally, visual aids were used with the programs. These included toy animals, original illustrations or appropriate pictures taken from books, and ceramic or wooden figurines. Music was always used in the program. Library staff time to produce the video story hour program was minimal. The library staff artist and a library page with artistic inclinations produced whatever visuals were needed and provided studio set arrangements. Occasionally, an outside artist was employed. The storyteller already had an extensive repertory of stories, so little time was spent learning stories.

The television station provided by contract all production equipment and program technical assistance. Purchase of video tape, the expense of studio production time, and use of the studio were assumed for the first series by the Finger Lakes Library System and for the second by the Friends of the Tompkins County Public Library, a member of the Finger Lakes Library System. This amounted to $1,400, not an impossible sum for many libraries.

The funding process led, however, to many of the problems that the program encountered. Funding was not based on long-term need projections but rather served to keep things going from show to show. It was left to the originator of the project to scramble for the funds required to support it. While no other library program was sacrificed to implement it, the video storytelling program did not become an identifiable system program contributing its own objectives to the overall goals of the system. Under these circumstances, the video story hour program was expendable, an experimental venture without solid roots. None of this, by the way, implies a desire on anyone's part to subvert the program, for nearly everyone agreed it was a fine idea. However, this agreement could not be translated into performance or permanence.

Attempts to coordinate the program with the school media program were built into it, and the city school system worked at stimulating interest in the program. Teachers were surveyed about the involvement of their students with the TV story hour and suggestions about other kinds of stories for children were made by them. While the tapes show some production problems, mainly graphics, lighting, and pacing of show, these could be overcome.

When you are trying to sell a product, the first priority is to know the market. This means for a television show: Who is watching? How often do they watch? Do they talk about it afterwards? Sometimes you have to *create* a market. Two thirteen-week sequences for locally based program are not enough to evaluate its impact or create a market. This takes time—time to attract and hold an audience; time to prove your worth.

A further obstacle to the acceptance of the video story hour by its natural audience of young children was that it was aired at 7:30 and 10:30 in the evening. While some young children might possibly see a 7:30 video story hour, it is unlikely that any would be in a 10:30 P.M. audience. With the growing emphasis on good after-school television offerings for younger children, the time period from 3:30 to 5:30 P.M. would have been more appropriate for at least one airing. A time slot in mid-morning for preschoolers is a possibility too. In fact, almost any time of day earlier than that at which the show was aired would have helped locate its natural audience.

Innovation does not always translate into success, performance, or acceptance. The innovative aspects of this video story hour are important and deserve careful attention. The cooperation of a public library system with commercial television to carry to the public an important public library service is significant. And the potential for forging cooperative links betweeen local and regional school and public library systems is illustrated clearly and provides another valuable program dimension.

The use of the video tape as a staff development tool used to teach other storytellers the best techniques is an exciting possibility too. Logical extensions of this could be made to other programs as well—from hobby and crafts information to career education and health guidance. The potential is enormous and should coax more public libraries into considering possible tie-in programs.

Program Objectives
1. To use the medium of television to introduce children to folk literature and cultures of other countries.
2. To use the medium of television to introduce children to excellent children's literature.
3. To use the medium of television to bring the story hour to large numbers of children.
4. To attempt to involve the public schools and member libraries in a cooperative educational activity.
5. To develop community talent and involvement in a television program format for young children.

Some Suggestions
1. Create evaluation and guidance instrument before program begins.
2. Identify before the program start-up the target group (teachers, children, and parents) to be surveyed.
3. Secure enough advance funding to insure program operation for long enough period to insure proper evaluation.
4. Arrangement for shows to be aired, if possible, once in the afternoon and once in the morning.
5. Make planning cooperative with schools and regional educational agencies prior to doing shows.
6. Consider funding for program through arts foundation or endowment grant. Or, try to secure commercial sponsorship.

ROCHESTER PUBLIC SCHOOLS
Rochester, New York

Staff
Professional: 1
Support: 1

Budget (1975-1976)
Equipment: $8,000

Target Population: 100 children, ages 9-12

For some time now, the Rochester Public Schools have held to some very specific expectations of what media programs can do to make a good school system even better.

In 1971 the Rochester City School District issued a *Statement of Philosophy and Goals*. It's a strong and impressive commitment to the kinds of things that still make for excellence in education. It is curiously unassuming, in that it recognizes that the school is "One (only one) of the most significant institutions in the life of the individual and the community." This same statement says that, "Individuals must develop good schools so that schools will produce better communities." This is a strong endorsement of the concept that a school, after all, is a community resource and that perhaps the best thing it may accomplish is to turn youngsters into useful productive citizens.

The philosophy projects a number of goals that, while visionary, reflect the kinds of principles that should be the proper concern of schools. Among other things, it pledges that every individual will have the right to an equal opportunity to acquire a quality education. The objectives for achieving this goal speak of the need to challenge students, to help them develop their talents, and to improve their sense of responsibility. Specific reference is made as well to the necessity of acquiring skills to help solve problems.

Another goal states a belief in the worth of the individual and in the need to individualize the instructional process so that continuous progress and evalution may allow each student to achieve different degrees of success. Yet another concerns the "Responsibility of the entire community to provide the means, conditions, environment, interest and support necessary for excellence in the total educational program." The achievement of this goal recognizes that the learning of each child must be "centered not only in the formal school setting but also use the available human and material resources of the community."

These and the other goals stated in the Rochester philosophy are unquestionably worthy. The real test lies in how possible it is to achieve them in a system that is urban in geographic and ethnic composition and suffers from all the dislocations and pressures found wtihin any educational setting today. Like many others, the Rochester Schools must deal (or cope) somehow with the reality of broken homes, dimmed aspirations, and clouded hopes when it comes to what education can really hope to accomplish for many children.

One best hope for this is the Rochester media program. Recognition of its successful attainment of goals as a system-wide program has come from a number of sources. One example, *Encyclopaedia Britannica* and the American Association of School Librarians recognized the media program of the elementary schools of Rochester as the School Library Media Award of the Year Program for 1975.

The media program of the Rochester schools provides for flexibility and innovation that should make districts with far greater resources and fewer problems envious. Inservice training, staff development activities, previewing of materials, curriculum involvement, the instructional use of professional staff, and a host of other related components give focus to the media programs fo the Rochester schools.

There is a specific outstanding program designed to help disadvantaged elementary school children upgrade their reading abilities by using media in a manner closely akin to producing a television show. This format has been so successful in the City of Rochester that the State Education Commissioner, speaking for the State Education Department, has urged its adoption in school districts across New York state.

The Video Graphics System is a reading skills program

operating in seven Rochester elementary schools, and is funded by E.S.E.A. Title I monies. Its purpose is to help children with identified reading skills deficiencies become proficient readers. The magic element, of course, is television! This medium has been cited as a prime reason why children do not read with fluency and high motivation. The idea that television could be a potential motivator or facilitator for reading is generally ignored. In Rochester, this is not the case.

GERIS is an acronym for Graphic Expression Reading Improvement System, the full program name. Participants in GERIS are children of ages nine through twelve and its focus is to make children want to read. The extra dimension—the encouragement factor—is that to produce a television show of your own making you *need* to read. For entry into the program a child must be deficient by at least two years in reading level. But GERIS is available for those students who have exhibited potential but lack the motivation to learn to read.

Some 150 children in Rochester participate in the program which uses six TV studios. Usually about twelve children work in a group. An eight-step process, carefully monitored and structured, provides the framework for the program. The steps are (1) selection of a topic; (2) research; (3) graphics preparation; (4) script writing; (5) script revision and practice; (6) practice run-through; (7) evaluation of the practice tape; and (8) final recording.

The only purpose of this media project is to reinforce basic reading skills. At step one, the selection of a topic, children are encouraged to select anything that interests them. The research section of the project has a special focus on outlining and note taking. It is designed to allow the teacher to capitalize on development of such related abilities as finding main ideas, recall of specific facts and details, sequencing, and other reference skills. Use of correct grammar and sentence structure is reinforced as children express in their own words what they have read. When children prepare a script on which to base their planned TV production, these skills are further reinforced.

As the children develop their scripts and move into the process of reading them, other important things must be learned. The ability to communicate effectively with others by using written materials is both art and skill and they are both best learned through repetition and practice. The oral expression sequence concentrates on word pronunciation, rate of reading, enunciation, and reading with expression.

The practice video tape which follows this process and its evaluation reinforces other skills. As the tape is played back, the child and teacher, working together, ask such questions as: Are words pronounced correctly? Am I reading with expression? Are my graphics conveying the ideas I want to express? This involves self-evaluation on the part of the child, but with a direct and sustaining relationship to the teacher.

Even the facilities that house the program are structured so that the skills that go into creating the final production may be reinforced physically. The room housing the program is partitioned to include a research area, containing appropriate print resources. The research area is subdivided as well to permit students to work with little distraction. Selection of a topic, research, and writing may all be accommodated within this area.

A graphics area contains the necessary art supplies such as paints, marking pencils, and the like. Next in line with the production sequence, a listening area with wet (electrified) carrels and cassette player-recorders allows children to practice reading and then listen to themselves. Finally, of course, there is the studio. The accent here is on the simple, the portable, and the easily moved rather than on an elaborate, fixed, and immovable television studio. The less complicated the studio procedure and the easier equipment is to operate, the more children, and their teachers, will be able to do it for themselves.

The Video Graphic Program at Rochester uses three video cameras, two stationary and one mobile; a video monitor; a video cassette player; and a simple special effects generator. That's it!

"Rewarding" and "satisfying," like "interesting," have become cliches with little meaning within the educational vocabulary. They don't have to be, if they are tied realistically to diagnosis, prescription, and evaluation. If television is seen in this perspective, perhaps it will play the kind of educational role its proponents have so fervently wished for it.

Children participating in the Video Graphics Program cannot carry out all the steps until the basic skills of word comprehension, word study, and vocabulary are used with some facility. Review and reinforcement of these skills are a consistent preoccupation of the program.

There is, too, a valuable degree of group interaction and cooperation in the process. The productions of the video graphic program can only be accomplished successfully as children learn to plan and work together. The benefits in terms of self-confidence and self-expression are an obvious and tangible result of this media program. They reinforce a philosophy that commits itself to "guiding students to develop desirable reading, viewing and listening patterns, attitudes and appreciations," and provide an extraordinary dimension to a media-learning program.

Program Objectives
1. To reinforce base skills of reading and writing by using a graphic and video production program.
2. To individualize the skill process of teaching reading and writing.
3. To allow children who have experienced a minimum of success with school to have a successful learning experience.
4. To improve reading scores, on a norm referenced test, by using a video format.
5. To teach effective use of video to reinforce good reading.

Some Suggestions
1. Relate program more specifically to media center resources, particularly in the research and evaluation process.

2. Involve senior high students who are taking video courses in the program to reinforce their skills.
3. Incorporate some volunteers in the program to work with children in the research and evaluation process.
4. Provide a listing of favorite and best tapes that could be used for other instructional purposes in the school.
5. Do specific follow up on number of books read for pleasure by children who are involved in the program before and after participation.

GEORGE BRUCE BRANCH
New York Public Library
New York, New York

Staff
Professional: 1½

Budget (1975-1976)
ESEA Title II: $60,000
(Special purpose grant materials)

Target Population: Uncounted, preschool through grade 7

The needs-assessment survey undertaken by the George Bruce Branch of the New York Public Library before developing a proposal for funding an exemplary media center for children was thorough, comprehensive, and provided clear program goals.

Located in Harlem, the George Bruce Branch has always attracted large numbers of children into its varied programs. It has plenty of space—some 3,000 square feet in the children's room. Attracting an audience was not the problem, for the branch has a tradition of heavy use by children; what was required was a program to relate to the special needs and interests of children, providing an extra learning dimension for their education.

Nearby are located a public elementary school and two Roman Catholic parochial schools. The initial needs assessment revealed that these schools had limited or nonexistent nonprint collections relating to the curriculum areas of science, social studies, and language arts. While the public school media center had a better collection, its resources were strained to meet the needs of the entire curriculum. And money could not be found to purchase the large amounts of materials necessary to support enriched learning programs.

The need was evident—provide an ungraded, expanded collection of nonprint items that could relate to the learning needs of school children for an entire inner-city area. This collection had to be accessible to each of the schools, easily used by teachers and children, and related to various curricula. The George Bruce Branch was selected to be the home of the special project.

A significant project innovation was the careful planning to involve teaching staff. The first objective stated for the program was "to provide an exemplary school and public library cooperative program." Already this objective has been met with success. The program is operating and makes the educational impact expected of it.

Built in 1914 as one of the earliest Carnegie libraries, the library building is unmistakably New York City, identified if only by the grafitti that adorn its walls. But pass through this indecorous facade, climb two flights of stairs, and enter a spacious, tastefully arranged, attractive room. The media center is found at the front of the room, in the former children's reading and reference area. A plus for this project is that little renovation was required to get it started. Additional electrical outlets had to be installed, and the carrels in use were donated by other libraries in the system. Minor shelving changes to accommodate some nonprint media were the only other structural changes.

Media selected with grant monies were 8mm film loops, filmstrips, cassette tapes, records, transparencies, slides, and videotapes. Three-dimensional realia (part of the science kit) included such objects as a plastic model of the human body and an electrified globe of the universe.

Equipment costs for the project amounted to a little more than $1,600. These funds came from a special endowment fund available to the George Bruce Branch. This equipment included cassette players, filmstrip viewers, record players, headsets, and sound filmstrip viewers.

The greatest difficulty in operating such a project is getting materials into the hands of the teachers for instructional use. The children gravitate to it on their own. One possible way to do this is to schedule teacher and class visits to the center. But will such scheduling necessarily fit the time at which information is needed? The answer, of course, is no. These visits are not so useful for research by children as they are to inform teachers about materials and how best to use them. Teachers are encouraged to take out materials, and they do. Teachers in the New York City public schools are familiar with this process, for scheduled visits to district media centers are normal routine here, so that teachers may take what they need for classroom use.

The public library and its school partners also scheduled orientation sessions with teachers to discuss mutual problems; how to use the materials for good instruction; and how to relate the materials to curriculum. Day-to-day program coordination is shared by the public school media staff and children's specialist at the public library.

A significant break-through for the program results from access to the New York Public Library's computer. The materials purchased for the program were ordered by the public library, received, and processed by its staff. As they become ready for use, computer printed cards are sent to each school media center so that building access to the project materials is assured. Soon, however, every teacher in *each* school will have an individual computer printed catalog of all available materials. The program will thus leap over the traditional problem of how to get teachers to use the card catalog as an instruction planning resource for their teaching. With a resource catalog in their hands, there is expectation that teachers will make much better use of the instructional resource.

In its first year of operation, interviews with teachers and checks of circulation figures show that teachers are using more nonprint media for instruction. This is especially noticeable in the nonpublic schools, with their severely limited nonprint collections. One of these schools reports that teachers are planning to purchase equipment that will permit even more use of the materials. An early spin-off appears to be strengthened building level media programs.

Unanticipated during project planning was something the staff has watched wtih interest and approval—walk-in business is up! The materials are attracting attention in the community, much of which is bilingual. Many of the books purchased for the project are in Spanish and French. But it is clearly the nonprint items that entice parents and children to use the materials. No formal attempt has been made to evaluate it, but this outreach into a community that needs information so desperately has to be considered a plus.

Continuity of learning opportunity must be recognized as an important program strength. Most New York public schools rely heavily on scheduling classes into the media center. Resources there are not always available to individuals or small groups of children when they need them. The open-access policy of the public library means that the media children need for learning is available to them outside of school hours. The increased opportunity to get at and use informtion is important. Demonstrated too is that public libraries and librarians need not shy away from direct learning involvement and teaching. In fact, they have an important role to play in many situations.

The interlinking and cooperation of schools and public library is the program's strongest feature. The teachers show this in their work. The ability of teachers to initiate projects in their classrooms and have them continued and developed at the public library was a project objective that is also being met. The coordination of human and material resources is an extraordinary enrichment component of the program.

Dilemmas caused by New York City's continuing fiscal plight have had their impact here too. Two professionals and support staff were planned for the program. Budget cuts did that in. The one professional children's librarian who works with the project gets some help from the head of the branch who is also a children's librarian. Clerical help is almost nonexistent. Hours of service have been cut as well. The branch now closes on Fridays in order that it may be opened on Saturdays so the children will be able to use the materials and resources of the project. Discouraging, yes! But the message comes through clearly that this program may be more important than ever for this community, and somehow must survive and grow. So while progress is slower than planned, it is happening.

The project is in an area where active parent support of educational programs and volunteering is uncommon. Every attempt should be made to recruit some volunteers into the program, for they could help.

There is hope that the project can carry on beyond the life of the funding monies, which were used only to purchase materials. The staff running the program is already in place and the program is on-going, a solid prototype available for expansion into other branches if the need is there and the situation appropriate.

Meanwhile, the project demonstrates (1) the advantages of purchasing materials on a shared and cooperative basis, (2) the in-service benefits that come from school-public library cooperation, (3) better teacher use of media in classrooms, and (4) increased learning opportunities for children.

Program Objectives
1. To provide an exemplary program of school and public library cooperation.
2. To provide access to information and materials for children after school hours.
3. To stimulate teachers to initiate more teaching with nonprint media on the expectation that the resources to support this would be available.
4. To provide specific school curriculum support through use of federal funds to buy materials for school use but to be housed in a public library.
5. To provide computer print-outs of materials available in the public library within the school.

Some Suggestions
1. Add at least one clerical support position.
2. Try to involve some volunteers from the community.
3. Do random survey-interviews of those involved in the project to track their use of the materials.
4. Consider some specific community programs that could utilize the materials.
5. Continue to schedule workshops with teachers to demonstrate materials and suggest use of them.

LEWISTON-PORTER PUBLIC SCHOOLS
Youngstown, New York

Staff
Professional: 77
Media
 Coordinator: 1
Curriculum
 Coordinator: 1
 Curriculum
 Coordinator
 (building): 3
 Support: 9
Volunteers: 3

Budget (1975-1976)
Print: $28,000

Nonprint: 26,000

Target Population: 2,000 children, ages 7-12

Most educators who give any thought to the relationship of media programs and reading programs seem to believe that it is one of time and adjustment. Time translates to mean that somehwere in its passage, media programs and reading programs will come together more or less spontaneously. Adjustment is really an euphemism, expressing only the hope and not the expectation that the two programs will somehow find the ways to work together to achieve common program goals.

Hoping is not going to make this happen, and if there is one thing that clouds the credibility of media programs and reading programs, it is the appallingly short-sighted way they relate to and work with each other. In fact, in many schools they don't work together at all! The victims of this are many: children who need the resources and help of both programs; classroom teachers who need the guidance and assistance of media and reading professionals; and parents whose taxes pay twice for programs that needlessly duplicate each other. And it is media programs and reading programs themselves that suffer the greatest damage; for their preoccupation with ignoring or downgrading the other saps their energy and ability to focus where they should—helping children gain the skills, interests, and attitudes necessary to become good readers.

Much of the failure to communicate and cooperate comes from our inability to plan or coordinate—even to talk together. Separate vocabularies, separate professional concerns, separate funding procedures, and separate preparation of professionals cannot but have a negative effect on both programs. It doesn't have to be this way. The steady growth and effectiveness of media programs that tie behavioral objectives and expected outcomes to other programs give greater hope than ever before that media programs and reading programs can "get it together."

The Reading Levels Programs of the Lewiston-Porter Schools is a carefully planned, systematic attempt to put together media programs and reading programs at the building level; it seeks to overcome some of these traditional problems. The program began over six years ago and continues to undergo refinement and modification. Designed as an individualized approach to the *reading skills* segment of the *total* reading program, the skills program seems, at first, complex and formidable. This is not so, for it is really only a management system. And effective reading systems management here involves media and reading programs and media and reading specialists working together.

Traditional attitudes and methods must be shelved in planning and implementing this program. Too many media specialists see their role as involving reading for enjoyment only with reading specialists consigned to skills teaching or remedial work. Thus, artificial and harmful boundaries are established; a reading center, or lab, for the drudgery of skill building, the media center for the fun of reading. But mastery of skills and reading enjoyment are not two separate functions. Media specialists have a responsibility to see that reading skills are incorporated naturally on a daily basis into media center programs. Together, media specialists and reading teachers have a natural, sensible mandate to do everything necessary to see that the end product of a skills program is a child able to use reading skills to read for information and pleasure. What other possible justification can there possibly be for the preoccupation we exhibit with reading skills and reading levels.

Within the Reading Levels Program, reading skills are sequenced by levels, there being twenty-four in all. Each reading level is composed of a number of skills classified in broad categories such as word recognition, vocabulary, literal comprehension, interpretive comprehension, dictionary skills, library skills, literature and appreciation, and psychomotor and social adjustments. Each of the twenty-four skills levels requires that a skills check list be maintained for each student. This skills check list allows teacher, reading specialist, media specialist, and aide to monitor the progress of every child, varying prescriptions and activities as appropriate or necessary. Diagnostic testing is an integral portion of the skills program. This testing program operates from the testing center and tests students for competency in specific skill areas both before and after they work through a skills sequence.

A main purpose of the reading center and the skills reinforcement program is to allow classroom teachers more time to work with individual or small groups of children who require additional help in other areas. Children work in the learning center under the direction of an aide whose job is to help the child find prescribed materials and supervise their use.

Several principles of the Reading Levels Program clarify the involvement of the media program. Among these are (1) that for each child, learning, though sometimes erratic, is a continuous process; (2) that children learn best when they are successful; (3) that responsibility and independence can be taught best by providing children opportunities to practice them; and (4) that students learn best when they have a positive self-image. There are other principles, but these principles any good media program will endorse, support, and use to extend its instructional-service role.

Some of the learning center programs incorporate a strand that ties together reading center and media center. This strand is an activity or learning experience that takes the child from the reading center or the classroom into the media center. Its purpose is to get children interested in, and involved with, using the best reading resource in many schools, the media center.

Potential tie-in strands from a reading center to a media center are really limitless. It may be a straightforward activity such as selecting a book. It could be to read books by a single author or develop activities around a single literary genre, such as poetry or short stories. And the reports which culminate these activities need not be the traditional written report on "Why I liked this book" but more imaginative, such as having one child sell another as to *why* a book should be read. The objective though becomes tying the reading center and media center program together in program activities rather than separating them into unique, distinct, and unrelated programs.

Media skills teaching can also be made more relevant when related to the reading program. The broad categories of necessary media skills used in this program are use of the card catalog; arrangement of books and nonprint materials; use of indexes, almanacs, dictionaries and other reference materials; and ability to use various parts of a book such as the table of contents and the index. The media program and reading program reinforce each other's activities to help children understand that effective use of information comes from an ability to use skills with ease to get at and use information.

The Reading Levels Program presents a ready-made opportunity for a media program to relate media skills instruction to learning needs. The process used is not looking up information to be recopied, but skills mastery relating directly to, and reinforced by, the sequential steps of the reading program.

The financial commitment necessary to carry a Reading Skills Center is considerable. Abundant resources, many prepared commercially, must be available. Language Master Programs, reading kits, study skills kits, developmental learning materials, controlled readers, audio cassettes, programmed readers, skill-pacing boxes, filmstrips, film loops, and reading comprehension programs are among the arsenal of materials and equipment used in the program. It is possible to select from only one or two of these commercially prepared reading programs, but this may diminish program impact.

Then, too, support staff must be available to release the teacher or media specialist for more concentrated one-to-one, or small group, work with children. Volunteers can help, and do, in this program but no program as tightly structured as the Reading Skills Program can rely to any great degree on volunteer staffing. Management, in the form of record keeping, pretesting, post-testing and continuous assessment can be a burden. But the support staff, with proper direction, is able to maintain the records used in the program.

For those looking, the Reading Levels Program is an unusual opportunity for the media program to piggy-back its way directly into the most important instructional program in any elementary school, the reading program.

Building an individualized media skills instruction program in the vacuum that exists in even the best elementary schools is frustrating and delivers only minimal instructional payoff. In this program specific instructional relationship is established and reinforced, for the media skills portion of the program is located right in the media center.

A visitor remarked about the skill with which the media program has been integrated into the instructional program and the enthusiasm with which this has been accomplished. A unified media concept, pervades the media program and relates it successfully to many programs including the reading program, showing integration of the media into the curriculum at its best.

Program Objectives
1. To integrate media program into a reading levels program.
2. To have such media-related tasks as the teaching of media skills and other skills relate to the reading program.

3. To apply principles of prescriptive learning to media programs.
4. To use media program to individualize student instruction.
5. To attempt to use a reading skills development program in the transition to reading for pleasure.

Some Suggestions
1. Establish more formal lines of evaluation between media skills program and Reading Levels Program.
2. State more specifically which media skills will be part of the Skills Check List.
3. Provide more specific activities relating to the literature for pleasure component to better involve the media program.
4. Consider some recognition tie-in to the program from the media center. Top readers, creative poetry, and the like.
5. Clarify budget responsibilities and costs for replacement of kit items. What are replacement costs?

FORSYTH COUNTY PUBLIC LIBRARY
Winston-Salem, North Carolina

Staff
Professional: 2
Support: 12

Budget (1975-1976)
Print: $7,500
Nonprint: 1,000

Target Population: 6,000 children, ages 3-18

The City of Winston-Salem and Forsyth County, North Carolina, have benefitted for over four years from a unique program called Public Library Action for Children's Education (PLACE). Representing wise use of LSCA funding and a fine example of outreach programming to persons not traditionally served by public library programs, it directly involves the local community in some basic decision-making about the kinds of programs needed to serve their information needs. A number of community institutions and agencies make a unified attempt to meet the needs of a carefully selected target group, disadvantaged youth. Project PLACE is the umbrella program and provides excellent examples of this kind of library service for other libraries. The program recognizes the responsibility of a public library to be an educational institution reaching out to people, involving them in finding and using necessary information and services.

Funded initially with federal monies, the program is now supported by allocations of budget money from the county government. A measure of program success is the willingness of local government to assume the costs of a special program that has proved its worth to the community.

Precise and sensitive planning marked the program start; it involved headstart programs, churches, and child development agencies and provided the basis for strong community support. Programs included in the PLACE outreach program are a morning preschool program, an afternoon and evening program for young adults, and some weekend programs.

The preschool program began first in eight preschool

centers. Weekly services included a rotating book collection, library instruction, storytelling, music, creative drama, and other education and enrichment programs utilizing a wide variety of community resources.

Staffing relied upon the combined resources of the library's professional and support personnel, preschool center personnel, and volunteers from the families of children enrolled in the preschool program. Service was to continue, even without a library representative, so the library conducted workshops on the program objectives and provided continuing guidance and supervision. A specific purpose was to train a core of persons at the preschool centers that could carry on the program while new programs were begun in additional centers. There are now thirty-two programs in housing projects, churches, and other early childhood centers.

The afterschool and evening program for children provides educational and enrichment materials and programs for children age six to fourteen through programs in two recreational centers, two community houses, and ten mobile stops. Special guidance, training, and information programs were to be available to meet the diverse needs of disadvantaged youth. These included orientation to library resources, reading guidance, resource programs (survival information), and other activities.

Local centers housing this program were established with the cooperation of Model Cities, the Housing Authority, and the Winston-Salem Recreation Department. Program coordination was accomplished by an advisory committee of library personnel, agency officials, and young people and adults from the community.

A multiplier effect was planned to maximize the impact of the library staff associated with Project PLACE. This was an emphasis placed on recruiting and training young adults from the community into the program; they would in turn extend the program into the community. One community house program is directed by a husky basketball player; the media mobile has a high school drop-out who studied as an aide in the library program and was motivated to study and pass high school equivalency so that he could become a library staff member.

Additional hours of service for children, resource programs for the general public, and training sessions for volunteers were provided with an extended hours (6:00 to 9:00 P.M.,) program Monday through Friday. Saturday, and occasional Sundays, would bring film programs, gallery exhibits, and lectures or demonstrations.

Mobility for the many parts of the program was crucial if it was to impact upon the local community. The Media Mobile Service provides maximum contact for a widely scattered population and allows some after-hours and weekend service. The mobile unit has books and visual materials and equipment and is manned by a specially trained staff. This highly successful outreach operation established its value early and has accomplished the purpose of bringing together people, dispersed over a wide geographic area, with important media resources. The media mobile reinforces the ties between the library and the community and it is a visible reminder that the library has credibility and can be trusted to do its job.

In assessing what happened with all of these plans many things have to be considered. First, some early assumptions had to be laid to rest. One assumption was that poor people, unaccustomed to library programs, would reject them unless they had a hard-sell effort to encourage their use. The PLACE staff discovered that once children and young people were convinced the program was really there for them, their involvement was enthusiastic and easily sustained. A second assumption, more unconscious than conscious, was that the library was doing something wonderfully praiseworthy in giving from its "bounty" services to citizens who had never had them. In fact, the library staff soon came to realize, the program was providing something that is the *right* of every citizen. Confusion between rights and privileges is a liability common to many outreach programs. A do-gooding approach can sink a program fast, particularly with people not used to trusting or to having their expectations met.

What else has been learned? The mixing of professional library staff and paid community support staff can be most successful. Only two of the nine staff members have professional library degrees; in fact, only one other has a college degree. The primary success criteria for personnel appear to be a love of working with children and a good relationship to the community. It is the staff that provides the glue that holds this dispersed multifaceted program together. New staff members receive two weeks of formal training and periodic special workshops to upgrade or train for special program skills.

The citizen advisory committees, organized to help plan the afternoon and evening program for children, have not been successful. Lack of interest and failure to find a real need for them finished them off. Attempts to involve teenage volunteers have also been unrewarding.

A variety of approaches backed by a wide selection of media used to entice and to educate are vital. Filmstrips, cassettes, paperback books, 16mm films, and 8mm film loops provide the backbone of materials support for the program. The relative ease with which they may be moved about and used, their high level of acceptability among children, their usefulness for entertainment and education, and their applicability to many situations make these media formats ideal for a program such as PLACE.

Interspersed with educational programs are beauty demonstrations, arts and crafts programs, story times, and film programs. Quiet time for study is provided and is a successful program.

A visitor reported that one typical community house library-outreach program occupied several small rooms on the second floor of a shabby frame house and was sponsored jointly as a center by the Episcopal church and a self-help association. Painting and clay-modelling, a pet turtle, games, lots of books (well used), reading and story times, help with homework, a lovely homey atmosphere, makes this a haven from the misery and hopelessness of much of the surrounding neighborhood.

The PLACE program has provided the disadvantaged child with media programs reinforced by personal contact with caring adult models. These have helped create positive self-images and promote learning where it did not exist before. The impact within the total community is equally important, for to many it is probably the only demonstration of an institutionalized community effort to be effective in meeting their specific needs.

PLACE program priorities are clear. They are to get as much service, program, adventure, recreation, discovery, and self-identity to the children as possible. If the cycle of apathy and noninvolvement in the public library programs can be broken in communities like these, then truly the public library can make major strides toward the realization of its proper role as an educational and informational resource, contributing to the enrichment of living, knowing, and learning throughout the community.

Program Objectives
1. To provide disadvantaged youths with outreach programs to create a more positive self-image and promote learning.
2. To promote the role of the public library as a concerned and active agency, serving a population usually ignored.
3. To integrate a wide variety of media into programs for preschool children and young adults.
4. To promote institutional cooperation in defining patterns of useful and effective service to the disadvantaged.
5. To improve motivation of disadvantaged children and young adults to use information to help their advancement.

Some Suggestions
1. Develop closer relationship with school programs to evaluate effect of PLACE programs on the achievement of the child in school.
2. Increase support staff to provide more employment opportunities as well as closer relationship to community.
3. Provide for increased continuation of PLACE program with other more established programs emanating from the public library.

4. Continue effort to attract more adult volunteers into the program to reinforce community ties.
5. Work at establishing clearer information programs useful to mothers (nutrition and health) as tie-in to preschool programs.

SCHOOL OF LIBRARY SCIENCE
North Carolina Central University
Durham, North Carolina

Staff
Professional: 1

Budget
Initial grant from various foundations for materials and salary: $392,400
On going for materials:1,000

Target Population: Student Librarians and parents

North Carolina Central University's School of Library Science offers a program of specialization in Early Childhood Librarianship. Among other things, it proposes to (1) train students to become effective practitioners of early childhood library methods; (2) provide an exemplary learning center for implementing methods and applying theories; (3) involve library science students in actual learning programs in community agencies; (4) provide students with some work experience wtih parents, aiding them to be effective change agents in the home. These objectives, and the activities that result constitute a unique program of specialized library education.

Underlying the program are a series of expectations and assumptions. One assumption, supported by research, is that proper selection and use of appropriate learning materials will increase certain foundation skills in young children. There is widespread and growing interest in "parenting," and this presents a real target of opportunity to library media specialists. The point is to get children and parents involved at the earliest possible time in using media to improve learning readiness. Motivation, guidance, and use of media to improve developmental skills for young children are at the core of the program.

While this program is designed for specialized preparation in early childhood librarianship, it exhibits other significant factors. One is the heavy financial support for the program provided by large corporations and foundations. These have included Xerox, Z. Smith Reynolds, and General Mills. Foundation contributions came from the Carnegie and Mellon Trusts. Another source of funding has been the United States Office of Education. Exemplary, then, is the program's ability to attract and utilize funding from disparate sources. As government funding for library programs recedes, private corporations (who do have a direct "enlightened self interest" concern in the quality of community library-information programs) must be pursued more ardently if new funding sources are to be found for specialized programs.

Recently the high level of funding provided for the Early Childhood Program has been reduced with a negative effect on staffing and acquisition of new materials. A program priority (concern) must be to establish a more predictable and secure base of funding from local or state government resources.

Both the Early Childhood Librarianship Program and the library school involve students in programs that enable them to transfer from theories about how children learn and what makes them want to learn to first-hand work with children in real life situations. Also receiving a priority is parent involvement. Attention goes particularly to parents of disadvantaged children who might, through increased understandings and expectations about their childrens' learning, increase home opportunities for this. Other community groups and agencies including nursery schools, day-care centers, and kindergarten groups come to the early childhood center library to use and borrow materials.

Initially, the program staff consisted of a full-time professional (paid for by foundation funds) who taught two program-related courses, a full-time secretary, and graduate assistants. Now, the librarian who directs the Early Childhood Librarianship Program is a member of the university staff and teaches other courses as well. While many professionals must assume multiple roles and double up on program assignments, this range of responsibilities does detract from the best possible service from the Early Childhood Library.

With secretarial and clerical reductions, other limitations and restraints are placed on the program. In spite of this, the library serves as a special kind of laboratory for students in university teacher education programs, for parents, and for others working directly with children. This multiplicity of uses strengthens and extends the usefulness and impact of the program. Despite staff limitations, a significant number of persons is reached and affected favorably.

Materials in the Early Childhood Library are used on site or loaned out, and staff development workshops for different groups and individuals are on-going program components. Materials from the library are used by library school classes as well. Finally, parents and organizations wanting to use these materials may sign them out. This accessibility to, and easy movement of, materials into different locations is a program plus.

Equipment and materials available include cassette player recorders, opaque projectors, flannel boards, filmstrip, and 8mm projectors and a camera. Materials are far too numerous to list completely, but a sampling includes art prints, dolls, globes, masks, puzzles, and a wide variety of toys. Many of these have been purchased, while other items have been made by students in the library school. They are an interesting, useful, and practical addition to the collection.

The library makes clear that it is not a baby-sitting or playpen operation. Children are not just dropped off to play for retrieval later. Directions for using the library state that the parent or adult accompanying the child is responsible for how the child uses the center.

Special effort goes to involving parents in the center programs. Parents accompany their children and while the children play with, browse through, or select the materials, the program participants work with parents explaining and stressing the importance of play to developmental learning and reading readiness. Many parents have become interested enough to chart their own child's progress in a kind of learning developmental sequence.

As part of their course requirement, students in the Early Childhood Librarianship Program plan some experiences involving children that take place at the center. Other adults are encouraged to become part of these programs and interact directly with the young children. The learning experience for adult and child is *expected* to be mutual.

Neither a complete catalog nor a thorough description of the materials in the collection is available. Accordingly, retrieval is random and depends upon the ability of the staff to locate materials and equipment as needed. Since the room housing the collection is small (about 500 square feet) and its use carefully structured in proportion of children to adults this is not a serious problem. However, when the Early Childhood Library moves to newer and larger quarters, as is now anticipated, complete organization, cataloging, and coding of the collection must have top priority. The collection is almost entirely nonprint items—realia and toys. The materials are organized into broad subject curriculum areas such as language arts, social studies, mathematics and science, and the arts. A color code is assigned to each subject area, and this allows a reasonably coherent method of locating needed materials.

Only a few books are to be found in the Early Childhood Library because of space limitations. Books that relate to this age group or have a professional importance are found in the library of the School of Library Science. It would, of course, be preferable to have both print and nonprint materials housed together at the center.

The program stresses the learning process rather than just playing with toys. Everything relates to developmental learning and learning readiness skills and serves as a training model for librarians, parents, teachers and others involved with early childhood learning.

Another valuable aspect of the program is that it demonstrates benefits gained from close cooperation between library schools and public libraries. While public libraries rarely have either the resources or capabilities to establish such model programs themselves, they are quick to grasp the important need filled by such a resource. A public library satellite operation provides direct access to children and parents here. This fosters close and continuing contacts between the school of library science and the public library, reinforcing further the value of the program to children, parents, and community.

The potential for a program like this acting as a regional or district evaluation center should not be overlooked. As many learning agencies, other than libraries, become directly involved with the education of the preschool child, there is a growing need to evaluate carefully the materials to be used in these library programs. Toys used for instructional purposes with children should be examined carefully and used under appropriate conditions.

Clearly, the Early Childhood Library is a valuable program, one with the potential to make outstanding contributions to the learning of young children. It has established that librarians and parents do have a shared concern and responsibility to involve themselves together in improving the learning possibilities for the very young child.

Program Objectives
1. To provide a laboratory experience to help parents understand the importance of play to developmental learning.
2. To provide library school students an opportunity to devise learning activities, using play and toys, for very young children.
3. To outreach into the community to provide headstart developmental learning programs for young children.
4. To develop cooperative preschool children programs between a library school and a public library.
5. To use a variety and combination of funding (corporate, foundation, government) to create a preschool learning program.

Some Suggestions
1. Secure increased local or state funding to maintain and

enrich collection and replace diminishing foundation-corporate support.
2. Place a full-time professional in charge of program.
3. Organize collection in such a way that it may be retrieved other than through "hunt and find" access.
4. Try to relate program more specifically to local school districts for clearer follow-through.
5. Use video tape to record play experiences for later seminar class use.

CHILLICOTHE AND ROSS COUNTY PUBLIC LIBRARY
Chillicothe, Ohio

Staff
Professional: 8 (includes school and public library staff)
Support: 2
Volunteer: 6

Budget
Not applicable

Target Population: 5,381 children, ages 5-18 (K-12)

If you're looking for a library program that involves large numbers of children in an educational program of resource oriented history, is based upon cooperative planning by schools and a public library, involves other community agencies and costs practically nothing, then consider a program going on in Chillicothe, Ohio.

It is no secret that we sought out for our survey media programs for children that were marked by efforts to develop such programs on an inter-institutional basis, with shared responsibilities for them. We looked for cooperation. Not considered here are programs coming from shared facilities; that's bound to provoke counter-productive debate that hides the real issue of how to provide the best possible media programs for children. The Chillicothe-Ross County program demonstrates that it is possible for disparate institutions to plan and implement programs serving children's needs by crossing over institutional boundaries.

The program relates specifically to history teaching in the schools and is used for either enrichment or basic instruction. The core of the program is an historical exhibit consisting of realia, print materials, pictures, and historical artifacts. The project began in 1976 as a special bicentennial program, but this does not limit the possibilities this kind of program has to relate easily to a nearly limitless number of social or historical events and issues. For example, a similar earlier program here consisted of a series of exhibits about the nations of the world that circulated among the schools and was used to provide instructional support.

The local historical society, with its access to historical artifacts and memorabilia, played an important role in program planning. Local historical societies often have a determination to show those elements and colorations that make local history the lively study it potentially is. Personalities, events, and local place and family names provide a reality and immediacy about local history so often missing for children as they study national history. Aside from memorabilia, pictures, pamphlets, and sometimes movies, slides and filmstrips, local historical societies provide important access to the resource people, who can add unique dimensions to teaching local history. They are a community resource that can provide an important program success factor.

Planning and some special staff and resource commitments were required for this program to accomplish valid educational objectives for the schools. In Chillicothe the public library provides certain services to the schools by contract. This contract, though, does not mandate cooperation or joint planning by the two institutions, important as this may be. Planning for the project brought together the public library head of School Services and the public school head of the Instructional Material Center. The public library with heavily print oriented programs and the IMC, more oriented to nonprint services, quickly saw the value of cooperation. Sometimes attitudes and "postures" of individuals in similar situations scuttle any such programs before they float. Not so here!

It was agreed the exhibits would focus on (1) early Chillicothe; (2) industrial growth; (3) transportation; (4) colonial America; (5) art, music, sports, clothing and life styles; (6) Revolution and founding the nation; (7) the Civil War; (8) schools; (9) natural resources; (10) immigration; (11) conflicts abroad; and (12) Indians in America. These themes could be adapted easily by any library or media program wanting to try a variation of this program. Limitations come only from the imagination and abilities of those planning. The potential number of historical themes, alone, is enormous.

And the exhibit theme may be built into most disciplines; environment and ecology, health information, and career education are other obvious possibilities.

The exhibit program was to extend and enrich the limited resources of the school media centers by providing materials giving a specific focus to historical events and personalities. A second objective was to stimulate teachers to improve their use of the services and materials in school media centers.

Artifacts, costumes, and documents were the main exhibit elements. The exhibits would be placed in cases and treated, in a sense, as museum displays. The humanizing-teaching element came from persons recruited through the historical society, who would go into the schools. Their purpose—to add life, and a personal dimension, to the display objects, making of them more than museum objects. They provided an important instructional dimension to the exhibit program, as they met and interacted with students while talking about the exhibit objects.

Scheduling the exhibits is an important consideration. Three weeks per school was agreed to, and the schedule was announced far enough in advance to give time for instructional planning within the building. Making a virtue of necessity, this schedule encouraged teachers, particularly at the elementary level, to plan ahead so that they did not all have to teach about Indians at the same time. By using the resource exhibits and rotating the displays, planning was better coordinated, providing positive reinforcement for teachers to be more rational and imaginative in planning their teaching.

Only teachers may use the exhibit realia items, and this could limit program value if the goal were for children to use these resources. The intent of this program, however, is to improve the teaching of certain history units by teacher use of these items. Other resources are available to students and are coordinated within the program to satisfy their learning needs.

A multiplier effect of the historical exhibit program has been to promote other additional PTA and community programs. Its success at the local level has also caused the State

Library to adopt a similar program that circulates displays of books and materials.

A positive program impact has been that children are stimulated to do more individualized inquiry, research, and investigation. The displays are intended to be provocative—to make the observer wonder and want to know. Reinforcement of the belief that learning can be acquired beyond the bounds of a single text book is a program asset too. Its use requires teachers and children to assume a more individualized learning style and to rely upon a variety of resources to provide necessary information. Field trips, use of resource persons, and a variety of media lead to a kind of learning that demands more involvement from the teacher and the child.

The cooperative planning continues as the program reassesses its directions. New dimensions are planned by adding either a storytelling or book-talk element. This reading tie-in will provide an enrichment aspect that will strengthen the program. An attempt to draw more volunteers into the program is underway too. As a program it is neat and simple yet it displays an effective capacity to improve instruction in the schools.

Program Objectives
1. To involve school media programs and public library programs in cooperative planning for joint programs within schools.
2. To involve community agencies in an instructional program administered by both a school and public library program.
3. To use artifacts and other items of historical interest to upgrade the quality of instruction in some schools.
4. To make teachers more aware of the value of using a wide variety of media to improve instruction.

5. To promote and stimulate use of existing materials and services without significant budget increases.

Some Suggestions
1. Provide more specific directions or programs for exhibits. A variation of a Learning Activity Package (LAP) is a possibility.
2. Provide more specific evaluation of materials and items used.
3. Involve more volunteers in the program to extend its impact while in a building.
4. Consider use of video to tape local historical sites or film interviews with local figures in oral/visual history approach.
5. Provide more specific building level staff development programs on using the exhibits.

OKLAHOMA

PUTNAM CITY HIGH SCHOOL
Oklahoma City, Oklahoma

Staff

Professional: 3
Support: 1

Budget (1975-1976, for career education project only)

Print: $2,400
Nonprint: 3,000
Equipment: 9,000
ESEA Title III:
First year: $25,000
Second year: 20,500
Third year: 20,000

Target Population: 3,000 children, ages 15-18

In the federal grant-projects world, career education programs are hot ticket items. The high priority placed on career awareness and world of work programs by national, state, and local education agencies is backed with big money. In schools it is not unusual to see nooks, crannies, and closets—even whole rooms—transformed almost instantaneously into career education centers. And cascading onto the market is a stupefying array of materials for use with career awareness programs. Local staff development leaders reassess their offerings to make certain that an increased ability to teach career awareness and work alternatives is provided for teachers. Media specialists and guidance personnel have ESEA Title IV B monies as their catalyst to plan programs in this area. It is unwise then to report media programs for the 1970s without reporting some programs that use media to implement a career information programs.

That some cynicism surrounds some of the current effort to marry media with career education is understandable. Like many new programs it may be oversold in its expectations and promised results. The concept, though, makes good sense, especially if the program focus lies in helping young persons to recognize and deal realistically with the array of options surrounding career or work choices. Options is an important word to this book and in our lives. We live in an age of options that allows us to *choose* satisfying living styles, desirable learning methods, and ways of working to name a few. Specific codes and rigid rules enforced by social pressure and psychological expectation give way to alternative life styles and increased freedom of choice.

Career education reflects these changes. It is reasonable to expect that many people will have several different careers and work experiences during their lifespans. It is impossible to think of anything that affects life so profoundly as work. From an early age, then, children need information to make them aware of career options, the things that can be done to maximize opportunities, to achieve ambitions, and to help make wise career decisions. The key to this process is access to the information.

The Putnam City High School Occupational Information Program has one major goal: To develop and implement an exemplary media support system for the integration of career education into the curriculum of the school through the library-based career information center.

A healthy characteristic of the Putnam Project is that it was not devised in response to the availability of money to finance it. The program reflects an ordering of priorities established within the district; priorities established by educators, students, and the community. An accountability approach to evaluating various educational programs fostered separate needs assessments in most of the Putnam school district. Requested at the high school was more up-to-date job opportunity information. Vocational awareness, said students, was their number one need.

The Career Information Center created in response to this was funded from a special ESEA Title III grant of $25,000. Additional grants of $20,500 followed for the second year and $20,000 (Title IV C) for a coming third year. The first grant provided salary for an occupational information specialist (a media specialist), a paraprofessional, and for the Project Director during one summer month. The Project Director also serves as head of the Putnam High School media center, more than eighty percent of the director's time goes to other parts of the media program.

Of the initial grant, about $15,000 ($10,000 Title III and $5,000 district) was used to purchase materials and equipment to create a well-stocked career information center. These materials included reference books, trade books, pamphlets, career briefs, films, microfiche, filmstrips, games, and other materials. Video and photographic equipment encourage production or recording of original materials, useful events, or information.

Program emphasis is on getting information into the hands of users. The vertical file, with its hidden "find-me-if-you-can" folders of yellowed clippings, is replaced by pamphlets and clippings located in well-marked folders, easily accessible in open tub files. Catalogs from colleges, universities, and trade schools are found in book and microfilm format. Print and nonprint materials are intershelved together, to invite browsing and facilitate use. Emphasized too is *understanding* the options of career choices by increasing awareness of alternatives. Going to college, for example, is not the end process in the decision-making chain. For some it is a useful alternative, for others irrelevant and unnecessary.

Involvement of people, use of materials, and evaluation of outcomes combine together in this program. Initial program objectives stated that the Center would involve at least eighty-five percent of the students by the end of its first year of operation, and that at least ninety percent of the school's professional staff would be aware of the Center and use its resources in their teaching.

The Career Information Center is the only one of its kind in Oklahoma, and so it was committed also to some involvement with that state's educational community in order to make that community more aware of the value of a career center. This program outreach capacity adds greatly to its dimension. It is also committed to work with students from a nearby university, orienting them to the Center. The Center has offered several workshops for Oklahoma educators about career awareness programs.

The precision with which the Career Center moved to

achieve these goals is noteworthy. Introductory learning activities to encourage student use of the center are done cooperatively with the English department in the sophomore year. This class also participates in a career planning activity by taking the Career Planning Program, a standardized test by ACT (American College Testing), in cooperation with the Guidance department. Junior students participate formally in the center by taking an Assessment of Career Development (ACD), another standardized test by ACT, in cooperation with the Social Studies department.

The highly structured involvement of the students in these initial activities is deliberate. From this beginning develops a sequence of activities including individual career planning assistance for seniors; mini-courses in career awareness; and, eventually, completely individualized learning programs.

For the professional staff, an objective of getting them involved with the Center to the point where at least twenty-five percent will try one career-related teaching activity begins with an orientation session. This includes a half-day workshop designed to acquaint them with career awareness, how to integrate career awareness into teaching, and how best to use the resouces of the Career Center.

Teachers and students serve on the project's advisory committee. Their suggestions and comments are considered carefully and exert an impact on the direction of the program. The program reflects meticulous planning to establish goals, specify objectives, and develop activities to provide successful programs. The staff is committed to the program and wants it to succeed. Super-graphics, posters, and displays add a sense of the with-it to the Career Information Center. A sense of involvement by the school and community is evident. Guidance counselors spread the word and elective career awareness courses emanating from the Center show a steady increase in participants.

The Career Center is an integral part of the media center program. It is one component of a media information program for the school, but it enriches the entire program. Reflected, too, are its success in integrating career guidance into the regular instructional programs. The Career Center sponsors an active teaching program, attracting students on a voluntary basis—a clear indicator of excellence. Such courses as college planning and financing, selecting a technical or business school, getting a job, and studying specific career clusters point to the contribution the media center and the Career Information Center make to the school. Its teaching and service roles combine to strengthen the entire instructional program.

Program Objectives
1. To develop and implement an exemplary media support system for integrating career education into the curriculum.
2. To show that a well-stocked and well-staffed career information center will make an impact on student awareness of career alternatives.
3. To provide for specific career related activities for classes of students, mini-courses, individualized career guidance, and special tutoring.
4. To increase teacher awareness of the importance of teaching for career awareness alternatives with the regular curriculum.
5. To increase the involvement of the broader education community (colleges, other schools, State Department of Education) in a media center based Career Information Center.

Some Suggestions
1. Increase number of mini-course offerings in broader range for more work orientation.
2. Use video to record job interviews and job situations within the work world.
3. Involve more volunteers from business and work world.
4. Use program as model for Title IV B or C cooperation between media and guidance programs.

OKLAHOMA COUNTY LIBRARIES
Oklahoma City, Oklahoma

Staff
Professional: 3
Support: 12
Volunteer: 25

Budget (1975-1976)
Arts in Park Program: $10,000

Target Population: 8,000 children, ages 3-12

Most urban parks today are not notable as neighborly gathering places. When Thomas Hoving was Parks Commissioner in New York City, he wanted to have "happenings" in the park. So Barbara Streisand, Ella Fitzgerald, and Duke Ellington sang and played and people came to the parks. In many metropolitan areas of this country, the pleasant notion of combining people, performing talent, and open spaces to create something to make the quality of community life better is not a unique idea.

It is not every day, though, that a public library program takes the leadership in planning and presenting a summer arts program for people in the parks. In Oklahoma City this is just what happened, and over the past two years some twenty city parks have been sites for a participatory art experience called the Neighborhood Arts Program. Sponsoring organizations for the Arts Program are the Oklahoma City Arts Council and the Oklahoma County libraries system. Program emphasis is exclusively on the performing arts.

It is impossible to limit the participants in such a program to children of an age of five to eighteen or so. They do, however, form a significant percentage of participants in the Neighborhood Arts Program. The ability of the program to attract and hold its audience shows a dramatic increase for each year of operation. In 1973 about 2,500 persons attended the Arts Program and by 1975, some 10,000 participants surged into the program. Numbers, like circulation statistics, sometimes tell only half a story and can even be misleading.

Here, though, they are a valid measure for a program that has attracted and held increasing numbers of people each year.

"Outreach," that all-purpose word of the profession, was the original driving force behind the Neighborhood Arts Program. After all, reasoned several people, if children would turn out for the always popular puppet show in the park, why not enrich the program to provide a more varied sampling of the performing arts? A music workshop, a movement workshop, involvement dramatics, and children's theatre became core offerings of the expanded arts program.

The "talent" involved in such programs would have to go beyond those of library professionals. A dance instructor was hired for the movement workshops, designed to increase body awareness. The music workshops were planned to introduce children to a variety of instruments with special emphasis on do-it-yourself musical instruments. Involvement theatre requires that participants don't just sit back and be an audience but that they be involved as characters and actors.

These are the primary offerings of the summer arts program. The potential for these programs lies not just in putting people into the parks but in helping to develop the senses, artistic perceptions, creative expression, and aesthetic appreciations. For children and young people this can translate to improved skills of viewing, listening, and speaking. These skills may be used to good advantage in sorting out the communications of the world, so there is both an instructional and entertainment program focus.

Generally, the program goals have been low-keyed but effective. Chief among these goals is to provide entertainment and learning through the arts for children and adults during the summer months. The program has sought to heighten and extend the participants' involvement. A clear purpose too has been to show that cooperation among a variety of community agencies could produce programs for the benefit of the entire community they serve. The cooperative approach to program planning is important and provides a model for other interagency cooperation designed to reach people.

Cooperating agencies in the Oklahoma City program are the Oklahoma County Libraries System, the Arts Council of

Oklahoma City; the Oklahoma City Parks and Recreation Department; the Community Action Program; Oklahoma City University; Oklahoma Theatre Center; and the National Endowment for the Arts which provides funds through the Oklahoma Arts and Humanities Council. It's a long list, but it illustrates the breadth of backing required to put together the support for this kind of venture.

Backing is important, for this is a program that costs money. The total in 1974 was slightly in excess of $10,000. The four major sources of income were the Oklahoma Arts and Humanities Grant (from the National Endowment for the Arts) $2,800; the Oklahoma County Libraries $2,600; the Oklahoma City University $750; and the Arts Council of Oklahoma City, Inc., $4,150.

This income was spent as follows: salaries (including a project administrator, field assistant business manager, public relations officer and promotion artist) $3,300; performing artists' pay ranges from $25 for a performance to a top of $150. Fees and salaries consumed more than half of the budget; the rest went for supplies, materials, and office expenses. A budget review shows that most of the staff salaries (with the exception of the field assistant) were assumed by the libraries; payment for the artists was assumed by the Oklahoma Arts and Humanities Council, the Oklahoma City University, and Arts Council. The remaining expenses were shared by everyone.

Steering the project is the responsibility of the cooperating agencies. An advisory committee of eight members was formed to represent the individual agencies. This committee does not participate actively in the actual planning or evaluation of the program; its function is liaison and information sharing.

Program staff is supplemented by field staff of the Parks and Recreation Department who receive special workshop training about the arts program so that they may be able to carry out and extend the ideas and programs presented by the performing artists.

While doing your own thing is an attractive notion to large numbers of entertainers, this is hardly the approach to take when putting together something that is both good entertainment and has learning values for the immediate participants. A park arts program isn't the Persian Room at the Waldorf Astoria or Broadway theatre, but attention to quality and audience satisfaction is the essence of any good performance. Artists must give thought to planning what they do. A form is used to describe the kind of program they will present. They are asked also to tell how the audience will be involved in the performance. Other questions concern the kind of facilities required, electrical needs, props, and the like. The intent is not to make all artists conform to a preconceived notion, but to help each artist plan activities that lead to maximum audience involvement. After a performance, an observation sheet is prepared by a staff member associated with the arts program which seeks to ascertain audience response to the program. A breakdown of the age group attending is recorded too.

Participation of ethnic groups is noted as is the presence of any organized groups such as day care centers. Additional comments by the audience concern the artists and whether follow-up activities are planned. As with any successful program, very little is left to chance.

While it is clear that some very specific expectations are part of the arts program, it is a measure of good sense not to demand that a program like this be placed always within a measurable objective/analysis approach.

A visitor who discussed the program with a staff member of the Oklahoma County Library System came away with these observations: The program is an exemplary summer neighborhood activity; while single-shot library sponsored performances or programs in parks are not unusual, a program that sponsors 130 performing program activities is unique. Further, the program is providing a free fine arts program for children and adults. Finally, the program provides a viable performing arts activity throughout Oklahoma City that is reaching effectively into outreach areas.

The arts program provides for increased particpation by children in a variety of art forms, and is widening participants concepts of creative expression. The attention to aesthetic sensitivity and the aesthetic qualities of the arts is a program accomplishment. And the involvement portions of the program sharpen reception and perception, two skills needing attention.

Big benefits stem too from a better involvement of the library staff with other agency staffs. The project demands understanding and cooperation to create a media program that makes a lasting impact upon the quality of life within a community.

Program Objectives
1. To provide quality art programs to children during the summer.
2. To involve children (and adults) in art programs such as drama, music, and dance.
3. To make use of federal, state, and local funding to present a program to enrich community life.
4. To extend and fully utilize the recreational facilities of a park system.
5. To involve a number of community social and educational agencies in cooperative planning and implementation of community programs.

Some Suggestions
1. Extend program into year-round operation by using indoor sites too.
2. Use some video recording capacity to extend the training aspects of program.
3. Consider other possible site locations for performances.
4. Extend program into some production kinds of activities such as painting or photography.
5. Tie other nonprint resources, particularly 16mm film, into the program.
6. Build in more library (probably branch) tie-ins and follow-ups.

MOUNTAIN VIEW INTERMEDIATE SCHOOL DISTRICT NO. 48
Beaverton, Oregon

Staff
Professional: 2
Support: 6
Volunteer: 2

Budget (1975-1976)
Print: $7,700
Nonprint: 2,500

Target Population: 967 children, ages 12-15

If you want to understand how the media program at Mountain View Intermediate Schools makes the extraordinary impact it does, first you've got to get a proper fix on what the school is all about. This, by the way, is the most positive program evaluation any school media program could hope for. We all know the gap that often exists between what we want to think a media center program is doing and what is really happening. It's the difference between the media program as spectator sport and the media program as a catalyst for instructional change and educational excellence.

The Mountain View School media program and educational program are deliberately intermixed to form a bold and innovative program entity. The school, opened in 1968, appears deceptively traditional, but throughout the building inside walls can be moved in modules allowing for team teaching and other instructional grouping arrangements.

The media center, located in the middle of the academic wing of the school, is divided into a series of rooms. These include a conference room, a viewing and listening area, a periodical room, a professional library, a work room, an office, and certain other media-related areas. The total space allotted to the center is slightly in excess of 8,000 feet. A 760-square-foot television studio is another design feature. However, it is not from the facility design that the Mountain View Intermediate School media program draws its ability to affect so positively the school's instructional program.

It is through staffing patterns that the media program has exerted its exceptional impact for instructional leadership and educational innovation. Eight staff persons, (two professionals and six support) work in the media center program assisted by a small number of volunteers. For a school of 967 students, this provides the "people power" for an unusually effective media program.

This staffing pattern was planned carefully to meet the educational program needs of the building and is a specially refined form of differentiated staffing. As a model for the future for a school and a media program it has some compelling ideas and effective practices.

The objective of the differentiated staffing program was to "Steer the way to an improvement in the education process in an effort to find the best road to travel for the future." The creation of the model was made possible by a large grant from the United States Office of Education, along with proportionate funds from the Beaverton District. Reflecting, as it does, an excellent mixture of federal and local funding, with a clear attention to specific local needs, the project began with important built-in success factors.

Appropriate funding, joined to an overriding belief that professionals should have a role in decisions about staffing, curriculum development, educational strategies, and other instructional policy decisions, will always be at the heart of good planning for outstanding educational programs. It is hardly news that considerations other than staff input into educational policy decisions have motivated the growing interest in differentiated staffing. More efficient use of staff, salaries commensurate with educational responsibilities, an attempt to equate competency with responsibilities, more flexible use of a professional's time, increasing productivity through larger amounts of student contact time, and more staff development time—all are important concerns now. They also spell greater economies in operating a school; so for reasons educational and economic, differentiated staffing is a very attractive idea.

Accordingly, a media center program operated with a kind of differentiated staffing needs close analysis as a model.

While the professional level staffing for the media program at the Mountain View School does not even approximate what is proposed in either the *Standards for School Media Programs,* 1969, or *Media Programs: District and School,* 1975, they represent, for this school, a number capable of providing the necessary direction for a program of proven excellence. Standards or guidelines notwithstanding, it may not take all those professionals to accomplish the purpose of the media program. The important requisite for the media professional is to be an excellent organizer of time and people, a keen surveyor of the educational terrain within the building, an able communicator and link between professional staff and administrators, and an educational leader capable of getting both teachers and children to try new ideas and methods. This requires intellect, skill, and stamina but one effective leader can have the impact of two or three if time is managed effectively and a clear program focus exists. What this kind of leader needs most is adequate support staff, in quantity and quality, to do the job well.

All paraprofessional assistants have certain duties that must be performed if the store is going to operate. These duties are so well known, agreed upon, and obvious that they are not listed here again. Rather, it is to the innovative uses of aide time that our attention is directed.

One of the support aides at the Mountain View Schools is an Independent Study Facilitator. As an observer who visited the program put it, "This is the one who keeps the kids on task when they come into the media center." An individual particularly well attuned to working with the junior high school age, a good listener and sympathetic too, this staff person is most responsible for answering the "where do I get?" questions, the kinds of things children need to get or know to complete an assignment successfully. Other aides, and volunteers, are available for this too, but here is a school that recognizes the fact that for a professional, the most costly and least productive time may well be spent in answering elementary and routine questions. If we believe that the main job of a media specialist is to work with teachers in instruction and curriculum development, then every effort must go toward increasing such contact time; only some form of differentiated staffing can provide reasonable assurance that this happens.

A second support position is a Community Resource Coordinator. This position, created by specific teacher demand, helps the staff tap into the resources of the community. This person helps locate guest speakers and people who have special talents and abilities that could enrich learning. This coordinator also acts as liaison for volunteer activities within the building. Usually if teachers have access to such services, they are performed at the district level and rarely satisfactory, since they do not relate specifically enough to the needs of the individual building. Reinforced too is the concept that a school media program is, if effective, a community information program and should draw upon the resources of the entire community. Thus, two key support positions have spurred the growth of a powerful media program within the school.

The range of services translated into educational leadership are extensive. A computer terminal, housed in a media center conference room, is used for mathematics and career education programs. Simulation games, educationally valid as well as entertaining, are popular. All school sports activities are video taped and enjoyed in rerun by a significant segment of the school's population.

The head of the media center teaches a mini-course in old-time radio that has roused student and teacher enthusiasm. Then too, the media center is involved in a telelecture program which allows students to go out into the community, to question and to learn, wtihout ever leaving the building.

An especially vital factor in the media program is the almost constant evaluation it receives from the teachers who participate directly in deciding what the media program should be. Since the media program and the total instructional program are so inextricably meshed this is a major continuing strength. Teachers are encouraged to use the video equipment to do their own self-evaluations and contribute to their own professional development.

This program illustrates the concept that some time in the immediate future we shall view the best media program as one that is not entirely discernable as being conducted through or by the media center. The entire building as media center may be the future.

Excellence manifests itself in many ways within the Mountain View Intermediate School. The integration of the media program with the curriculum, the wide range of services, including a computer terminal, TV production program, and printing facilities all demonstrate the wide impact of media. Add to this a strong involvement in the school's reading programs through the best possible use of print and nonprint media and you have a program that is "making it" in ways that indicate what the media program of the future may be.

Program Objectives
1. To integrate media program into curriculum development program.
2. To use differentiated staffing patterns to permit maximum professional media staff involvement in curriculum development and teaching.
3. To provide a full range of media support services to increase teacher and student use of media programs.
4. To involve the media program in reading improvement program through use of laboratory.
5. To increase individualized learning potential through use of media center resources.

Some Suggestions
1. Involve more student users in selection of materials and production activities.
2. Increase program coordination with senior high school level.
3. Offer more staff development opportunities on use of media center and its resources on planned and systematic basis.

MONTGOMERY COUNTY-NORRISTOWN PUBLIC LIBRARY
Norristown, Pennsylvania

Staff
Professional: 1
Support: 1

Budget
Not applicable

Target Population: 50 children, ages 3-5; 30 parents

Despite inflation, restrictive budget cuts, and limited resources, it is still possible for professionals with imagination, energy, and determination to develop programs that have a maximum community impact.

The Children's Service Department of the Montgomery County-Norristown Public Library provides an important community-wide program particularly for children and mothers of preschool children. The request to start a preschool program came from the director of the Central Montgomery County Mental Health and Mental Retardation Center. He saw the need for these programs for parents, to provide information to them and guidance to increase their understanding of their children and how to help them develop better habits of exploration and learning.

An exemplary program component is the excellent cooperation between these two community agencies. While initial contact for the program was made by the mental health agency, the public library quickly took the initiative in its development.

Careful attention to specific learning objectives and knowledge experiences provides excellent program foundations. Having fun is wonderfully evident, but this is accompanied by carefully prepared objectives and creative teaching methods that would do any excellent school system proud. Reinforced is the concept that while learning can be fun, it must have structure, content, focus, and clear objectives to be of lasting value.

Among program objectives are (1) introducing the child to a group relationship and to participation in an institutional program involving sharing and relating to others; (2) introducing the child to the world of books and preparing him for a lifetime of appreciation of books; (3) providing a visual and listening experience that reinforces the interrelationship of talking and reading, viewing and listening; (4) assisting in lengthening the attention span of children as a method of helping them concentrate; and (5) providing an entertaining and creative learning format that allows the young child to experience and feel that entertainment can lead to learning.

Among program units that have been developed are Learning through Play, You and Your World, and Learning through the Senses. These programs tie learning to the senses and emotions that touch children most at this age. It is simple, direct, and effective learning strategy.

These learning experiences are increased through excellent use of a variety of media. There are three-dimensional objects to touch and manipulate; swatches of material for matching pairs and color; pictures in envelopes; an accordion and a tambourine, to hear and play; and posters to stimulate and promote discussions. These objects are easily available and to an inspired teacher can provide all that is necessary for a provocative learning experience. Add to these rich mixtures of slides, cassette recordings, records, and 16mm film to promote viewing and listening accuity. Finally, provide an array of exciting beautiful picture books that stimulate interest and satisfy it too. The end result, a beautiful media mix that stimulates the child's desire to learn, while guiding it into productive and constructive channels.

A clearer understanding of what's going on is found by examining some of the individual programs of the Learning through Play Program. Individual sessions last for an hour and extend over a six-week period. Participation is limited to twenty-five children who must be preregistered by their families.

Session I concerned the Five Senses. The film, *Me and My Senses*, was reinforced with such books as *Find Out by Touching*, by Paul Showers; *The Very Hungry Caterpillar*, by

Eric Carle; *The Listening Walk,* by Paul Showers; *Bear's Picture,* by Monus Pinkwater; and *A Fresh Look at Flowers,* by Laura Allen.

Activities for the session related to the specific topic of the senses, and the materials used reinforced this topic. An example is the touch-and-tell or "feely" box, an enclosed box, with a hole in one side into which a child places a hand. Within the box are placed a number of articles, a sponge, a spoon, a scarf, a toothbrush, a straw, and a paper cup to name only a few. Since the articles cannot be seen, the child tells by touch what is in the box. It appeals to a child's naturally curious instincts and is even a bit scary. But it has a specific learning objective: to heighten the acuity of recognition through touching rather than seeing. It is never too early to understand that while the eyes are the primary source through which learning is received there are other modes for this process.

Other learning activities that support this lesson are matching pairs such as squares of foil, sandpaper, velvet, and terrycloth. For the tasting sense salt, sugar, lemon, and lime cubes are used. Even at three and one-half the sense of smelling the difference between perfume and mothballs brings important learning experiences. Finally, using a cassette to identify such sounds as clocks ticking, water running, a horn sounding, and an egg-beater whirring heightens the ability of the young child to listen to and sift and sort out the sounds that are so much a part of life. Talking about and describing what is touched, tasted, or smelled are vital elements in developing language and reading readiness.

While it is fun, the ultimate purpose is serious. Research shows that reading skills are not single or isolated skills attained at some chronological age. The child who does not read well may not hear or see well. He may not be able to focus his thoughts or relate ideas to words, either. The senses that permit the child to read with ease and comprehension, to listen with clarity and understanding, and to see with acuity and definition relate, one to the other, and must be developed cooperatively to produce a reader. The Norristown program recognizes the importance of these interrelationships and acts to reinforce them in direct and subtle ways.

Another session in the Learning through Play series used creativity and self-expression to develop self-esteem. Books used included *Frances Face-Maker* by William Cole; *Just Me*, by Marie Hall Ets; *What Have I Got*, by Mike McClintock; *Peter's Chair*, by Ezra Jack Keats; and *Andy*, by Eleanor Schick. The film used for reinforcement in this sequence was the *Golden Fish*.

Capacity for self-expression within the program was developed a number of ways. Music to march to, to hop-in-time with, to clap to and to dance to provided one expression. Charades, the game of statues, and paper bag masks, each is used to help the child become aware of who he is.

When the imagination is allowed to play in the fields of creativity, results can be exciting. How many ways can you whistle? How many ways can you laugh? How many ways can you say goodnight? It is fun and it is a form of emotional release through performing. Finally, though, it is reinforcing the concept of self-identity and self-esteem through the use of creative play.

Other individual lessons in the preschool series are language development (using riddles, jokes and participation books), counting and measuring, sorting and classifying (using the sorting of screws, nuts, bolts and washers into egg cartons), problem solving and imagination (seeing what's inside—shelling a nut and cutting an apple). A final session dealt with physical growth and self-awareness. Here, a participation game of animal imitations such as crawling like a snake, or walking like a duck, helps the young child become aware of the body and how it may be used to express important needs.

Money isn't the essential ingredient for a program like this. More important are a lively imagination, an understanding of good teaching methods for very young children, an understanding of how physical activities can reinforce patterns of mental development, and a desire to relate the creative imagination of children and their ability to learn, to some specific learning objectives.

The cost of this program is hidden in the amount of staff time it takes to develop and implement it. Initially this time factor is considerable. Once in motion, though, this lessens considerably. For the program, two professionals devoted some time to this planning. These professionals also selected books from the adult department that relate to various phases of child care and development which may be borrowed from the library. Bibliographies and booklists were also prepared and distributed. Some volunteers have been recruited to help wtih the youngest children and they are helpful, but volunteers working with preschool children must have extraordinary patience, stamina, and understanding.

Coordination, too, is required with the Community Health agency, for while the children have their program, parents are involved in discussions or lectures. For example, during one awareness session for children the parents met with a child psychiatrist. At Norristown, the health agency has taken the responsibility of providing for the parent instructional hour. The two programs must, however, be carefully coordinated.

For any library looking for a low cost program that will establish cooperation between two community agencies and focus directly on the improvement of learning by children, this provides a fine example.

Program Objectives
1. To provide a specific learning program for children age 3½-5 that will increase their awareness of self.
2. To help children age 3½-5 understand and accept their own uniqueness of self, while relating to a group.
3. To increase, through appropriate activities, the ability of the child to listen and to see with understanding and clarity.
4. To use a variety of media, professionally and locally produced, to help the child of 3½-5 appreciate the art of reading a book.

5. To introduce the child to a library program that involves him or her directly in activities that promote the enjoyment of the library.

Some Suggestions
1. Consider some programs involving the physically or mentally limited child to be coordinated with interested agencies.
2. Offer similar programs through day-care centers or other neighborhood locations.
3. Plan some coordination of program with school programs to show that for the earliest age group, the school media programs and public library programs do relate and mutually reinforce each other's goals.
4. Involve more fathers in the program by shifting hours or times so that they could attend some sessions.
5. Videotape the sessions so they can be used by teacher training institutes, day-care centers, and health centers for staff development.

WARWICK PUBLIC LIBRARY
Warwick, Rhode Island
and
CACHE PUBLIC LIBRARY
Logan, Utah

Staff (Warwick)
Professional: 1
Support: 3

Budget
Not applicable

Target Population: Uncounted, ages 7-12

Staff (Cache)
Professional: 2
Support: 1
Volunteer: 6

Budget
Not applicable

Target Population: 600 children, ages 5-7

As the crow flies (cliche intended) there are a lot of miles between Warwick, Rhode Island, and Logan, Utah. Miles themselves don't mean much, distance being a relative matter when your interest is in children and how to develop within them an appreciation and understanding for the relationship between people and their environment.

Marjorie Kinnan Rawlings in her book *Cross Creek* has written, "The earth may be borrowed but not bought.... It may be used, but not owned." This conveys a special understanding that living within the bounds of nature means always hardship and hope. Despite urbanization, a feel for the tug of the land is still strongly evident in this country. There remains a feeling that the wild and the untamed hold beauty and harmony with nature. These attitudes transcend regionalism, landscape, or location.

The decision to combine two library programs that seek to bring children to an appreciation and respect for the relationship they must build with their environment is appropriate. A kind of neo-romantic involvement with the land is chic just now. This infatuation lends enchantment to the notion that closeness to the land purges society of corrupting influences. But culture is not defined so easily nor are our relationships with nature explained so naively.

Here is how two public libraries are trying to establish programs for children that increase their appreciation of nature and respect for the environmental balances between humans and their surroundings. At Warwick, the program is a pet loan. The pets include such domestic varieties as rabbits, hamsters, guinea pigs, and gerbils, plus more exotic varieties—two boa constrictors, a hedgehog, a chinchilla, and an armadillo. The domestic pets are loaned for a period of two weeks with the objective of stimulating an interest and concern for animals by children. Pet ownership is well established in the American way of life and a program that brings children to an early awareness of their *responsibility* in owning and caring for a pet is appropriate.

At Logan, the Cache Public Library seeks different results, yet uses a similar approach that finds its basis in an understanding that we are the products of our ability to deal with the nature of nature. The Logan area abounds with a wildlife population that reflects a way of life, mostly ranching and farming. Easy stereotypes about the dangers of wildlife and fears about the economic implications of its destruction of domestic animal life led to the creation of the program. Its objective was to bring children to see and touch this wildlife in a friendly situation. Children and wild animals were brought together in this attempt to help children appreciate their environment and the balance of nature.

For example, many children are exposed early to a hatred of coyotes because they prey on domestic livestock. This program introduces the coyote from a different viewpoint, explaining his role in nature. Children pet and hold a baby coyote and gain an understanding and respect for this animal.

Such a program could only take place in areas similar to Logan. Close by are wildlife experts, mostly graduate students working the departments of Wildlife and Biology and the College of Natural Resources at Utah State University.

These students volunteer their services and bring the animals. Their involvement in research projects and grant programs makes them experts in wildlife ecology.

Culturally, Warwick and Logan are worlds apart. Warwick, a city of 80,000 population, is a densely packed urban area. A demonstration of man's interrelationship with wild animals would be hard to sustain here. Yet both programs find their purpose in a concern and commitment to more rational and responsible relationships with nature. Both represent locally developed programs to deal with local needs. In Warwick it is probable that a child may assume the responsibility of caring for a pet. In Logan the presence of wildlife in its natural state requires a program to meet these special needs. A purpose underlying both programs is to promote respect for animals and to encourage their conservation and well-being. This process is supported by an educational effort that emphasizes the place of the animal within the total environment.

The Warwick Animal Awareness Program includes exhibits of wild animals and the pets that may be borrowed. For these pets-to-go, the library provides a cage, food, bedding material, and an instruction sheet about caring for the pet. This is supplemented by appropriate books, pamphlets, films, film loops, and displays selected carefully to create feelings of interest and concern for animals by children. Expert advice comes from the staff of the Roger Williams Park Zoo in Providence, and professors in the Division of Biological and Medical Sciences at Brown University.

A concern in programs like this must be the contention that a cage or pen is not, after all, a natural habitat for animals. Some maintain that there is nothing cute about the rabbit caged or the hamster in his exercise wheel. Why argue? These people are probably right. But to what end? Our concerns about the rights of animals to live in a natural state must balance with the reality which perpetuates the domestic pet. It is better to educate well those who will care for pets rather than outlawing pets. The one approach deals with the world that is; the other, fantasy.

The Warwick and Cache programs have in common the involvement of professionals in animal life and care. These experts have provided direction and advice and have helped make adjustments as they became necessary. Both programs demonstrate that an interest in animal life is a legitimate concern of a media program for children. In a sense animal programs for children cannot fail. They are like having Easter egg rolls on Easter Sunday! Their purpose is to make a child's relationships to animals, as wildlife or domesticated pets, be based upon understanding and respect; this provides these two programs with exemplary dimensions.

In both, a specific objective is to get children to read about or experience some interaction with a live animal. Stories about animals are told; films and other media about animals are used. Adults and children talk together about animal life and pets. A result of the Warwick program is that parents and children together have reached decisions about the readiness of children to assume the responsibility for a pet.

Animals and media programs for children can find a compatible home together if we recognize that such programs are means to ends. Means to attract young children (and concerned adults) into library programs; means to understand that animals are not "objects" but exist and have feelings and habits that relate to man's environment.

Control of emotions in these programs is important. Pets, animals, and exotic menageries will always attract hordes of enthusiastic children. This can obscure serious program intent. The Cache Library found that an animal involvement program could attract as many as 100 children. This is too many. A mob scene inhibits the personal experience necessary to program success.

Of course, there is a good deal of fun in these programs, but their ultimate purpose is to have a lasting effect upon children's attitudes toward animals, making them more tolerant, more understanding, more appreciative, and perhaps more thoughtful. Even more important such programs may help them to learn about themselves.

Diverse judgments and opinions about both programs are inevitable. But the programs, with their good sense in using local human resources, their low, almost nonexistent budget demands, and the obvious educational value they bring, recommend themselves for consideration by other public library and school media programs.

Program Objectives
1. To dispense information on pet care in an attempt to help parents decide readiness of children to care for pets (Warwick).
2. To acquaint children with local wildlife in an effort to decrease hatreds and stereotypes (Cache).
3. To involve local resource persons, expert in animal care, in teaching children about animal life and care (Cache and Warwick).
4. To draw children (and adults) into library service programs not usually associated with public libraries (Cache and Warwick).
5. To promote a respect for animal life and to encourage its preservation (Cache and Warwick).

Some Suggestions
1. Use videotaping to increase impact of programs on audience as well as limiting repetitiousness.
2. Establish more cooperation between school and public library programs to extend the impact of the program.
3. Involve other community agencies and move locations of programs as appropriate.
4. Establish a more complete program of print and nonprint educational tie-in materials to strengthen programs.
5. Establish list of 16mm films to tie-in to programs. These would be both enrichment and educational.

DALLAS PUBLIC LIBRARY
Dallas, Texas

Staff
   Professional: 2
   Support: 2
   Volunteer: 2

Project Budget
   Federal grant: $36,300

Target Population: 150 children, ages 10-13

While project "Look at Me" is no longer in operation, as a program it is so easily replicated by most libraries or school media centers it deserves consideration.

Project Look at Me was funded under provisions of the Emergency School Assistance Program, and the Dallas Public Library finished its participation in the program in March, 1973. In several ways, however, the program continues to make useful, important contributions. It is used as a model by several organizations, particularly for summer programs, and the 16mm film that resulted from the project provides suggestions for other communities and organizations considering a similar project.

Another legacy is a book, *Look at Me*, about the experiences of the children of Dallas, told by themselves. The book recognizes that as children speak about themselves, "They want to be noticed, understood, and accepted." *Look at Me* is a polished, professional publication containing many excellent black and white photographs of children at play, in schools, working with their families, and in their neighborhoods. The photographs are accompanied by a narrative text that reflects the moods and feelings of the children in the picture. One, for instance states, "I think I can succeed in anything I want to do. Myself, I am a surprising human being."

A number of purposes were outlined for the project when it began. As the Dallas schools were ordered to desegregate, possibilities for community-based projects to help smooth the desegregation process were considered and developed. These aimed at developing the accepting attitudes so essential to accomplish peaceful desegregation or integration programs. The public library expressed, early and in a forthright manner, its commitment to acting as a community resource agency and contributor in helping the desegregation plan. An expectation of project *Look at Me* was that it would help develop in participants and the community attitudes of self-esteem and confidence that would permit an openness and acceptance of a new and changed way of life.

Improved literacy, including listening, speaking, and viewing as well as reading, was also a program priority. These skills would be related to an improved ability to read and a more positive attitude about books and reading. Improving communication skills through use of carefully applied media programs is by now a validated learning experience. If this is related to an affective program that aims to help children of varying ethnic backgrounds talk to and learn from each other, an excellent program can result. The relationship of viewing literacy to reading is underscored by the fact that Look At Me continued a second year after being incorporated into a youth photographic program.

Community outreach and service dominated the program planning from the start; site locations were YMCA centers serving specific ethnic groups. Indians, Mexican-Americans, and blacks were the major minority groups reached by the project. One of the main reasons for the success of the program is that it operated from these neighborhood centers, becoming a part of other neighborhood activities. About ten children from each center were selected to participate in the program. They were recommended by the center directors and were contacted by the program staff, with invitations to participate.

For this kind of project, staff is far more important than facility. Initially, the staff consisted of a coordinator from the library staff who had other responsibilities within the library program. The working director of the program was a professional photographer. Four part-time employees, community college students, were hired too. Three volunteers later became involved.

The photographer was essential, for photography was to be the primary focus of the project. The singular ability of the camera to capture and stimulate self-expression made it a natural for this program. The cameras need not be expensive or sophisticated for this type of project; for project Look at Me the photographs were taken with Instamatic cameras. These photographs, taken by the children, were used to illustrate books the children wrote about themselves, their community, and their own experiences.

Emphasis went always to upgrading and improving all communication skills. Seeing themselves and their world helped the children develop the ability to explore, experience, and learn. Belief in self was the thing to be reinforced, for the child conditioned by expectations of failure will probably fail.

Self-expression provided a built in success factor as children shared their world through a variety of media experiences. Tape recorders were also used to excellent advantage. With these, the children were able to express their feelings and thoughts about themselves and their community. Not only did this improve another communication skill but it fostered increased understanding of their community as well.

A high degree of participation by the family unit was developed during the project, and this had an important multiplier effect. As the children took photographs to be developed into slides, these slides were used to produce media shows for parents and the community. The interaction of parents with children, sharing their feelings and talking about experiences, hopes, and expectations, contributed to the success of the program.

Increasing cross-cultural understanding was a crucial component of the program. Eventually the total number of participants in the project rose to 150 children *and* their families. Other activities were incorporated as well. An example was a tutorial enrichment program that added a direct learning sequence and helped children with their studies as well as giving them the security to move ahead in other ways.

The culminating activity of Look At Me was the books the

children made out of what they had photographed and what they wanted to share of that experience. Provocative and creative, this project reinforced the pleasurable aspects of reading and books. The "afterword" of the book *Look at Me* says it nicely: "Once you've made a book your own, you're not afraid of books anymore."

As it operated in Dallas, the program was well funded with the resources to pay for a project director and other assistants. This money paid for the production of some extraordinarily handsome work. The program could be mounted, though, for a minimal outlay. Instamatic cameras are inexpensive and easy to operate, even the price of the Polaroid camera has decreased to the level where it is generally affordable.

Sponsorship for such a project could come from a local camera club, a high school photography club, even from the staff of a library or a media center. It is the *idea* that is most important here, the attempt to get children to express themselves through media in an effort to increase their positive feelings about themselves, books and reading. A project like this responds to the literacy needs of any community. In Dallas it was an outreach program planned to help ease that city through the traumas of school desegregation. However, a program relating photography to personal feelings, self-expression, and reading has no particular limits of time or occasion. It is adaptable to different age levels and may be used for several purposes.

The Dallas project received significant amounts of film from the National Association of Photographic Manufacturers. Film purchase and cost of developing it is an important budget consideration in setting up such a project. If regular budget monies are not available, it is possible that sponsorship could come from local business or community groups.

A program like this ties in beautifully to field trips or other improvised activities, but it should emphasize feelings and self-expression through photography, not how to operate cameras or develop photographs. These skills may be built into the program but they should not be its purpose.

In Dallas the program would have been strengthened with

better ties to the schools. Coordinating two governing agencies (public library and the Emergency School Assistance Program) presented problems too, but these did not prevent a successful program. When it began, Look at Me had some difficulties with some local community members who feared the photography might be used as a form of negative social commentary on a particular ethnic life style. Good staff work within the community put this fear to rest. And the eventual involvement of the community through the sound-slide community presentation was a great plus for the program.

The program promotes the natural desire of children to want to be noticed, understood, and accepted by adopting a specific library effort to improve the child's ability to communicate and become involved in the world of books through photography.

Program Objectives
1. To improve children's ability to communicate by using photography and tape recording.
2. To reinforce positive attitude in children about books and reading.
3. To help improve community attitudes and feelings during a period of school desegregation.
4. To improve communications skills of children through self-expression activities.
5. To increase cross cultural understandings and awareness within a community.

Some Suggestions
1. Relate program more specifically to schools to improve impact.
2. Involve more community volunteers with an interest in photography in the program.

3. Build in some special program follow-throughs to see if individual participants actually do more reading.
4. Include Super 8mm filmmaking as another program component that also stimulates creativity and self-expression.

TEXAS

FORT WORTH PUBLIC LIBRARY
Fort Worth, Texas

Staff
Professional: 4
Support: 3

Budget
Federal funding: $125,000 two-year grant for materials and equipment

Target Population: 1,000 children, ages 2-5

The terms "outreach" and "service to the disadvantaged" are sometimes overworked to the point of meaninglessness. At Fort Worth, Texas, however, some useful and unusual programs that reach out to serve the disadvantaged are making important contributions. These programs and the activities they use to accomplish their purpose deserve consideration.

An unusual focus of the Fort Worth program is that it includes in its target audience persons at the extreme ends of the age scale: the very young and the very old. While the purpose of this book is not to report library programs serving the elderly, their combination within the Fort Worth early childhood outreach program is significant and important to that program.

In establishing its objectives the program recognized that a disadvantage shared by the very young and the very old is lack of easy access to transportation to get to the facilities and resources of the public library. So bringing resources to these people became a high program priority: fundamental to the program operation is moving people and materials about in ways that maximize their contact where the need is greatest.

Two fifteen passenger vans were purchased from federal funds. The vans are used to transport residents of nursing homes and children from day-care and nursing centers to the two branch libraries selected as target sites for the program. These branches were selected on the basis of their proximity to certain population target groups in areas where the largest numbers of disadvantaged were located. The vans are also used to take programs to the nontransportable senior citizens in nursing homes. General criteria used to define this target population were multi-ethnic mix, elderly whites, Mexican-American, or black; bilingual population; and inner-city residents. Within these target populations were large numbers of the age groupings to be served.

To achieve its goals the early childhood program uses as a main resource people of the community. They are brought into the program in an effort to accustom children early in their lives to using public library services. Generally, these resource programs feature performing artists, puppet shows, or musical presentations. While their main purpose is to entertain, their educational role is fundamental, for they bring the preschool child to an early awareness of public library resources as interesting and meant for him.

Program staffing patterns provide a clear understanding of the acute sensitivity the program shows for its community role. Its director is not a librarian, but rather brings to the program a background of experience in community relations, lobbying, and governmental administration. While this is a library program and its operations, plans, and procedures are directed by the library, community outreach is the main preoccupation. Professional librarians are, however, very much involved in planning and carrying out the program, assuring that it remains always very much a part of the total program of library services for the city.

Other staff consists of one professional librarian in each of two branch library sites serving the program, one professional outreach librarian working from a library extension office, two parttime equipment operators who serve also as van drivers, and one full-time equipment operator who drives the bookmobile. Staff roles have been established so that they interrelate to foster a program of library services that goes out into the community rather than creating and operating a static site library program. Community involvement activities are encouraged by all staff members.

The largest part of the initial federal grant of $77,900 went to purchase equipment necessary to use the nonprint materials. Generally, this equipment is small, easily maintained, and transported to various sites. Cassette players and recorders, 16mm projectors, filmstrip projectors, and filmstrip viewers are typical. Equipment and materials are intended to be used either by individuals or in group sessions.

Film programs used in combination with books or learning activities are important program components. Every effort is made to reinforce the relationship and compatability of print and nonprint media by using them together. This emphasis establishes in the mind of the young child that the two mediums both complement and reinforce each other and that while each has an entertainment capability, each has a specific educational purpose, too. The continuous effort by the staff to emphasize the compatability and interrelationship of print and nonprint resources is one of the strongest aspects of the program. Its usefulness to children in terms of attitudes about different kinds of learning materials and their use is another important factor.

The programs conducted at the branch libraries generally follow a similar format. While the librarian works with the children, the teachers from the day-care center select appropriate materials, including games, toys, filmstrips, and cassettes, to take back to their centers. Thus is begun the subtle but effective process of creating a new generation of library users.

Another important service of this outreach program is its use as a resource center for professional materials useful to those who work with preschool and primary school children. Materials about child development, the operation of day-care centers, and related topics are available. These special collections are used by all day-care and library staff members to upgrade their understanding of the young and their abilities to work with them.

Efforts to involve staff members of day-care centers have included not only access to professional collections but workshops on how to use nonprint materials with children. These workshops were conducted for day-care center personnel by members of the library outreach program staff. Heavy emphasis on materials used in the program goes to nonprint media. In the preschool program special attention is given to selecting materials that relate directly to reading readiness, health care, and science. An exhibited program strength has been its ability to work its way into the ongoing programs of day-care centers and other community agencies, becoming really part of the warp of an entire array of community service activities.

Most day-care and child care centers operate on limited budgets and do not have the resources or staff to operate a full program of media services for children and teachers. Yet we know, both by research and intuition, how important it is to reach these children at the earliest possible age with sound educational-learning programs using library services and personnel. Not only does this have a beneficial impact upon children but it can involve their parents and other community adults in a number of ways. One of the central purposes of a program such as this is to change attitudes of the community and to create new expectations and demands for library use and service.

Day-care centers are found in every city and town, and the materials used in this kind of program are generally available in most public libraries. The effort needed is to bring together the materials and human resources through the public library and make them available where they are most needed, at the same time creating an appetite for services that feeds on itself.

At Fort Worth excellent use of substantial federal funds channeled through the State Library Agency made the program possible on an ambitious scale. The potential, though, is available without much outside funding, providing libraries are willing to establish priorities and redirect toward innovative uses of professional and support staff.

As with many outreach programs a positive multiplier effect noted by the library staff has been the growing involvement of parents, concerned about their children's learning, in the program. And, with many of these parents, involvement in this program leads to use of other library programs, as attitudes are changed and new user expectations are established.

Program Objectives
1. To establish an outreach program aimed at preschool children.
2. To use print and nonprint media separately and in combination to improve early learning program for preschool children.
3. To make transportation of preschool children to selected branch libraries a component of the outreach program.
4. To serve as a professional resource collection for staff members of day-care centers to help them improve their abilities in these programs.
5. To cooperate with a variety of community agencies to create a community public library day-care program.

Some Suggestions
1. Consider involving some community volunteers in the program.
2. Consider allowing some equipment (filmstrip viewers and cassettes) to circulate to homes.
3. Establish some separate but related programs for parents of preschool day-care center children to increase their involvement.
4. Keep contact with public schools in effort to assess if children entering the public schools from the day-care program do read more and exhibit a wider range of interests and language skills.
5. Make plans for adequate local support for program to continue after federal funds cease. Efforts might include a new funding source related to early childhood programs.

DIXIE HIGH SCHOOL
St. George, Utah

Staff
Professional: 1
Support: 1

Budget (1976-1976)
Print: $4,200
Nonprint: 3,000
Special funding from
ESEA Title II and NDEA
Title III to assist
program development

Target Population: 762 children, ages 15-18
(35 students enrolled in IMC course)

The State of Utah recognizes the media program at Dixie High School as "exemplary." This designation means first that the media program shows a high level of cooperative planning, among teachers, administrators, and media professionals. Recognizing that facilities, materials, furniture, or equipment do not make an effective media program, emphasis here is on a philosophy of service and an operational method that exhilarates the entire school.

It is still possible to speak of goodness wtihout embarrassment, and a visitor to the Dixie High School program says that its philosophy has added a dimension of goodness not often seen in school media programs. It is based on mutual respect (among members of the school community) that places confidence and faith in the student. Here one expects that young people will develop respect for themselves and for others and for the ability to live and work cooperatively together. This expectation is reinforced by dominant community attitudes of this Mormon region.

Cooperation with people and respect for property are essential for any media program to operate. A silent issue in the profession is that many school media programs cannot function properly because of the high degree of vandalism to, and theft of, materials and equipment. For many this problem has reached crisis proportions. Media programs must be built upon a philosophy of service that is open to all and trusts individual integrity. Thus attitudes, in addition to facilities, materials, equipment, and personnel components of media programs are fundamental. Only in an atmosphere of respect and trust can an excellent media program proceed. The Dixie program exhibits clearly the importance of respect by students for materials, equipment and people, for good program operation to proceed.

Excellent cooperation between the State Department of Education and the local district also strengthen this program. In 1971, the State of Utah committed itself to funding a media program that would totally integrate media into the curriculum by helping teachers plan units of instruction based on media use. Learning would also improve as students became better users of media. It was established that media personnel would work directly with teachers in creating programs that established course learning objectives. There is follow-through, for teacher evaluation involves an assessment of how well the goals are being met.

Some school districts now evaluate media professionals on their ability to conduct instructional planning with professional staff. Few districts, however, ever evaluate *teachers* on their ability to incorporate media effectively into their teaching. For most the road runs one way, forcing media professionals to spend too much time begging, selling, threatening, pleading, and persuading others to use media. Evaluation of how effectively teachers use media is one great hope for fostering better use of media.

At Dixie the evaluation of teachers on their use of media has strengthened the media program. This is properly conceived, nonthreatening evaluation because teachers and administrators together established agreed-upon goals and the strategies to achieve these goals. This cooperation and planning among the professional staff involves the entire school and forces commitment to the improvement of instruction through good media use.

A powerful motivating force for this media program is its ability to involve students. Again, attitudes and a commitment to provide instructional help are essential. The media center is open during the school day to any student at any time; extended hours keep it open until 5:00 P.M. and evening hours are available too. Abundant, easily used production facilities and materials stimulate good use of this area. All equipment may be checked out for home use, and this includes calculators and 35mm cameras.

The availability of nonprint materials and equipment for use outside the school helps keep parents aware of what is being taught and how their children learn. This increased understanding of the school program translates into community pride and support for it. There is an annual Spring Film Festival which shows student produced media including 8mm films and 35mm slide shows. A Fine Arts Week is held for display of student art work.

Student involvement in the media program is fostered too by a credit course in producing and using media. These classes are limited to five students for each seven hours of instruction. Admission is by permission and the student chooses one or more unit objectives to pursue. In some instances media personnel conduct the teaching. Many times, though, students teach other students the mastery of skills or process. Units include processing of materials, use of reference materials, operation of equipment, lettering, filing, use of the 35mm and 8mm cameras, copy stand work, and the appropriate utilization of various media in pursuit of individualized learning goals. Students establish specific learning objectives and use media to achieve these objectives. A proficiency test is administered when the unit is completed.

Students are assigned to designated areas within the media center and are directly involved in the day-to-day operation of the media program. Some professionals maintain that it is wrong to use free help, that schools should pay for adequate support staff. These responses geared to a philosophy of "using" student help completely miss the point in today's media programs. Students are an important "people resource" to advance media programs. Their potential for helping others *and* themselves is generally undeveloped and largely ignored in most schools. And the purpose is not to provide a free labor force but rather to establish in youngsters an ease about working with and using media to accomplish certain tasks or objectives. Here, the media program shows the excellent results of this kind of student participation.

For teachers, mini-units, variations of Learning Activity Packets (LAP), provide instructional support for a variety of instructional activities. The media professional and staff together prepare these instructional mini-units which are based upon prescriptions to meet learning needs and require the use of media resources. Used for learning reinforcement, make-up work, or enrichment, these units are a core component of the media program.

In-service and staff development programs are part of the media program and include alternatives ranging from proper equipment operation to the establishment of learning objectives for various courses. Two-day workshops for selected teachers in the production and use of media are common. These programs effectively integrate the media program into the curriculum of the school.

An evaluation component is built into the program providing a process that is constant, comprehensive and self-correcting. Teacher attitudes toward the media program are surveyed on a yearly basis. The involvement of administration, professional staff, and students in establishing program goals and learning objectives provides continuous evaluation as well.

The definitive structure for evaluation is provided by the State through its publication, *Media, How Are We Doing? Guidelines for the Development of an Instructional Media System*. The guidelines give measurable objectives that encourage individual school buildings or districts to set priorities for media programs. Sequentially, these look at the present, the expectations for one year ahead, and for four years in the future. School districts receive an evaluation team from the State Board of Education once each year to determine if the priorities established are being addressed.

The guidelines are flexible and allow districts or schools to establish sensible program priorities, while providing specific directions to help establish these priorities. The media program at Dixie is vibrant and has carefully meshed student productivity, administrative commitment, staff participation, and community involvement into an exemplary program.

Program Objectives
1. To provide a full media resource program for a school and a community.
2. To integrate a media program into curriculum development program.
3. To involve students directly in the day-to-day operation of a media program.
4. To work with teachers to help them establish instructional goals and objectives in which using media is required.
5. To demonstrate the benefits that occur from close cooperation and planning between a state department of education and a local school district.

Some Suggestions
1. Increase parent volunteer program within the media program.
2. Increase local funding to expand print and nonprint collection of materials.
3. Provide clearer definition of working relationships with area public library resources.

AMELIA STREET SCHOOL
Richmond, Virginia

Staff
  Professional: 1
  Support: 1
  Volunteer: 3

Budget (1976-1976)
  Print: $1,200
  Nonprint: 1,000

Target Population: 127 children, ages 4-21 nongraded

There is a simple and direct focus to the media program at the Amelia Street School in Richmond, Virginia; this is that children are capable of learning regardless of intelligence level. In many ways the Amelia Street School is a very special school, for the 127 children who go there are all trainable, mentally retarded (with an I.Q. between 30-50,) or physically limited. The program is a part of the Special Education Program of the Richmond Public Schools.

In the old days, which really weren't so very long ago, children with I.Q.'s of 30-50 were shunted aside. They were placed in institutional caretaking situations which served primarily to assure that the already deficient capacity to learn would be permanently and completely sealed off. Removed from the sight and caring of even their families in many cases, these children were truly the living dead.

It doesn't have to be this way. The Federal Government through the provisions of the "Education For All Handicapped Children Act" has recognized the importance of seeing to it that mentally and physically handicapped children have opportunities equal to their normal peers. These include opportunities to develop their individual potential as far as possible and learn the skills and competencies necessary to insure a useful life in a home living situation, a sheltered workshop, or a supervised job.

Many states were in advance, both in philosophy and practice, of this federal legislation and already boast of extensive special education programs. It seems probable that while federal and state funds for many educational programs are disappearing, funds for early identification of handicapped children and their education in regular public school systems will increase. Media program planners need to be far more aware of the realities of this development than they have so far shown themselves to be. Media programs, operating in either a school or public library setting, are bound to be affected by these special programs.

For many professionals and institutions first encountering the process of work with physically or mentally limited children, the experience is at best unnerving and, at worst a fiasco. The Amelia Street School has developed a philosophy that undergirds its program for these special children. This philsophy states that, "Each child is an individual with talents, needs, problems, and experiences peculiar to him, and although he may be lacking in mental, physical, and sometimes emotional capacity and development, his similarities to normal children are greater than his differences."

All well and good, but where does this philosophy meet the reality of trying to make the life of a child who is limited as normal as possible? At the Amelia Street School the media program has a great deal to do with helping a child adjust successfully to life through a school experience.

The program was begun in 1973, almost as an afterthought, it seems. As so often happens, a bright and dynamic individual was available and expressed an interest in this type of program at the time the center for the trainable mentally retarded was being moved to larger quarters. The media center staff consists of the media specialist who is there two days a week, and an aide who covers the other two days. The media center is closed on Fridays because of special activities of the school.

Right away, a lot of professionals are probably going to get very nervous about a program working with children with only a part-time professional in charge. Generally, the arguments against this are valid. After all, how can a part-time professional hope to cope with planning learning activities, as well as selecting, ordering, and seeing to the processing of all materials? In most public school situations this concern is justifiable and proper.

In a situation like Amelia Street, however, most preconceived notions and standards or guidelines about what constitutes service must be set aside. A school media program for the mentally or physically limited child demands very different patterns of service and staffing. And, while staffing with a full-time professional is still a desirable program component, sometimes it may not be the essential ingredient.

Generally, too, professionals judging a fine media program in a public school point to as much unstructured, free access time for children as possible as a sign of an excellent program. This criterion cannot be applied to the kind of program found at the Amelia Street School. Structure, and sequence, and an orderly progression of events and activities are vital to the learning of the mentally handicapped. This structure, in the Amelia program and others like it, means important support so that children may maximize their assets. For these children, structured learning means an opportunity to learn the skills that literally mean survival.

The innovations of the Amelia Street School media program are many. Most important, it is the first media program in the State of Virginia designed especially to serve the needs of students and teachers in a center for the trainable mentally retarded. Previous to its establishment, it was not thought that a media program would be of any use for these children. To those trained in the use of media and its application to a wide number of learning situations and conditions this is incredibly mistaken idea, but it is not an uncommon attitude in many school situations.

A visitor to the media center observed two groups of children. Five mentally retarded students came to watch a sound filmstrip and look at picture books. Physically limited children also used the center, choosing their own books, and signing them out. The remainder of the period was spent in reading and working with puzzles and other manipulatives. For the normal child, this is a pretty traditional use of a media center. But, remember we are talking here about children to whom access to any information would have been denied just two years ago. All the classes are accompanied by a teacher and an aide. The visitor noted that the teachers used the time in the center to preview and select materials for use in the classroom. That, of course, is something to be desired in any school media program.

The unified media program at the Amelia Street School means access to both print and nonprint materials. The collection has periodicals, and as one might expect, the book collection is oriented heavily toward picture books. There is also an elementary (K-8) book collection arranged according to the Dewey Decimal System and used chiefly by physically handicapped children. The materials used with the trainable mentally retarded children are chiefly to nonprint media.

In both media formats, the pioneer program at Amelia Street highlights a problem area of great concern for schools trying to provide some sort of media program for the physically or mentally limited. This is, that the commercial producers have generally ignored the needs of this particular market. At present, there are few appropriate materials available to these children. Doubtless, as an increasing amount of federal and state monies become available for such programs, this situation will be remedied. But it is likely that the media program that is a part of special education will always have to rely, to a great extent on locally designed and produced materials.

While the Amelia Street Schools has no production center of its own, its media staff, and the school staff, have ready access to a district materials center. In an effort to "make it" with what is, the school also shares the production facilities of nearby schools. While a highly sophisticated production center is not a necessity for a special education media program, access to production facilities for such activities as laminating, ektagraphic photography, and simple tape recording is necessary. None of these activities, by the way, demands an elaborate facility, and thousands of schools across the country are already demonstrating that many an old book closet or store room can be converted easily and cheaply into a very effective production center.

In one sense, the limited clientele of a school like the Amelia Street School provides an instant and welcome focus for the program. Whereas in many schools media programs must try hard to be all things to all people, the special education media program has some very specific goals established within it. In a learning program for the trainable mentally retarded and the severely physically limited child, the media program must help train the child in self-care skills, directional skills, and such others so that he will find it possible to work in sheltered situations and become a reasonably responsible citizen.

Both the print and nonprint collections for these media programs must aim foremost at promoting an awareness of relating beyond self. These materials must be selected and used in ways that will help prepare children for coping and making successful adjustments to daily living. And they must help trainable mentally retarded children master the physical, social, emotional, and intellectual skills necessary to their well being.

The professional collection, often the poorest step-child in a media center, is a vital program component for the special education program. So much is happening in this field, so much must be learned, and unlearned, about teaching and learning in these programs; the professional collection must reflect teacher resource materials and other special resources available.

The heart of the Amelia media program is a belief that children can learn regardless of intelligence. It is the degree of learning that is important. The media program in seeking to support this goal is doing an impressive job in helping public school teachers, administrators, and the community recognize the crucial role that media programs can play in the proper education of the mentally or physically limited child.

Program Objectives
1. To provide print and nonprint learning resources to teachers of the trainable mentally retarded and physically handicapped.

2. To provide print and nonprint resources to help the trainable mentally retarded and physically handicapped children learn how to be good citizens, to be aware of their responsibilities to themselves and to others, and to care for themselves.
3. To help educate the community and parents to the special needs of the trainable mentally retarded and physically limited student.
4. To provide resources and advisory service that will permit teachers to be more innovative in their teaching.
5. To provide a special teacher resource collection of materials to enable teachers to be more effective in their teaching.

Some Suggestions
1. Extend professional coverage to full-time (e.g. four-day week).
2. Increase local production facility for greater use by teachers and, where appropriate, children.
3. Use of videotaping with children so that they may observe their own actions and learn from this experience.
4. Involvement of more volunteers, who have been carefully selected and trained, in the program.
5. Preparation of resource file of commercially prepared materials, suitable to the trainable mentally retarded and physically limited, that are of high quality and an effective teaching device.

VIRGINIA

RICHMOND PUBLIC LIBRARY
Richmond, Virginia

Staff
Volunteer: 1

Budget
Not applicable

Target Population: 20 children, ages 12-15

How to carry out successfully, with diminished staff and restricted budget support, a full library program of community-related activities is a preoccupation of many libraries today. Obviously, this cannot be done to anyone's satisfaction, for fewer resources cannot be made to do the work of more. Productivity, enthusiasm, optimism, and desire have carried many programs a long way but these too have their ultimate limits.

In the search for help to maintain library programs for the community and its children, the resource represented by the volunteer must be utilized as never before. It is not encouraging that many of the surveys returned for this book stated emphatically that no volunteers were used in their program. Putting it straight, programs that claim to serve the community but are unwilling to involve the community directly in the program are diminished programs. If one accepts that media programs for children will come to them increasingly from a variety of locations and involve many people other than media professionals, the need to examine the role of the volunteer is essential.

The arguments against using volunteers are unrelenting and make a persuasive, albeit specious, litany. Volunteers detract from the integrity and role of the professionals people might even conclude that volunteers can supplant professionals. Volunteers do not bring to their job the objectivity of a professional, and good will or good intentions cannot replace the training of the professional to design, implement, and evaluate programs. Then too, volunteers can be nosey. They can try to second-guess you; they ask too many questions;

they make emotional observations about people; and they *always* disappear when you need them most.

But just as a web of circumstantial evidence can be broken apart by proven fact in court, so do many of the common myths about the volunteer fail to hold up under careful analysis. We allow ourselves to be manipulated by a series of incorrect variables if we debate the merits of the volunteer service on any of the foregoing grounds, for these are not the real issues; they are true or false only as they apply to a particular situation. Debating them will not allow us to judge honestly what volunteers can contribute to media programs for children.

The Richmond Public Library has made a specific effort to deploy the volunteer in an important instructional role. This is a volunteer who does not shelve books, stamp out materials, erase pencil marks from book pages, unpack cartons, or serve as a free babysitter. Here the volunteer actually directs a library program. True, it's a modest and discreet program; almost an afterthought it seems. The program doesn't cost the public library one penny from its operating budget, and it doesn't involve any elaborate facilities for the production of materials. No reading labs, poetry corners, puppet shows, or media mobiles are needed. What it takes to operate the program is one person who cares a lot about children and what makes them want to create by expressing themselves through writing.

To be sure, the creative writing program sponsored by the library has more going for it than just the creativity of a volunteer and the high interest of its participants. The Richmond program deals with an important, growing national concern, that many children are educated or schooled but are alarmingly deficient in their ability to communicate in writing. Indeed, writing may be coming to reflect the results of exposure to a mediated pattern whereby information is communicated in fragments, quickly perceived and eliminated. However, our purpose is not to debate that issue. But it does require careful attention by library-media professionals.

The volunteer in charge of this program is a retired teacher in his seventies, working with children who are twelve, thirteen, and fourteen years old. Without a sermon, there is something very healthy in helping the young people understand that age need not, does not, dim creativity or dull the ability to think and help others think. So many aspects of this single volunteer program come forth to recommend themselves to other libraries! The program itself is so unpretentious that it could be easily overlooked. And this would be a pity, for there is hardly a community in this country that would not have the resources to support this kind of volunteer venture within its library program.

Walter M. Gladding, Jr., the volunteer at Richmond recognizes that "we are all artists until art is taught out of us...." What this man seeks is to bring young people together with each other and a friendly guide and then to let creativity and artistry happen.

The principles behind the effort are those found in any good creative writing course, but by reaching children early Mr. Gladding hopes to make a more significant and lasting impact. The first direction is for the children to write about what they *know*. He suggests, "Look at your own self, your friends, your family, your home.... This is the story material you *know*.... Your reader cannot see the exact scene you write about unless you have seen it first." In other words, for the child, write about what could happen in *your own backyard*. It is not chance then, that provides the title for this program, "Backyard Stories."

Other suggestions and directions to participants are important when planning a program like Backyard Stories. These include the use of specific details to provoke reader interest, the use of the senses—sight, smell, hearing, touch, and taste—to provide short descriptions that do not bore. Show, don't just tell, suggests Mr. Gladding, "Instead of saying a man is mean or nervous or scared, have him kick a dog or do something that shows his feeling." A suggestion to base all story writing in conflict is made too. "The conflict may be very gentle, but it must be there or the reader will not be eager to see what happens next.... Conflict is most interesting when it is *inside* you yourself.... If you make your character squirm over a difficult choice, your reader is going to squirm too." So it goes, with simple but good directions on how to approach this kind of creative writing.

In evaluating programs, one looks always for the spin-off or multiplier effect of various activities. The media, which so incessantly bombards us, almost forces many of us not to pay attention to details. Many people appear to function much of the time as though they had no hearing, speech, or sight, even though their senses may be in perfect physical working order. While no formula or program or teacher can guarantee an increased ability to see, hear, and respond with clarity and understanding, this kind of program can help in many important ways to educate and strengthen these senses in children.

The program at Richmond has undergone significant changes since it began. Its original purpose was purely entertainment, a response to coping with the needs of minority children brought into the main library from community action centers. The original role of the volunteer was to entertain and interest—frankly to babysit. The volunteer began to work with these children, trying to get them to write about things they knew about and were interested in. This initial club (as it has come to be regarded) fluctuated from between six to thirty children.

The club now meets in two separate sections: holdovers from last year meet on Monday afternoons; the newly formed group meets on Saturday mornings. Club meetings last just an hour. The original purpose of the club, to help minority children express themselves through writing, has not been sustained and most of the children now participating in the club are clearly avid, eager readers. Possibly a more specific and planned approach, involving a greater number and variety of children in the Backyard Program, would stimulate a more comprehensive and meaningful outreach program. The library also needs to think through more clearly its commitment to the program. It is possible that its essential integrity, its sensitivity with regard to channelling creativity in children toward positive outcomes without overstructuring learning, can be accommodated within a more structured library situation.

The importance of the program remains, though, its acceptance of a volunteer to serve as a program leader. The use of older persons, many with excellent professional careers, experiences, and capabilities behind them, offers many libraries extraordinary opportunities to extend library programs for the community. The Richmond experience supports the significant impact the volunteer can have on improving library services for children and young adults.

Program Objectives

1. To involve a volunteer in an instructional type program sponsored by a public library.
2. To increase the ability of participants to describe, with specificity and style, their feelings and the sights, sounds, and smells around them.
3. To operate a library service program without any extra expenditure of regular funds or professional personnel.
4. To reinforce the positive aspects of older people serving as good models for younger children.
5. To present the positive reinforcement of a public library learning program as a supplement to a school program.

Some Suggestions

1. Involve more than one volunteer in the program to enlarge the number of groups.
2. Move the program into local community action centers to involve more minority group children.
3. Provide for a method of retaining for use in the library program the work of the children involved in the Backyard Story project.
4. Open the program up to children of both a younger and older age.
5. Clarify and specify the interest and purpose of the library system's commitment to the program.

ECHO GLEN CHILDREN'S CENTER
Snoqualmie, Washington

Staff
Professional: 1
Volunteer: 3

Budget (average year)
Print: $1,500
Nonprint: 2,000

Target Population: 120 to 160 children, ages 8-18

The usual criteria for media program evaluation have to be put aside when evaluating the Echo Glen Children's Center program. First, the program is directed by a media specialist who works for the local school district and also reports to the librarian in charge of county institutional libraries. In addition, the professional must also relate to the Director of Institutional Libraries for the Washington State Library. A good example of line/staff accountability, it isn't! For Echo Glen, just put away the case books on administration, they will only make you lose sight of what the program is all about.

Analysis of media program effectiveness somehow always considers setting. "Institution" is the setting here, for Echo Glen is part of the State Bureau of Juvenile Rehabilitation. The media program serves young people committed to Echo Glen because they are juvenile delinquents, or who are unable to be contained within the bounds of a normal society for other reasons.

A pamphlet issued by the Center states, "The goal of treatment is to reduce delinquent and destructive behaviors and to increase socially adaptive behavior." Objectives to achieve this goal focus on experiences and activities for children that encourage normal social and intellectual development. The center seeks to provide an environment condusive to the kinds of behavior that will allow children to lead normal lives. And, finally, in a statement that should underlie the philosophy of all schools, the Echo Glen Children's Center *promises* to "Do no harm to the children committed here." Other institutions immunized from accountability and held to no standards whatever in such concerns might well consider this promise.

At Echo Glen the media program has a job to do, with goals and objectives to accomplish, and like any other media program to justify its existence it must prove its worth to the overall program of the school. These objectives do not differ significantly from those of any effective media program. Service and leadership sum it up. But here service and leadership relate always to the institutional purpose of rehabilitation.

At Echo Glen rehabilitation is a high priority. Media to support the program are available and used heavily. Special emphasis goes to career information materials, classroom sets of paperbacks, field trip resource guides, microfiche, pamphlets, paperbacks (almost fifteen for each child), puzzles, educational records, slides, television guides, and vertical file materials.

The program puts these materials into use in ways that show a naive ingenuousness that could be embarrassing but is appropriate here. The program accepts as a first priority that it must reach out to find new ways to involve children who do not have a high trust level for persons or programs.

Successful product advertising is a useful evaluative measure for any good media program, and advertising at the center is constant and effective. "Midnight Media," a newsletter of sorts issued by the Echo Glen Media Center, is an example. The idea for the newsletter was hatched at midnight and it hard sells all the information, services, and materials of the center.

For instance, "How about a freebee box? Come investigate," says the newsletter—"anything you find in the box is yours." Pictures to show "action in the center" are announced for a future date as well as a repeat of a popular slide show with a speaker. And, a healthy program sign, seven students and five staff persons took exactly thirty-three minutes to spend over two hundred dollars for twenty-six record albums, eight games, and one calculator. Having students and teachers participate directly in the selection/acquisition process clearly strengthens the media program in this school.

A later edition of "Midnight Media" announces that over 300 slides of the center have been taken showing staff and students using the facility. Eventually the show, with dialogue, will be used for orienting students, staff, and visitors to the program. A birthday book, scratch and smell boxes (orchids, onions, and lemons), and recorded ghost stories on Halloween—these are all used to entice children to use the media center.

A student aide program, suspect and neglected by many media programs, is a crucial program component. Aides are mentioned by name frequently in news items; they like this recognition. Learning responsibility about sharing and using materials and helping others is something most children are expected to learn in transit through school. At the Children's Center this attitude is crucial, for the ability to do this reveals much about the ability of the child to cope with larger social demands. At least three student aides work each period, and they are paid fifty cents for a work hour. The aide program reinforces the concept of responsibility for people and property, increases motivation to become involved in a school program, and allows the child to achieve the self-respect which comes from earning money for productive labor.

To become a student assistant, children fill out an application form that inventories their assets and capabilities. The "applicant" must be endorsed by another student, a teacher, and a staff person who is in charge of the residential cottages for children scattered around the center. Evaluation sheets are used to assess the aide program. On these sheets students make suggestions about the work program, their assignments, the media specialist, favorite materials they have used, and things about which they would like to know more.

The main goal for the Echo Glen media program is to "Create and organize a learning environment for staff and students at [the school] so that they have access to information, resources, materials and people to meet their needs." Measures to achieve this include using students' names for positive interacting, providing staff development and inservice workshops for teachers and children, and bringing many community resource persons into the program.

A visitor to the Echo Glen program remarked that a strength of the program was found in the way it *makes* good things happen with children who have frequently had little but bad happen to them in their short life spans. Innovative programs in a simplistic but not simple mold, availability of a large and useful collection of print and nonprint materials, an attractive and inviting room, and the personality of a media professional and her concern and care for children account for program success. A final measure is that any media center program that involves 95 to 100 percent of the student body in learning activities during a week is clearly making an important contribution to a total learning program.

Program Objectives
1. To provide an open access media program for delinquent children in an institutional setting.
2. To develop an effective student media aide program that provides both service and rehabilitation.
3. To promote interest in reading by children who are not necessarily readers by habit, by adding significant numbers of paperbacks to the collection.
4. To provide a media program that will encourage positive social change and attitudes on the part of children.
5. To create and organize a learning environment for staff and students to have access to information, resources, materials, and people to meet their needs.

Some Suggestions
1. Provide more production facilities for increased student production of materials.
2. Involve more community volunteers within the program.
3. Provide for at least one paid paraprofessional staff support position.

4. Provide for more specific involvement in selection of materials by teachers.
5. Provide more production facilities for teachers to produce useful learning materials relating to local needs.

EISENHOWER HIGH SCHOOL
New Berlin, Wisconsin

Staff
Professional: 4
Support: 4

Budget (1975-1976)
Print: $10,000
Nonprint: $4,000

Target Population: 1,650 children, ages 7-12

The Wisconsin State Department of Public Instruction considers the Eisenhower High School media program exemplary and the Office of Education of the Department of Health, Education & Welfare states that the school "possesses a creative media program." A visitor described the media center as "Exciting—with open doors, open attitudes, open minds, open smiles—from every direction." These are times when progress for many school media programs is easily measured in thimbles, but the Eisenhower media program produces an abundance of excellence in programming.

How? The best reason is that those who created this program understand that principles and theories about media must be put into practice for successful program results. The integration of all print and nonprint materials in a single shelving area, the arrangement of the card catalog unit for ease of access and use, the arrangement of reference materials to relate to subject areas, the capacity to produce a wide array of materials—each of these reflects the paramount media program goal. This goal is to assess the needs of students and teachers and produce the most efficient and effective delivery systems to meet these needs. Here, the media program has confronted and solved (or made manageable) many problems facing many media programs. The attitude is, "Show us a problem and we'll give you a solution!"

A staff program evaluation states the belief that the exemplary program results from (1) a comprehensive facility where print and nonprint programs are combined, providing maximum instructional involvement for students and teachers; (2) differentiated staffing, with the media staff operating within competency areas, such as selection of materials, equipment use, production of media and teaching but understanding responsibility to the entire program; (3) integrated media shelving with all print and nonprint materials housed together on open, easily accessible, shelving; and (4) in-service and staff development programs whereby a wide vareity of skills, knowledge, and experiences are continuously introduced, mastered, and reinforced by students and teachers.

Organization and operation are buttressed by a philosophy compelling in its commitment to "Make *all* materials openly available to students and teachers," providing students and teachers *easy access* to as much equipment as possible. The media program further commits itself "to provide media production possibilities where students and teachers can, by using a variety of production techniques make the materials and products necessary to support their own learning needs." This direct no-nonsense approach to providing services and leadership gives energy and purpose to the media program. And programs rooted in outworn assumptions and no longer valid cannot exist in this atmosphere.

Integrated shelving of media is guaranteed to provoke fruitless but passionate dialogue since most persons prefer not to be moved from their bias by new information. It works well at Eisenhower High School and it deserves consideration by others. Media formats shelved together include filmstrips, all books, tapes, sound film, strips and some realia. Slides, transparencies, 8mm film loops, and 16mm films, are not included in this open shelving arrangement. They are excluded because of their costliness or because of quantities involved or special storage problems. Microforms are located near the machines required for their use. Storage of nonprint is done in commercially made boxes designed for this purpose, available from most library supply houses.

The media staff states that intershelving of media "increased astonishingly" the circulation of all materials. They report, too, better use of the card catalog as a resource for locating materials, rather than as a pure bibliographic reference tool. Some 7,000 nonprint items are cataloged and intershelved with the rest of the collection.

Visibility, which permits easy access and quick retrieval, is cited most often by persons who support integrated media shelving. This is obviously true and it is sensible not to debate that point. A less appreciated but equally important benefit is that intershelving media generally enforces higher standards for weeding nonprint collections. For many professionals, weeding useless print items is difficult but nonprint weeding causes even greater pain! When they are housed or hidden away in storage cabinets, these items often don't get the visibility or use needed for proper evaluation.

What of the negative aspects of integrated media shelving? Among these is the contention that integrated shelving encourages stealing or mutilation. This school's experience does not support this, and for the 1975-76 school year the staff reported that eight filmstrips (from a total of 1,520) were missing or damaged beyond repair. That same year, eighty-six cassette tapes were missing; the cost to replace them was about $62. Staff judgment is that this is a small price to pay for having these materials so easily accessible.

Production of instructional materials is an important component of the media program. The sequencing of production to meet instructional goals dominates the program. For instance, in the television unit of a mass media course, career education and work experience are combined and students electing to produce a television program for class projects learn to operate equipment, do lighting and sound work, direct, and edit. Observers remark on the ability of the staff to carry on a "continuous, superorderly, hands-on student training program." There is an abundance of production materials, but they must be used with a purpose. Production must support expected outcomes expressed most often in the form of a "contract." And some media produced is added to the materials collection if quality and content warrant. Diazo's, simple transparencies, photomodifications, handmade filmstrips, slide shows—whatever, once produced, are considered to be part of the school media program. They are processed, cataloged, and used within the instructional program. While this does not guarantee absolute quality control or prevent waste, it does lift the production of materials above the level of fun-and-games.

A further excellent quality of the media program is its determination to involve faculty and media staff in selecting nonprint materials in ways that stress accountability. Nonprint materials are not selected only by the media center staff. The intent is for the media specialist to serve as an "informtion generalist" rather than subject area specialist working with teachers to help them select appropriate materials. Making departments *accountable* for purchase of instructional materials encourages better methods for getting media used well. Rather than selling the teacher media selected by the media specialist, the specialist can suggest creative and innovative ways to make better use of materials which the teacher selected.

The media staff spends at least ninety percent of its time working directly with students and teachers. An adequate support staff permits this, but really it happens because the staff *makes* it happen. Routines are analyzed and made responsive to school needs. For instance, paperbacks used extensively here (some 18,000 have been acquired over several years) are given minimal or no cataloging and seen as expendables.

A program budgeting format used in the district mandates thinking and planning about the future, necessary to any excellent program. Program review (including successes and failures) is on-going and continuous. This forces the media program to assess not only itself but its contribution to the entire school instructional program. Program budgeting requires direct staff involvement in the planning and evaluating process, strengthening staff commitment to achieve goals.

Staff development programs leading to better utilization of all materials, increased competency in equipment usage, and skill in media production are other examples of the instructional force of this program.

Finally, the worth of any media program is its effect on the quality or excellence of teaching and learning within the school. This measurement is met and surpassed here by a program providing exceptional leadership in creative and innovative ways.

Program Objectives
1. To provide an integrated and unified media program designed for instructional leadership.
2. To assure that ninety percent of professional staff time is spent in work with children or teachers.
3. To provide integrated open shelving of print and nonprint media.
4. To make all materials and equipment easily available to students and teachers, and to provide a media production program that permits students and teachers to produce their own media projects.
5. To have teaching staff directly involved in selection of media materials by making final decisions on what is to be purchased.

Some Suggestions
1. Involve students more specifically in selection of materials; use student preview form.
2. Involve more community volunteers in program, thus providing even more service.
3. Expand collection of professional materials and resources.

RACINE PUBLIC LIBRARY
Racine, Wisconsin

Staff
Professional: 1

Budget
Not applicable

Target Population: 600 children, ages 3-12

When it began, the "Yankee Doodle Dandy Library Program" was an almost casual attempt to put together a summer program for children that would capitalize on the Bicentennial, use a unifying theme to introduce children to library services, and do some cooperative community outreach by combining public library and school media program resources.

In Racine, Wisconsin, a number of thoughtful and committed people saw and acted upon the opportunity to put together an uncomplicated, unsophisticated, and people-oriented program, planned to enrich community life by combining the best components of two separate library-media systems. If it accomplished nothing more than to bring together public library and school media programs in cooperative, systematic, community-oriented planning this activity was a success.

In the summer of 1974, ten of the Racine School media centers were opened to community use. Community access to school media centers during summer vacation periods is in itself unique, since most schools close up tight for the summer. In many cases, school media center collections are superior to those of nearby libraries. Nearly always, they are more accessible to the public, for neighborhood schools still exist in greater numbers than branches of the public library.

One part of the 1974 school program that was a big success was the story hour program. The modest but distinct success of the school programs prompted the public library to suggest that the two plan joint story telling programs. From this came the "Yankee Doodle Dandy Program."

Most public libraries plan some summer programs for

children. These programs may involve crafts, performing arts, film, creative dramatics, and a host of other offerings depending upon the resources and imaginations available. Nearly all of these programs are built upon the expectation that involvement in them will encourage children to read for pleasure and enjoyment—certainly a shared concern of both schools and public libraries. This was a specified intent of the Racine program.

Eventually, the Yankee Doodle project involved not only the schools and the public library but the City Parks and Recreation Department; the playground programs; a migrant camp program; and a host of parents, who, from curiosity and interest, got involved. Planned as a one-shot performance, designed as a storytelling festival, the program quickly added dimension and became more of a travelling library show. What had been planned to be one or two super spectacular festivals built around the Yankee Doodle theme became instead a fast-paced offering to be show-cased in a variety of ways to different audiences.

The result, a ten-performance Yankee Doodle Festival presented over a two-week span. It was a kind of saturation effort emphasizing and reinforcing summer library program offerings of the public library and school media centers.

None of the animosity or apprehension that can mar the relationship of school media and public library programs intruded here. In Racine, history is against this kind of nonsense, even though the school media program must necessarily be oriented to curriculum support and the public library oriented to the community. Dual program sponsorship did not threaten the separate responsibilities or obligations of the two. In fact, the programs show that access to information and community service programs for children can comfortably be a shared responsibility of both institutions.

Does anyone need another lesson in the economics of reality? For library-media programs, this reality means that the information turf is not something to be fought over for control but shared by two institutions which need each other in order to serve a common public adequately. Also the Yankee Doodle Project shows that there is no budget expense in cooperation. At least not in terms of materials, equipment, or other resources used within this program. All that was required was to put together existing resources and personnel.

Once a basic program format was established it could be moved easily to any location. Requiring the service of two persons, and such volunteers as could be recruited when necessary, and using materials already on hand, the program operated with no overhead. Programs usually ran for thirty to forty minutes and were always a cooperative venture. Each program was introduced by the school representative who talked with the audience about American folklore, and this was followed by the film *Room for Heroes*. Public library personnel did the storytelling program which followed. Such stories as *John Henry* or *Paul Bunyon and the Popcorn Blizzard* were used most often. If time allowed, group singing of American folk songs or the telling of some American riddles was included.

The simplicity of the program permits its easy adoption and use almost anywhere. Its pay off is an increased understanding, appreciation, and use of community library services by the public. Nearly fifteen percent of the audience for the Yankee Doodle programs were adults attracted to them and finally involved because of their children. Bookmarks, individual flyers to promote future events, puzzles, and other handouts were used in the program and provided enjoyment, instruction, and publicity.

It may be that the most important contribution this model summer program makes is not its content, but its experience in planning and working together. Cooperative program planning and implementation between school and a public library programs is necessary, sensible, and can be, as here, refreshing.

Program relationships to heroes and heroines of American folklore and the celebration of a unique American historical event provided a focus in 1976. Other possible themes are numerous and depend upon time, personalities, and talents of the individuals involved and the program goals they establish. Time frame for the program may be expanded or contracted and locale may vary. Personalities and talents may be changed as well according to theme or purpose.

To cooperate costs nothing. Of course, some sort of in-kind cost for staff time to plan and carry out the programs must be allocated. The only real requirement is the willingness of public library and school media programs to take the leadership and risks involved in breaking down barriers to establish new patterns of service to children. While in many ways a modest effort, this cooperative program is miles ahead of what most school and public library programs do together. And once begun, the continuation of cooperative public-oriented programs will doubtless continue.

Program Objectives
1. To provide a cooperative summer program for children sponsored jointly by school media programs and public library programs.
2. To prepare a mixed media presentation suitable to children focused on a thematic issue (American folklore).
3. To provide young children with an early understanding of library-information service available to them through school and public libraries.
4. To involve adults in library programs for children.
5. To use special cooperative programs to encourage reading by children.

Some Suggestions
1. Extend time period and location of programs to involve more children.
2. Involve more community persons as volunteers or program resource personnel.
3. Devise a continuing program to provide specific programs for minority group populations.

4. Consider more activity oriented programs to specifically involve children in the program, e.g., crafts, arts, etc.
5. Provide evaluation form for participants to check off to improve program evaluation.

MEAD PUBLIC LIBRARY
Sheboygan, Wisconsin

Staff   **Budget**
Professional: 1
Support: 1 $1,100 (for program)

Target Population: 200 children, ages 5-12

For many, the end of 1976 meant surcease from an unending Bicentennial bombardment. Planned as a celebration and renewal of the character and spirit of the Nation, the event almost disappeared beneath piles of bicentennial souvenirs, tacky pageants, and overdone rehetoric. But among the many good things that emerged were many childrens' library programs that sparkle with personality and purpose, promising continued life beyond the Bicentennial Year. They will survive as effective on-going programs because they were shaped with understanding of children and how their special interests may be related to "special event" programs that entertain and educate.

"America's Birthday and Yours, Too! 1776-1976," a program of the Mead Public Library, Sheboygan, Wisconsin, is representative of such programs. It was conceived and carried out with a simplicity that makes it easily adaptable to most libraries. Program purpose: To make the children of Sheboygan aware of the anniversary of American's Independence by relating America's birthday with their own birthday.

Initial funding for program start up makes it a particularly attractive prospect. A $400 grant was provided by the Wisconsin Bicentennial Commission and additional small amounts came from library endowment funds. The total cost then is minimal, easily affordable by most libraries. Equally attractive, the program requires the attention of only one staff person to be implemented successfully, and it is possible for this person to maintain other responsibilities. Planning the program, selecting appropriate materials, and stage-managing the birthday party program take time, but one can manage with occasional limited and irregular help from others.

In the program, simplicity and spontaneity do not equate with time-filler activities. It is natural for a child to want recognition on MY birthday! Ego aside, there is an easily made transition to increased understandings and appreciations for significant historical events. Here is the program adaptability factor, for it can be related to a great number of historical events and personalities, providing usefulness far beyond an initial purpose to celebrate birthdays and the Bicentennial.

Program audience ranged from kindergarten through grade six. This is a wide age range, but a program visitor reported that on an evening when one of the birthday celebrations was held, forty-six children, age four to teenage, were present, attentive and involved. Their attitudes, responses, and involvement show that it is possible to encompass a wide-ranging age group if the program can be made relevant and satisfying. A further helpful aspect of the Bicentennial Birthday Party Program is that it follows a pre-established format, using similar materials and activities each month. Once the program is operating it is reuseable on a continuing basis. Libraries with limited staff to plan childrens programs will be particularly interested in this.

Program format goes thus: the children assemble and are given brief introductory remarks by a children's librarian, for this program they include comments on the significance of the Bicentennial celebration. This was followed by an original play, with a birthday theme performed by drama students from a local high school. When the program was visited, the twenty minute play consisted of a series of mildly irreverent historical vignettes, scripted by a former library page. Relating the program to a community resource, such as a high school drama club, provides additional dimension and interest. The drama club presented twelve programs and received a $300 honorarium.

The Walt Disney film, *Ben and Me,* was a regular program event. A classic in either print or nonprint format, it is always a success. Irreverent is an apt word to describe the film too; what child can resist the whimsy of Ben aloft, clinging to a kite during a thunder and lightning storm? Many 16mm films of high quality and tested value offer possibilities of relating historical events and personalities to high quality programs. Selecting the best of these presents the only problem.

The high point of the birthday celebration was the appearance of Uncle Sam. He went about the audience, shaking hands, congratulating birthday celebrants, getting and giving answers to historical questions. Audience involvement was always high for this portion of the program.

There were take-away gifts too. These are important to the child and can carry visible advertisements for library programs. At Mead the gifts were buttons saying "America's Birthday and Yours Too." Available also was a printed booklet describing children's books relating to the Bicentennial. An attractive offering, it provided clear title and location sources for a selected list of fiction and nonfiction books for children in primary and intermediate grades. Its eight pages list mostly print items but contain entries for some recordings available in the children's room. It has further use as a bibliography for parents and teachers.

A program offering gave parents the opportunity to request a cassette tape be made of their child's favorite story. Requested in advance, the tape could not exceed fifteen minutes and cost sixty cents. It was presented as a special gift to the child at the party. Request forms for the service were available at the children's room desk. The number of these requests was low and it is possible that the advance time to fill the request and the single location for the request form inhibited its use.

The idea, though, has excellent public relations and educational possibilities and should be developed. Part of the program publicity involved the placement of handsome posters in such locations as schools, grocery stores, and service clubs. If request forms for the taping of favorite children's stories as a gift had been available in these places, too, quite probably more requests would have been generated. Before this step is taken, though, it is best to be certain that adequate staff (perhaps community volunteers) with enough time and the ability to read well are available to tape the stories.

Community involvement in programs like the Bicentennial is a natural and lends it a particular strength. At Mead, a committee of parents and friends of the public library served this purpose. They helped prepare refreshments and set-up for the party and were always on hand to help. A number of adults always attended the birthday programs which were held at seven in the evening, on the first Tuesday of each month. The program's ability to stimulate adult use of the library and involvement in its programs provides another commendable program feature.

The visitor also made an observation that a fine facility, particularly one newly built, is no guarantee of excellent program. The Wisconsin State Library Agency keeps an ongoing file of patterns of successful programs. The file for the Mead Library already contains some sixty-five patterns, including back-up materials. The birthday celebration is only one of many activities for children involving animals, puppets, children's art work, instructional media, and equipment. It is an impressive array of programs designed to educate, and involve children in many creative ways. The thrust of this particular series though gives it an especially appealing dimension because of the ease with which it involves community and children in a personal way in an outreach program.

Program Objectives
1. To make children aware of a particular historical event (the Bicentennial) by relating it to their own birthdays.
2. To demonstrate to children a number of enjoyable and educational library activities.
3. To involve parents of these children in library programs.
4. To develop a program to serve as a model for other related programs to follow.

5. To combine a number of media experiences into a specific program format.

Some Suggestions
1. Consider using additional or other films in related programs.
2. Seek sponsorship, if necessary, from community-related programs.
3. Increase story taping aspect of program through more request locations and use of volunteers.
4. Involve a variety of performers (musicians and dancers) in the performance aspect of the program.
5. Include some specific learning activities, such as crossword puzzles or quizzes, to involve children in program. Perhaps offer a prize for the contest winner.

PART III

Interpreting the Surveys; Implications for School and Public Library Media Programs

It is probable that no two people, however professional both of them are, will come to exactly the same conclusion about the effectiveness of any given media program. Accordingly, some will not agree with some of the conclusions about the programs reported in this book.

When judgments and evaluations are based on information gained from a survey instrument, even though buttressed by the perceptions of an on-site visitor, there are even greater obstacles to formulating specific conclusions with which everyone would agree. In her book, *The Disadvantaged and Library Effectiveness,* Claire Lipsman states that "survey research involves systematic observations of particular variables in a variety of settings and with formal controls such that certain hypothesis can be tested...." The limitations to the survey approach to gather information about media programs are obvious immediately in that it is, after all, frequently impossible to collect adequate and varied data from many locations. Added to this is the difficulty of relating survey data to the actual conditions prevailing at any institution on the day and time that a visitation is made to observe and find out more about the program. We all know how a program, a plan, or a procedure may be altered in some way on a particular day due to circumstances beyond the control of anyone.

In a survey based approach, a very human element enters in; this is the way people respond to forms and questionnaires. George Gallup, who certainly should know, has discovered recently that it is becoming increasingly difficult to get Americans to respond to the questions of survey takers. It is possible that we are simply polled and surveyed out. The times make it difficult to provide the "right" answers to many questions and apparently people do not feel comfortable unless they can provide these "right" answers. Of course, this is not always possible or even desirable, but it seems especially true of the responses made to survey instruments that people receive unsolicited through the mail. They want to respond in the way that will be most pleasing and satisfying to the questioner. This can skew the validity of responses to the survey. After all, our successes, real or imagined, are infinitely more pleasing to relate than our failures.

There may also be feelings of anxiety associated with filling out forms and surveys. Many people are reluctant to commit themselves to specific statements. No matter how reassuring or nonthreatening the approach to gathering data may be, anxiety is sometimes present. At a certain level this anxiety means, quite simply, that the form will not be filled out at all; anonymity preserved is ego unchallenged.

At quite the opposite extreme the respondant feels compelled to report the most outlandish or nonexistent programs in a fashion that would indicate revealed truth. In the recent past too many of our governmental, social, and educational institutions have been exposed too often publicly in this process of myth making. But, this continues and to the extent that deception and myth making are products of these times, they too must be considered in evaluating responses to surveys.

Survey instruments have built-in limiting factors—the turn of a phrase, the positioning of sections being surveyed, the request for statistics and quantitative reactions—these, and others, condition response. A few (very few) persons responded to the survey taken for this book with annoyance. Some said it was too long (it probably was); others said that it asked for the wrong data (possibly it did); and others said it did not permit them to express what their particular media program was accomplishing. These few were more than balanced, however, by those who felt encouraged to pour out problems they were experiencing with staff or with the federal government or with parents, and they reported a number of other aspects that, in one way or another, marred their program. One conclusion that can be made, with little fear of challenge, is that there are still a great many humans "out there" who really want someone just to listen to their problems, their hopes, and ideas. The need to seek advice while providing information remains strong. If so, the column "Action Line" which has appeared recently in *American Libraries* is needed badly and will find a ready audience.

The point of this is not so much an "apologia"—the perfectly balanced survey instrument has probably yet to be devised—but an effort to help the reader understand the complexity of interpreting correctly responses to the kind of broadly based survey that was used to gather information for this book.

Considering all this, the response (both in numbers and in quality) was heartening. Eventually, over four hundred individuals or institutions responded in some way to our request for information. Those who found the survey most difficult to respond to were public libraries operating media programs in more than one branch or location, and schools wishing to report district programs as opposed to individual building programs.

The intent of the survey was to locate as many individual location media programs as possible. It seems clear that many persons are still convinced that the physical facitlity is more vital to program than it really is. In fact, the evidence shows that while the facility housing a program may be a factor in the success or failure of the program, it is not the crucial factor. Of course some facilities may be so substandard, so depressing, and so inhospitable that they actually inhibit programs, but the program that is truly having a salutary impact on children transcends poor facilities.

There is a certain arrogance in the term "media center." It implies a point, or pivot, the axis around which everything else must revolve. As an attitude, this is infuriating; in program terms it is impossible. Far too often it has led to the construction of school media centers and public libraries that, while beautiful to look upon, fail to perform anything like the purpose they arrogate to themselves.

A clear trend, one that will probably have significant bearing on the future of school media programs, is a growing recognition that the truly exemplary media *program* cannot physically be contained in a media center. Already, some of the more creative thinkers about media programs see that the ultimate realization of the media program will be when there is no longer need for a media center in a physical sense. Rather, every classroom, every instructional area, every place where children gather or come as individuals or groups to learn has the potential to be a media center containing a media program no less valid than that now assigned to the media center. None of this means, by the way, that there will no longer be a need in schools for media centers and media professionals. A central area, or areas, for housing and using instructional materials is essential; and a return to the era of the "classroom" collection is not advocated here. Rather, it is concept, or practice—a media program working *throughout* the school (and community) directed or managed by a media specialist who functions as an instructional consultant and learning facilitator for children and teachers. A corollary of this must be that every teacher, every aide, every principal, every child has within himself or herself the potential of becoming a media specialist. Why not? If a major purpose of the media program is to help people learn to sort, sift, and select sensibly from the vast array of alternatives, it will lead surely to true independent learning no longer controlled totally by a school, a teacher, or a program. Does it really take a Delphic oracle or a futurist to see this? No, for it is already abundantly clear and manifested in a variety of ways that teaching and learning have changed fundamentally.

It appears that the public library may be both more flexible and adept at changing its concept of media programs and what their purpose is than is the school. Over a long period of time many observers have noted that the quality that most distinguishes the American public library from all others in the world is its close identity with its community. While it is true that too few public libraries as yet plan their programs and services in relationship to the total needs of their communities and the total resources available, they have been shaped in general by a need to respond to and be involved with the community.

If the concern for providing information that has so characterized excellent public library programs could be combined with the emphasis by school programs on encouraging the use of this information, then a great step ahead would be taken.

In doing this, both institutions and the programs they generate would demonstrate that ideas, access to information, and the nurturing of the will to act by an informed populace are much more important than the form in which the ideas are presented, or the facility from which they emanate. To satisfy these needs will demand every bit of the cooperation, responsibility and desire to make things work that are so characteristic of our culture.

A survey instrument cannot make all of these needs explicit. But this does not make it any less important to try to assess the attitudes and the breadth of vision behind the media programs described.

Other intangible hard-to-measure qualities entered into our conclusions; for instance, the ability to change course and be flexible in the face of shifting demand, to create priorities and to cut off unproductive elements before they damage a program are key factors that consistently separate the excellent program from the merely good. Assessing these traits can be a very subjective business.

The "quality" of life is now a much discussed contemporary public issue. Ecology, concentration of economic power, family planning, and other concerns relate in one way or another to this general topic. The quality of media programs that affect children and young people should be considered as well. Quality means here that programs using media must respect the sensitivities and the instinct to learn, directing these into productive, satisfying end results. Media contribute for good or for ill to the quality of life. They are an important motivating force in establishing our value system.

The media are a powerful force, but measurement of their impact through specific programs is again often subjective.

If the virtues ascribed to the programs selected for this book seem consonant with those of any historically excellent public and school library programs, they are meant to be. Winston Churchill once said, "If these stories are not true, they ought to have been." To paraphase Churchill, if all of the virtues and successes ascribed to the programs described before in this book are not so, they ought to be. For they represent what should be the essence of excellent programming in any era.

Public library and school media programs have rather different notions of how to best use staff within a program. Using professional rather than support or paraprofessional staff to accomplish a program objective seems a less emotional issue in the public library field. The reason for this may be due to something always to be kept in mind when considering the differences between the school media specialist and the public librarian. The school media professional is by virtue of training, instinct, and, most important, certification laws first a teacher—an educator. It is rare for the certified school media professional not to have been through at least some sequence of courses that prepared for certification as a teacher. The quality of this preparation is not central to the concerns of this book and not possible to assess here. Inevitably though, because of this preparation, school media professionals generally consider themselves first as teachers and secondarily as librarians. This attitude and job focus is not shared by the public librarian who has frequently shunned, by intent, the very courses the school professional sought or was required to master.

There have been at best only vague and unrealistic attempts to bridge the gulf resulting from these differences in self-identity and professional preparation. This separation by preparation does have a fundamental impact on shaping the attitudes of personnel and the programs generated by the two institutions.

Because of this, professional relationships from time-to-time become visibly uncomfortable. Sometimes this remains hidden and sometimes it explodes publicly.

The relationship of the American Association of School Librarians to its parent the American Library Association remains always uneasy and at times deeply troubled. While trying to maintain some sort of home within the only organizational structure it has ever known, the American Association of School Librarians is compelled by many forces, ranging from membership concerns to government funding programs, to seek alliances and cooperative relationships with other associations and professional organizations.

State associations and regional groupings, (the New England Educational Media Association [NEEMA] being one), have merged separate audiovisual and library associations into unified *educational* media associations. These newly merged associations frequently recruit into their memberships such divergent, but related, educational personnel as principals, curriculum consultants, and even classroom teachers interested in using media.

The trend is evident and its implications are inescapable. State association mergers leave the national leadership of AASL in an exposed position. It is rarely good policy to let constituent action be too far in advance of that of leadership. While the prospects for any merger between AASL and the Association for Educational Communications and Technology (AECT) or other allied educational associations are somewhat remote (and perhaps not even desirable), the momentum for fundamental change continues to build at the state and regional level. Yet, the growing role of the public library as educational institution may foster second thoughts among school media specialists as to where their interests will be served best.

The growing development of the unionization movement within the National Education Association, while upsetting to many members of AASL, probably will not in the long run deter the course of natural events. If the trend of educators to organize themselves into unions continues, if school media specialists grow to think of themselves more and more as curriculum consultants and educational leaders, if national associations become less cooperative with each other, if public library and school media programs grow more competitive over control of programs for children, then we are in the midst of some unstable times.

No responses to any survey instrument received for this book indicated any prejudice on the part of school media or public library personnel toward each other nor any mistrust of the motivation or programs of one another. Rather, what came through clearly was a basic trust and respect, one for the other, that could be enhanced by joint planning and implementing of sound media programs. The citation, as exemplary, of some programs that involve a sharing of staff program and perhaps facilities was deliberate and planned.

Too often facility or site location becomes confused with program. A branch of the public library is not analogous to an individual school media center. At present, attitudes, programs, individuals served, administrative structure, and a host of other factors constitute differences between the two.

The public library sees a branch, housed in a building, as just that: a branch program. The staff to develop, implement, and evaluate branch programs may be shifted to other locations with relative ease. Likewise, the materials to support the program are moved about a large or medium-sized public library system with an ease that is incomprehensible to a school media specialist. In the sense that public libraries have understood, accepted, and acted upon the reality that programs seek out persons and use their materials with these persons in a variety of ways and in a number of potential settings, they are advanced considerably beyond the attitudes found in most public school systems where the individual building program is powerful and paramount. In education the notion of building autonomy has often retarded the development of effective and progressive media programs.

If public school educators and media specialists have something to learn from public libraries about attitudes and practices concerning the use of materials with people, public libraries have much to gain from closer attention to the effect of objective program evaluation, a process in which school media professionals have led the way.

As with most reform movements in education, the entire

process of measurable program planning and evaluation exemplified by such operations as program planning and budget systems (PPBS) and management by objectives (MBO) will not have the impact (either for good or bad) their proponents or opponents predict. Educators continue to display a distressing tendency to be misled by "experts", and in many cases evident today applications of PPBS and MBO to educational programs verify this truth.

Undoubtedly there is much that is right with the goals/objective-measurability approach to planning programs that has generated the "accountability movement" now so much with us. As a process for delineating and systematizing measurable skills and assessing expected results, these systems can't be beat. But, in his wonderfully wise little booklet, *Educational Accountability: Beyond Behavioral Objectives,* Arthur Coombs points out that the entire accountability movement may be a danger in that it may be only party right. It *assumes* always that the objectives being measured are important ones; that the behavior modification to be achieved is desirable; that the means of measurement are valid. That accountability is based on a logical, systematic, and rational approach to assessing a program's contribution and results cannot be denied. The possibility must always be allowed, though, that this same logical, systematic, and rational approach can lead to some wrong answers. Logical conclusions are not always right solutions. Expressed another way, there is a maddening tendency on the part of many of the objectivist/assessment proponents to provide us with all of the answers to our problems, but none of the solutions.

Despite its obvious limitations and techniques, the process of program assessment and evaluation will be a part of all institutional life for the forseeable future. Unfair as it may be, the enemies of public expenditure for any public program will insure the continued life of the accountability movement. To some of these persons any public expenditure beyond minimal police and fire protection reeks of socialism. It is useless to argue with such people that it costs a great deal of money just to keep information and media programs at their present level or that if education is expensive, ignorance is far more costly.

Somewhere between the crazy fringes that contain those who would dismantle the entire tax supported public institutional life of America and those who support the notion that everything ought to be taken care of by the government lies a substantial number of thoughtful, clear thinking persons who question, with vigorous assurance and correctness, continued large amounts of public expenditure for information programs that have not had their worth validated.

Our failure to recognize these legitimate concerns and the public's right to expect some measure of real accountability for programs financed by their taxes could have disastrous consequences.

Many of the survey instruments returned for this book spoke positively about the high degree of community involvement in their programs. Such involvement has always been an indicator of the good health and viability of any public program. The surveys seem to mirror what many other pollsters and survey takers have found recently: that even though there is readiness by many to identify any and all institutions as examples of costly and meddlesome bureaucracy, at best self-serving and at worst ineffective, the vast majority of Americans retain a basic respect and esteem for the institutions of this country.

Our critics are louder, more articulate, more powerful, better informed (by the media of all things), and more disputive than ever before. There remains, however, a large number, probably still a majority, of persons who want to be convinced that media programs for children and young persons need not be destructive to the care and nurturing of beginning readers; will not contribute to the idleness of youth; will not reinforce a totally permissive atmosphere in which there are no rules for children; will not create a learning environment that fails to involve children personally and specifically in their own learning; will not create a learning environment that is irrelevant to the needs of children; will not enhance the kind of institution that permits children to leave it poorly trained to find a place in the world of work; and *will* help children to use their minds effectively in managing their own and other larger problems. It is to this constituency, skeptical of our claims, knowledgable of the gap between our stated goals and failed achievements, yet still supportive of our efforts, that media professionals must find ways to demonstrate the worth of the media.

Here the schools have much help to offer to public libraries, the result of their recent experiences. All educators are confronted, almost daily, with demands for more and better program accountability. It is a healthy sign, clearly evident in many of the survey instruments returned by school media programs, that schools have moved far in the last decade toward greatly improved program evaluation procedures. Often, these evaluative criteria were properly built directly into a program from its inception. And many times these evaluative criteria were developed by media professionals, not imposed from without. The surveys indicate that the evaluative process is no longer the trauma for school media personnel that it was during its early years.

The same willingness to evaluate, which must be founded on an understanding of what the evaluation process is to be and how it should be structured, is not reflected in most public library survey responses. It was rarely mentioned and, when it was, usually in a casual and offhand way. This is not a good sign, for the public library as an institution has much it could learn and should coopt from the public school experience with program assessment. This opportunity for cooperation and help should not be overlooked.

It is inconceivable to many public librarians that such standbys as a children's story hour or phone reference service could be evaluated on the basis of strict program outcome or budget cost accountability. Can the public library, using tax money to support a children's story hour justify that program expenditure? Does the program contribute to an improvement in reading as quantified by number of books read? Does the program increase the ability of participants to select relevant reading materials? Does the program involve the participants in learning as assessed by a number of independent variables?

These are some obvious kinds of evaluative criteria that could be applied to these programs. They might not be the best ones but they could be used to establish program framework providing specific goals and objectives to be achieved by these programs. In fact, for many public librarians they are negative measurement factors. Yet, they are the kind of easy measurement devices that appeal to many racing toward their own notion of program accountability.

The use of goals and objectives to produce prescribed behavior and measurable results will confront public libraries. It is not just possible, but probable, that a well informed public will demand such measurement criteria to assess program value. In public education the initial impact of this was, quite simply, devastating. Programs folded ignominiously at the first challenge; personnel could not cope with the demands made of them to justify their programs. This need not have happened.

Hopefully, several of the public library programs used as examples in this book will serve to show how to do at least a beginning form of program evaluation. This process does not have to be initially a sophisticated model based on flow charts, perted outputs, and processed inputs. But it must be more than a simple recitation of the obvious. Most institutions have professional staff members quite capable of dealing effectively with this process. School media programs and public library programs could make this process less time consuming and far more productive if their expertise could be shared.

Survey responses indicate that many professionals in schools and public libraries are bemused, indeed baffled, by such terms as "exemplary" or "innovative." Apparently many still feel that unless there is a pot of money and an elaborate facility no innovative or exemplary programming can occur. What a job, therefore, to find some programs that required almost no money, needed no special facility, and were being done through the efforts of one or two individuals. These programs prevail because they have often made a virtue of necessity. That necessity: the need to reach out, to touch positively, and to change for the better the lives of one or many; this may still be accomplished even if tempered by lack of funds, poor facility, or understaffing.

It is this *attitude* of prevailing, of fulfilling a mission and overcoming the obstacles, that remains as one of the chief guarantors of excellence in programming. Conditions which are simply too hostile, forces that are too overwhelmingly negative, or resources that are always nonexistent can prove too destructive to carry on—this is obvious. Equally obvious, but frequently overlooked is that an abundance of resources, a multitude of staff, and rich facilities cannot guarantee program success.

Each of the exemplary programs described in this book have accommodated another fundamental truth, one often recognized but rarely understood by many media programs. This is that the best learning is that which makes the learner take an active part. Such learning *involves* rather than merely *serves* to interest. Passive listening to sounds or viewing of images does not mean learning. It is a simple fact yet fundamental truth—communication that translates to learning must be a two-way process. This, by the way, does not mean that learning always is expressed verbally. For the child, learning is often an internal, private experience. But no learner simply receives images to store for later retrieval. Something has to happen, involving the learner as respondent, only then are ideas translated into action, understanding—knowledge.

Too many media programs still do not reflect an understanding of this process. Thus, the media are still regarded by many as the ultimate pacifiers of our time. Television to amuse the class from 1:00 to 2:00 P.M.; a movie to soothe from 2:30 until dismissal; a trip to the media center to "look at" a filmstrip or "listen to" a cassette; the use of the popular recording at the public library branch to "involve" the children. For many persons working with media programs, it is a list monotonous and discouraging in its familiarity.

It is right here that our will to redirect and to redeploy the enormous resources available to us will be tested. After all, if we do not take these steps who will? Someone has to assume the responsibility; immediate attention to this issue should be a top priority. Public librarians and school media specialists together have the greatest possible interest in seeing to it that the media are applied productively and so as to encourage the kind of two-way communication that means excellence in learning opportunities.

The survey instruments provide ample reason to support the belief that the day of reckoning in terms of both preprofessional preparation and continued learning while on the job fast approaches for both the public librarian and school media specialist.

No position is taken here on the issue of how well library schools are preparing their graduates. A series of necessities have forced some library schools to adapt very traditional programs to meet better the demands placed upon them for preparing school media professionals. Is there anyone concerned about the preparation of school media professionals today who would seriously maintain that having that second or third reference course really adds to their preparation as educators? A review of the 1975 *Media Programs: District and School* or the final report of the AASL committee that prepared a national *Certification Model for Professional School Media Personnel* makes clear that the prevailing future demand must be for instructional leadership. If the library schools now preparing school media specialists choose to ignore guidelines created by the profession itself, then probably they will lose their clientele. This tends to support a conviction held by many that the preparation of school media specialists will be accomplished best by schools of education. For those who have had much contact with schools of education and their preparation of teachers, this may be an unacceptable alternative to existing library school programs.

It is disturbing to realize that this eventuality might widen the gulf now separating school and public library media programs. If the focus of both our efforts is to help develop active participants in their own learning; to integrate new methods of learning with traditional forms of knowledge; to help ourselves and others undertake to use media to enhance the quality of life; to help close the gap between the institution and the larger world of ideas; then we must consider other alternatives relative to the preparation and on-the-job learning of *all* media professionals.

This means in-service, continuing education, staff development, or some other method to improve professionals already holding positions. And it certainly means new varieties and methods of training before professionals begin work. It is sad when we want to change everybody but ourselves! Yet, to do what we have come to recognize as necessary, many of us must make basic changes in attitudes, competences and concerns, this is a process of change that will have no end.

The field of education seems to have perceived and acted more sensibly on the need for professionals to become more effective in their jobs while they hold them. Recently, specific resources, materials, and personnel have been focused upon the need for staff development in education. There have been in this process notable successes and some bad failures. Public library professionals have done little in the past to meet these important needs.

Cooperative efforts to develop staff programs for both systems must recognize that it is the future that is important. If staff development programs dwell on sharing what has happened in the past to shape better our ability to deal with current or future problems, they will fail. Our concern must go to upgrading the competencies of professionals to deal with new materials, new methods of communication, and new modes of learning. Staff development then must help professionals deal with the variety of futures that await. Otherwise they will remain a process of the past imitating the past.

In completing the survey instrument no one actually admitted a failure to attempt to develop new program operations to meet immediate and future needs; after all who would? But evidence of this failure or lack of concern appeared in a variety of ways. In some responses there was a startling attitude that present programs because they were "good" or "popular" (both undefined) would satisfy into the future. Evident too was the notion that a successful program now would guarantee a successful and continuing future life. Neither position is realistic or conducive to good program development.

Our profession has to become conditioned to expect more exact, specific outcomes from programs. Alas, the contradiction, for this is not the pattern of the future. Our emphasis on a search for answers and quantifiable results is clouded by ambiguity. It will require the most careful planning and the ability to absorb setbacks as we develop our abilities to think through, plan, and evaluate that which will help us be more effective in using media with chidren.

This need absolutely transcends the boundaries of a school media center or a public library building. To reiterate, if media professionals allow program location, preservice professional training, or any other of the usual reasons to prevent them from jointly preparing for the maximum sustained effort to create and change their own abilities to cope with the future, we will fail before we begin.

After all, when we talk about the need for unified media programs and shared informational activities, we are talking specifically about the needs of people to get at and use these resources. A common shared need is to translate media programs that are not necessarily people oriented into ones that are.

The story hour at the public library children's room; the toy lending library that emanates from a store front branch library; the video cassette program that seeks to improve consumer education and attitudes; the public library tutoring program that complements rather than competes with, the school; these and a multitude of others are the media programs most needed now by people. By dictionary definition, the media convey or transmit something from one place or person to another. The purpose of this book is in harmony with that definition, for it points out, wherever possible that conveying information from person to person is best done by programs that stress the humanizing capacity of media.

Whenever as professionals we communicate with each other or our public this humanizing dimension for media should be uppermost in our thinking.

It is not that we don't try. An enormous amount of time and energy is spent devising programs that serve to bring us together to plan and prepare better media programs and services. Perhaps the reason these meetings and conferences so often lead to increased frustration at our failure to do what we say we want to do is that we start with fixed and established outcomes in mind. For example, we agree that we want a certain number of people to learn how to read, or read more, or read faster. We impose solutions, fixed before any dialogue begins, that place a restraining influence around all discussion and eventual decisions. We overlook the fact that solutions only present themselves as a natural consequence of the process of concerned and creative people working and thinking together.

During the last decade, public librarians and school media specialists showed that they can be adept activists in fomenting social change and intellectual dissent. But we have not carried these attitudes into the 1970s. Specifically we neglect the most critical issue facing us: How to best manage media use?

Hopefully, the attempt of this book to identify and describe some specific program in schools and public libraries that use media with children will promote some of this necessary dialogue.

Emphasized in this book are programs that can be adopted and adapted by other library-media programs. In every instance, the unpretentious was selected over the exhibitionist; we sought restraint rather than excess. And we searched for and selected programs that placed contact with people (as persons) over the sophisticated, but often pointless, interfacing with information systems.

There was a little saying making the rounds some months ago: "Blessed are they who know what they are going to do for they shall know when they have done it." This nicely sums up what media programs should be in their service to children. Media programs must not be used to obscure or blur meaning, serving to distract rather than enlighten. It is the program that *knows* where it wants to go before it starts and what it wants to accomplish along the way that we most need to study.

The relationship of the media to reading will doubtless continue to engage much of our thinking and condition many of our responses. Here we must try to avoid focusing on invalid expectations or obsolete standards. Literacy is still too often defined in this country as little more than the ability to read and write one's name, or to score at some low grade level on a standardized test. There is a widening gap between the level of literacy people require in this society and what they actually need to achieve success. This demands our professional attention.

The emphasis in this book has been upon programs that recognize the need to commit media resources (singly or in combination) to help children become proficient in those skills that are requisite to adult competence. How obvious, again, that the schools and public libraries of America have a tremendous *shared* interest in bringing people, from the earliest possible age, to such competence. No one person, or program or institution can do it alone; it requires a community effort and commitment. To serve jointly or with other institutions as fulcrum for this community effort can be the greatest opportunity ever presented to school and public library media programs.

We know now that the child's ability to learn, the patterns by which he will learn, and the conditioning of his quest for learning are pretty well molded by the age of three. The evidence mounts, in impressive fashion, that the very earliest years of childhood, perhaps from eight to eighteen months are the most important learning period in the entire life of a person. It probably means that parents, not teachers, perform the primary educational-instructional role with their children. If that parent chooses to abdicate this responsibility to a television set, there is serious doubt that we can develop a literate, capable, and competent population.

Schools and public libraries must work together then toward developing not only those programs which help children begin to learn early but which also help parents accept with confidence the tremendous responsibility they must accept as teachers. Programs that help parents understand the motives and curiosities of their children and capitalize on them in evey way possible may well be the wave of the future for all media programs. Researchers have found that the mothers of the most competent children excelled in three key ways: (1) They were able to design and organize the physical environment in such a way that the child would wish to explore it and learn from it. (2) They were able to set limits early to dangerous or annoying behavior. (3) They were able to act as "learning consultants" to their young children at a time when the child had come into contact with something particularly exciting that caused him to want to explore more or further. If the transfer could be made, these are precisely the elements we would ascribe to a good media program as well.

Of course, programs cannot be ascribed the characteristics of people. But, media programs can facilitate the ability of people to maximize their capabilities in many desirable ways. While learning, for the very young, tends to be episodic rather than sustained, media programs for them must be more than a series of disjointed, sound, and light exposures designed to titillate rather than teach.

It is possible that the diminished funds available to public institutions will force unification or collaboration in some aspects of school media and public library programs. In both public education and public libraries the smallest share of funding is usually allotted to programs and services for the very young. How exciting it would be to put together jointly a program for the very youngest child, perhaps at a year to eighteen months! Imagination, initiative, a willingness to do things in new ways will all be necessary to overcome administrative barriers and make this happen.

Thus, we have a review of some of the things that might be possible in terms of cooperative programming and services by schools and public libraries. I do not say media programs, for the final mark of our success will be when we no longer confine the work of the media program to the media professional. This is the day we will be able to accept that while the media pervade our living patterns, they do so in a constructive, sustaining, and nonthreatening manner.

The future of media programs for children is everywhere, not just in media centers or public library children's rooms. Essential to our ability to manage this future well will be the recognition that every child is raelly a media specialist. The ability to perceive, to be stimulated by, to learn from, and to adapt to, is present in every child from birth. It is how to contain and direct this process so that it has the most beneficial and excellent results for children that must provide our focus for the future.

Afterword

Throughout *School and Public Library Media Programs for Children and Young Adults* we have tried to provide some suggestions, observations, and recommendations as well as to draw some conclusions about what it is that makes a library media program go beyond the bounds of the ordinary, seeking to accomplish excellent results for children, young adults, or the community it serves. Descriptive characteristics of such programs were detailed in Part I.

However, some final words are perhaps appropriate to serve as a distillation of summation of the factors of excellence found in each program described in this book. These are principles and are not intended to define a particular program of excellence or tell how to innovate.

For a program to be a "success" it is not necessary that each of the following fifteen factors be present. But it is unlikely that any program will accomplish much of lasting value if only a few of them are visible.

In one way these factors that define and describe success provide a kind of index for the library-media programs reported in this book. They remind us of some basics. They show up the fact that all successful programs have in common a strong bias toward the common-sense approach to program planning and implementation. Their simplicity can be a problem, causing them to be overlooked, or ignored, by those "planning" programs. While it is a safe bet that knowing about these success factors will not in itself guarantee success, ignoring them will probably insure failure.

They are intended to provide a rational and sensible framework for developing and implementing library-media programs, whatever their content or wherever they are located.

We include among these factors the following:

1. Successful library-media programs display an ability to recognize targets of opportunity; they react quickly and "ride on" opportunities to achieve their goals. "Opportunity" may take unusual forms, ranging from the trauma of integrating public schools to providing alternative learning programs to fill idle hours. But the exemplary library-media program recognizes a contribution it can make and moves quickly to take the initiative. Planners are alert to opportunities, keeping a close watch to recognize and to use them when they appear.

2. Successful library-media programs display an effective management and organizational style. This is not to be confused with bureaucratic structure, for this organization is lean and healthy, responding quickly to "opportunity" as described above, receptive to new ideas and able to experiment with reasonable confidence of success because administrative and management techniques provide the framework that sustains this process.

3. Many successful library-media programs serve as a transition link between the old and the new. While exemplary programs often use innovative methods or advanced technology to accomplish their purposes, they tie these to traditionally satisfying ways of involving people. Thus, their credibility level is high and is reflected in trust and the willingness of participants to become involved.

4. Successful library-media programs are most often truly unified media programs. In them the media are seen as

carriers of information to be used in different combinations, variations, and applications to accomplish program goals. These programs have long since departed from the concept that learning is acquired by a single medium of communication—segregated learning if you will.

5. Successful library-media programs have broad yet well-defined goals to inspire and guide them. They recognize that the process by which goals are achieved is often built upon individual—sometimes child-by-child—success. And they reflect an understanding that to achieve these goals, staff and participants must feel an identity with the program's success.

6. Successful library-media programs usually display an ability to incorporate the work of diverse personnel (professional and support), while providing them with clear understandings of the goals of the program and the abilities to achieve them. Paraprofessionals, or volunteers working twenty, ten, or even five hours a week, have contributions to make. Often these persons have important ties to the community the program serves and they help "sell" a program in ways that professionals cannot. In schools, the adult and student volunteer have an important role to fulfill and, with good direction, they can do this. The end result is an increased awareness and acceptance of the program *and* an improved ability to achieve program goals.

7. Successful library-media programs know how to live with their success. This means they never get too far in front of those with whom they serve or work. And while they display a healthy "program ego," showing pride and confidence in their ability to accomplish and produce, successful programs always relate well to or reinforce other library programs. While the successful program sparkles with its own personality, it works to fulfill other important institutional goals. And while the force of an individual personality may provide an extraordinary program dimension, no healthy program depends ultimately on a single personality for continuing life.

8. Successful library-media programs are effective teaching programs. They demonstrate fundamental principles of excellent teaching by involving the learner actively in searching for, finding out, and using information. They reflect the understanding that the end purpose of learning should be the improvement of the individual's ability to think well for himself. They are successful teaching programs because they present alternatives to learners and provide the structure by which the individual chooses from these alternatives.

9. Successful library-media programs are able to translate theoretical concepts about learning, teaching, and using the media to practical day-to-day individual needs. They demonstrate a proper concern with the theoretical concepts that provide the framework by which programs find their purpose. But, more important, the successful program knows when to leave off theorizing and to make useful application of the media.

10. Successful library-media programs generally display a lack of concern for location or site. Successful programs show in common an extraordinary ability to get to people no matter where they are found. In fact, it is evident that many programs are successful through their willingness to move out from a static site location, finding where their services are needed most.

11. Successful library-media programs have "a way with money." They display an ability to find and use "big" money, such as federal or private grants, with a sureness that advances the program; yet, they also display an ability to stretch limited funds to achieve their goals. No one can say that money doesn't matter—it does! The point is that the successful program searches out and uses financial resources with purpose and without waste.

12. Successful library-media programs have goals to which they are committed and which they expect to be measured objectively. Having clear goals and using measurable objec-

AFTERWORD

tives to evaluate the achievement of these goals is not restrictive or confining. Rather, they provide the method of judging how well the job is done. These goals and objectives are not so complicated that they dominate every decision. Successful programs have "internalized" goals that are often "sensed" rather than stated; they "find" and use the proper balance.

13. Successful library-media programs show that for the professional contact with children is always a process of learning and renewal, undertaken with pleasure and anticipation. Yet, professionals who manage or work within successful media programs understand too the important management ability of delegating authority, allowing others to carry out important program operations with children.

14. Successful library-media programs often display an ability to use advanced forms of technology (computers, video cassettes, transistorized communication) in creative ways to put persons in touch with the information they need or want. The ability to humanize technology is important now and will become increasingly essential.

15. Successful library-media programs can be adopted or adapted by others. The successful program is a model; one which inspires others to follow its example while permitting these program parts to be adopted relatively easily by others. While its "personality" bespeaks its own uniqueness; its procedures, goals, and activities are adaptable to other situations.

These, then, are factors that are most constant within successful library-media programs for children and young adults identified for this book. These fifteen points summarize the excellence that we found in the library-media programs serving children and young adults.

APPENDIXES
A. Survey Instrument
B. School Library Media Programs Reported in this Study
C. Public Library Programs Reported in this Study
D. Instructions to Site Visitors

Appendix A

Survey Instrument

APPENDIX A

A SURVEY OF EXEMPLARY
PROGRAMS FOR CHILDREN USING
MEDIA IN SCHOOLS AND
PUBLIC LIBRARIES

AUGUST, 1975

D. Philip Baker
Box 2070 C
Stamford, Connecticut 06906

DIRECTIONS

This is a preliminary survey to identify school media programs and public libraries using media with children in innovative, creative or other significant ways. Media are defined to include books, or other print materials, or audio visual (nonprint) materials; used separately or in combination in program work with children. Exemplary programs are defined as being excellent in all respects. These programs should serve as models for other districts, schools, public libraries, or other agencies with similar resources and goals.

Programs are defined here as any planned or sequenced activity involving children and professionals and volunteer or paid support staff. These programs should be planned specially for some identifiable goal and measurable objective. Children may be considered as ranging in age from 3 to 18 and professional means individuals with a certificate, license or other document or degree stating that they have successfully completed work in either the field of library science or instructional media.

Please fill in answers to the following questions to the best of your knowledge. Thank you for your cooperation.

NAME OF PERSON FILLING OUT SURVEY _____

POSITION _____

INSTITUTION _____

ADDRESS _____
(Street)

(City - State - Zip Code)

TELEPHONE NUMBER _____

I. PERSONNEL

1. Number of professionals involved in program _____. Number of paraprofessionals (clerks or aides) involved in program _____. Number of volunteers involved in program _____.

2. Do the professionals and paraprofessionals work full time with the program? Yes ___ No ___. If no, please explain.

APPENDIX A

3. Please provide the highest educational degree of the professional in charge of the program _____.

4. Name and title of professional in charge of program:

   Mr., Miss, Mrs., _____

   Title _____

   Is mailing address the same as the institutions? Yes ___ No ___. If no, please provide preferred mailing address:

   _____
   _____
   _____

5. Is there a district or department supervisor to whom the professional reports? Yes ___ No ___. If yes, please provide this individual's name and address and telephone.

   _____
   _____
   _____

6. Number of children served by or participating in this program _____.

7. Number of teachers, other professionals, parents or citizens involved in this program _____.

8. Are you willing to have a visit by no more than two individuals to this program? Yes ___ No ___.

9. Which of the following best describes the kind of community the program serves? Rural ___ Suburban ___ City (over 100,000) ___.

10. What is the predominant age group of the children served by the program? Check those most appropriate.

    | 3 - 5 _____ | 12 - 15 _____ |
    | 5 - 7 _____ | 15 - 18 _____ |
    | 7 - 12 _____ | other (please specify) _____ |

11. Under whose auspices does the program operate?

    Board of Education _____   State Agency _____
    Public Library _____   City or Town Agency _____
    Combination (please clarify) _____

12. Is the program a part of the regular program of the school or library or is it a separate and distinct program? Integrated ___ Separate ___. Comment _____

II. FACILITIES

1. What is the approximate age of the facility housing the program? _____.

2. Does the facility meet existing national standards e.g. <u>Guidelines for Media Programs</u>: <u>District and School</u> (ALA 1974) or Public Library Standards? Yes ___ No ___. If no, please clarify _____

3. Was the facility designed specifically to house a media program serving children? Yes ___ No ___.

4. Is the facility adequate to house the program? Yes ___ No ___. If no, please state briefly how the program has accommodated itself to the inadequate facility. _____

5. If the facility is a new one, was it planned cooperatively by library/media professionals and an architect? Yes ___ No ___. Comment _____

6. Has the facility received any award for excellence in design? Yes ___ No ___. If yes, please cite award and date. _____

7. Are any production facilities available to the program? Yes ___ No ___. (Production facilities would be dark rooms, areas for slide making, dry mounting or laminating, vidio or audio taping.) If yes, please describe these facilities briefly. _____

APPENDIX A

III. BUDGET
(Please provide all figures for last <u>full</u> budget year)

1. Dollar amount spent on print materials (books, pamphlets, etc.) _____.

2. Dollar amount spent on nonprint materials (filmstrips, tapes, 16mm film records, etc.) _____.

3. Were outside (Federal or State) funds used to finance the program? Yes ___ No ___. If yes, please describe briefly the source of funds. _____
   _____

4. Was any special source (above regular budget) local funding used for the program? Yes ___ No ___. If yes, please describe briefly. _____
   _____

5. How many years has the program been funded? _____

6. Is the program still in operation? Yes ___ No ___. If no, please provide details and last date of operation. _____
   _____
   _____

7. Has the budgeted amount increased ___, decreased ___, or remained stable ___ over the past three years?

8. What is the total budget for the <u>entire</u> <u>library</u> <u>or</u> <u>media</u> <u>center</u> program (excluding personnel)? Include all print and non-print items and equipment. _____

9. Is the staff for this program paid from regularly appropriated library or media budgets? Yes ___ No ___. If no, does one of the following categories apply: special local funds ___ special state funds ___ or special federal funds _____.

10. If you have checked one or more of the above, please describe briefly the source of funding. _____
    _____
    _____

11. Was the program begun originally as a special purpose program? Yes ___ No ___. If yes, please check the group to which service was most intended.

    Physically limited children _____   Minority groups _____
    Exceptional children _____   Other _____

Please clarify if you have checked any _____

12. How was the program initiated originally? _____
_____
_____
_____

IV. RESOURCES/MATERIALS

1. What are the total number of materials that support the program? Please provide approximate figures:

   Books   _____   Slides   _____
   Sound film strips _____   Transparencies   _____
   Audio tapes   _____   Phamphlets   _____
   16mm film   _____   Realia   _____
   Video tapes   _____   Other (specify)   _____

2. Do the materials circulate outside of the media center or library? Yes ___ No ___. If yes, please explain _____
_____

3. Are new materials added to the collection on a systematic regular basis? Yes ___ No ___. Comment _____
_____

4. Please check those involved in selection of materials, i.e., teachers ___, pupils ___, supervisors ___, laypersons ___, community groups ___, other ___. Please clarify other _____
_____

5. Is there a selection policy for materials? Yes ___ No ___.
   If yes, what is the date of the policy? _____

6. Is there any systematic evaluation of the materials used in the program? Yes ___ No ___. If yes, please explain _____
_____
_____

V. INNOVATION

1. What are the three major innovations you believe your program has accomplished to be termed exemplary?

   A. _____
   _____

B. _____
_____
_____

C. _____
_____
_____

2. What are the three most important results your program has brought to the school, library, or the community it serves?

A. _____
_____
_____

B. _____
_____
_____

C. _____
_____
_____

3. Has the program ever been evaluated by an independent non-involved individual or group? Yes ___ No ___. If yes, please clarify. _____
_____

N.B. If a copy of the evaluation is available, please feel free to return it with this survey form.

VI. RECOGNITION

1. Has the program ever received an award or recognition for excellence from a professional group, a community group, or other such group? Yes ___ No ___. If yes, please explain
_____
_____
_____

2. Has the program ever received publicity at the local, state, or national level? Yes ___ No ___. If yes, please explain _____
   _____
   _____
   _____

   Please include below any other comments, statements or observations you would care to make relative to the program and this survey instrument.

Return to:

Mr. D. Philip Baker
Box 2070 C
Stamford, Connecticut 06906

Appendix B
School Library Media Programs
Reported in This Study

CALIFORNIA	Saratoga—Saratoga School (elementary)
Program:	Use of carefully evaluated multimedia materials to advance specific educational objectives.
Contact:	Mrs. Charlotte Hoyer, Librarian
COLORADO	Arvada—Stott School (elementary)
Program:	Use of facility as year round school. Bonus learning program.
Contact:	Ms. Jan Cain, Media Specialist
COLORADO	Adams County Schools—District #12
Program:	Integration of health education project into curriculum. Staff development program.
Contact:	Janice Smith, Media Specialist
DELAWARE	Newark—Central Middle School
Program:	Resource Center; Integration of resources into curriculum.
Contact:	Mrs. Estelle Smith
FLORIDA	Boca Raton—J. C. Mitchell (elementary)
Program:	Exceptional child educational program, use of school as community resource.
Contact:	Ms. Ruth Flintom
FLORIDA	St. Petersburg—Azalea Middle School
Program:	Behavior modification program using games, records, puzzles, and other items.
Contact:	Ms. Carlene Aborn, Media Specialist
FLORIDA	Tallahassee—Astoria Park (elementary)
Program:	Student production of media. Photography and Cinematography Workshop.
Contact:	Mrs. Shirley Shiffman

GEORGIA	Atlanta—Spring Street School (elementary) Carter G. Woodson (elementary)
Program:	Project SEEK, EXPLORE, DISCOVER (SED)
Program:	Project LEARNING, EXPLORING, ACCOMPLISHING, DISCOVERING (LEAD)
Contact:	Mrs. Gay Dull (Woodson School)
GEORGIA	Norcross—Peachtree (elementary)
Program:	Open space arrangements. Open scheduling. Planning with teachers.
Contact:	Miss Anne Hale, Media Specialist
ILLINOIS	Riverside—Riverside-Brookfield (High School)
Program:	Use of media laboratory approach to instruction
Contact:	Ms. Dawn Heller, Coordinator, Media Services
KANSAS	Topeka—Topeka West High School
Program:	PASSPORT—Integration of program into curriculum.
Contact:	Mike Printz
MAINE	Waterville—Waterville High School
Program:	Use of federal funds. Involvement of program in curriculum.
Contact:	Ms. Judy Powell, Media Specialist
MARYLAND	Middletown—Middletown High School
Program:	Use of video cassettes to instruct in consumer education.
Contact:	Mrs. Joann Horine
MASSACHUSETTS	New Bedford—New Bedford High School
Program:	Use of student area resource centers. Television courses.

APPENDIX B

Contact: Mr. Robert Maucione

MICHIGAN Livonia—Buchanan Elementary School
Program: Prescription Learning Program
Contact: George Bageris, Coordinator IMS, Supervisor of Media

MICHIGAN Spring Lake—Spring Lake Junior-Senior High School
Program: Coordination of skills instruction with curriculum. Use of Renovated Space.
Contact: Mrs. Bernice Lamkin, Director of Media

NEW JERSEY Sea Grit—Sea Grit Elementary School
Program: Living Literature Program
Contact: Mrs. Shirley Norby, Media Specialist

NEW MEXICO Albuquerque—Sandia High School
Program: Freshman orientation unit including production of media units.
Contact: Dr. Pauline Jones, Media Center Director

NEW YORK Youngstown—Lewiston-Porter Central Schools
Program: Reading Levels Program.
Contact: Ms. Joy Casadonte, Media Coordinator

NEW YORK Rochester—Rochester Public Schools
Program: Relationship of reading improvement to video programs.
Contact: Doris A. Hicks, Director of Learning Resources

OKLAHOMA Oklahoma City—Putnam High School
Program: Occupational information program. Integrating career education into the curriculum.
Contact: Janelle Kirby, Head Librarian

OREGON	Beaverton—School District #48—Mt. View Intermediate School
Program:	Use of differentiated staffing. Design of Center.
Contact:	Tom Meir, Media Specialist
UTAH	St. George—Dixie High School
Program:	Complete integration of media program into curriculum program.
Contact:	Mr. Jay Andrus, Media Coordinator
VIRGINIA	Richmond—Amelia Street School
Program:	Relating media program to special education (Trainable mentally retarded)
Contact:	Ms. Dolores Pretlow, Librarian
WISCONSIN	New Berlin—Eisenhower High School
Program:	Use of mixed media shelving. Production program.
Contact:	Ms. Patricia McCarthy

Appendix C

Public Library Programs
Reported in This Study

CALIFORNIA	Huntington Beach
Program:	Children's Resource Center. Use of media materials.
Contact:	Marcia Donat Lewis
CONNECTICUT	Bridgeport
Program:	Tutoring program, Alternate High School
Contact:	Harriette Brown
FLORIDA	Orlando
Program:	Sharing literature with children. Workshop programs with adults.
Contact:	Carolyn Sue Peterson
HAWAII	Honolulu (Liliha Branch)
Program:	After School Project,—art and music
Contact:	Ms. Nancy Mott, Head Librarian
INDIANA	Indianapolis Marion County
Program:	Sunday program for children, including Sunday Kaleidascope.
Contact:	Ann Strachan, Coordinator Children Services
LOUISIANA	New Orleans
Program:	Your Child and Books: A seminar for parents
Contact:	Ms. Angeliki Hutchinson, Coordinator
MASSACHUSETTS	Fitchburg
Program:	A.V. Licensing
Contact:	Ms. Elizabeth Watson
MICHIGAN	Jackson County (A Phillip Randolph Branch)
Program:	Kangaroo Tracks: use of grant from A. Phillip Randolph Institute
Contact:	Susan Cattell, Head of Child and Young Adult Services
NEW YORK	New York Public (George Bruce Branch)

Program:	Cooperative school-public library program
Contact:	Barbara Rollock, Coordinator of Children's Services
NEW YORK	Finger Lakes System
Program:	Use of video to recreate original story hour.
Contact:	Mrs. Mary Carey
NEW MEXICO	Albuquerque (Esperanza Branch)
Program:	Preschool program to develop skills in social interacting, manual dexterity, math, and verbal development
Contact:	Ms. Norma Bobotis, Head Librarian
NEW MEXICO	Clovis-Carver
Program:	Parent/child toy lending library
Contact:	Mrs. Ruth Wuori, Head Librarian
NORTH CAROLINA	Winston-Salem Forsyth County
Program:	Community Outreach Program.
Contact:	Ann Gehlen, Head Outreach Services
NORTH CAROLINA	North Carolina Central University
Program:	Early childhood learning program.
Contact:	Dr. Annette L. Phinazee
OHIO	Chillicothe-Ross County
Program:	Cooperative Bicentennial program between schools and public library.
Contact:	Luvada Kuhn, Head of School Services
OKLAHOMA	Oklahoma County System
Program:	Neighborhood arts: A summer art program.
Contact:	Sharon Saulmon, Coordinator of Public Services
PENNSYLVANIA	Norristown-Montgomery County-Norristown
Program:	Mother's discussion group and preschool programs.

APPENDIX C

Contact:	Mrs. Marian Peck, Head of Children Services
TEXAS	Dallas
Program:	Project "Look At Me"
Contact:	Linda Allmand, Chief Branch Services
TEXAS	Fort Worth
Program:	Activities for preschool children to encourage use of facilities and services. Relationships to community action agencies.
Contact:	Mary Harding, Director Outreach Project
RHODE ISLAND	Warwick
Program:	Pet Program (Animal Loaning)
Contact:	Mrs. Alice Forsstrom
UTAH	Logan-Cache Library
Program:	Animal story hour that teaches appreciation for wildlife conservation.
Contact:	Ms. Judith McMahon, Director
VIRGINIA	Richmond
Program:	Use of single volunteer to teach writing of "Backyard Stories."
Contact:	Ms. Barbara Gregory, Coordinator Special Projects.
WASHINGTON	Snoqualmie
Program:	Involvement of media program in juvenile rehabilitation.
Contact:	Ms. Wilma Daniels
WISCONSIN	Racine
Program:	"Cooperative school-public library program" "Yankee Doodle Library Festival"
Contact:	Mrs. Nancy Elsmo, Director Children's Services
WISCONSIN	Sheboygan-Mead Library

Program: "America's Birthday and Yours, Too!"
Contact: Kay Knauer, Children's Librarian

Appendix D
Instructions to Site Visitors

SITE VISITATION—WHAT TO LOOK FOR

STAFF
1. Professional training—attitudes (toward other staff, children). Enthusiasm for program.
2. Support staff—numbers (paraprofessionals, volunteers, etc.) how are they used? Are they necessary to the program?
3. General responsibilities of the staff within the program—Adequate staff available to the program? How is the staff deployed?
4. Are other institutions or groups cooperating with, or involved in the program?
5. Are there volunteers in the program? What is their role?
6. Names of persons interviewed.

FACILITY
   (For some programs this section may be of minor importance, but please consider this section.)
1. Age of the facility? Is the facility important to the program or not relevant?
2. General upkeep—is it attractive, colorful, decorated with imagination?
3. Cost of facility and any special design information. Has the building been written up? If so, where? Any other information available. Cost per foot?
4. Is there any renovation of space involved in the program?
5. Are there production facilities e.g. video studio, dark rooms, sound-proof rooms, an art department available?

BUDGET
1. Do budget funds appear adequate to support the program?
2. Are there creative combinations of funds used—e.g. foundation, federal, local, or other?
3. Has budget increased in recent past? Or, is it decreasing?
4. Has any other program of the institution been "sacrificed" to keep this program going? Is this a priority program?

5. Is there any program analysis or budget cost accounting being used to develop future budgets?

RESOURCES/MATERIALS
1. How are the resources/materials organized? Are they immediately available for use?
2. How are the resources/materials being used on a daily basis?
3. Is there a good balance of print and nonprint items available?
4. Any attempt made to evaluate the results of the use of materials?
5. Are any unique resources necessary to support the program?

INNOVATIONS
1. Is the program innovative or exemplary? What is unusual or excellent about it? Have you seen a program like it before?
2. Does the program have an impact beyond the institution or its target audience?
3. Can you find out community or other attitudes about the program? Are other community agencies involved with this program?
4. Is the program making a significant contribution to learning? Improved teaching? Helping parents to take part in their children's learning, helping children in other ways?
5. Is there any spin-off or multiplier effect visible? Has the impact of the program multiplied itself beyond the original target audience?
6. What technology is in use? Computers, dial access, tie in to state or regional networks, data base?
7. In what ways could this program be adopted or adapted by other institutions?

RECOGNITION
1. Has there been recognition? Local, state, professional, community, national, other?

APPENDIX D

2. Is there an on-going PR program for the particular program or is it self generating?
3. Can you locate any newspaper or journal articles about the program? Photographs or other write-ups should be included as well. Please provide exact citations, dates, pages, name of Journal for any write-ups available.

ADDITIONAL SITE VISITATION QUESTIONS
1. Are there any specific documents or statements that relate to either long or short range goals for the program? Secure if possible.
2. Is the staff (paid, professional and support and volunteers) involved in the evaluation and reassessment of program goals and objectives?
3. Is it possible to identify one or two *specific* program activities that are truly innovative?
4. Have the numbers using the services of the program increased or decreased in recent years? (2-3)
5. What has been the major impact of the program?
6. What failures has the program experienced?
7. In retrospect, what would they do differently, if they were starting again?

Appendix E

List of Site Visitors

Aaron, Dr. Shirley, Assistant Professor
    Florida State University
    School of Library Science
    Tallahassee, Florida
Ahlers, Ms. Eleanor, Professor
    University of Washington
    School of Librarianship
    Seattle, Washington
Alexander, Ms. Mona, Library Supervisor
    Kansas State Department of Education
    Topeka, Kansas
Bender, Mr. David, Assistant Director
    School Media Office
    Division of Library Development and Services
    Maryland State Department of Education
    Baltimore, Maryland
Cookston, Dr. James, Supervisor of School Libraries
    Louisiana State Department of Education
    Baton Rouge, Louisiana
DeAngelo, Ms. Rachel, Professor Emeritus
    University of Hawaii at Manoa
    Graduate School of Library Studies
    Honolulu, Hawaii
Eidson, Ms. Barbara, Instructor
    University of Georgia
    Department of Library Education
    Athens, Georgia
Falsone, Ms. Ann Marie
    Development and Administration Unit
    Colorado State Department of Education
    Denver, Colorado
Field, Ms. Carolyn W., Coordinator
    Office of Work with Children
    Free Library of Philadelphia
    Philadelphia, Pennsylvania
Grazier, Ms. Margaret, Professor
    Wayne State University
    College of Education
    Department of Library Science
    Detroit, Michigan

Gregory, Ms. Dorothy, Consultant
  Maine State Library
  Augusta, Maine
Griffis, Ms. Joan, Library Supervisor
  Portland School District
  Portland, Oregon
Harris, Jewel, Associate Director
  Gaylord Professional Publications
  Syracuse, New York
Kreigh, Mrs. Helen, Supervisor
  Children's Services
  State Library of Wisconsin
  Madison, Wisconsin
Land, Ms. Phyllis M., Director
  Division of Instructional Media
  Indiana Department of Public Instruction
  Indianapolis, Indiana
Long, Ms. Sara
  Library Development Consultant
  Children Services
  State Library of Ohio
  Columbus, Ohio
Lowrey, Ms. Anna Mary, Assistant Professor
  State University of New York at Buffalo
  School of Information and Library Studies
  Buffalo, New York
Mathews, Ms. Mary, Librarian-media specialist
  Prince Georges Public Schools
  Bowie, Maryland
Mathews, Virginia H., Director
  Gaylord Professional Publications
  Syracuse, New York
May, Dr. F. Curtis, Director
  Educational Resources Center
  San Mateo County Schools
  Redwood City, California
Phillips, Ms. Luouida Vinson, Director
  Library Services
  Dallas Board of Education
  Dallas, Texas

Smith, Ms. Lotsee, Assistant Professor
  University of New Mexico
  College of Education
  Albuquerque, New Mexico
Stephens, Ms. Elizabeth, Director
  Educational Media Center
  Pinellas County Schools
  Clearwater, Florida
Stevenson, Ms. Maxine, Director
  Learning Resources
  Administration Center—District #11
  Alton, Illinois
Tolman, Dr. Lorraine, Assistant Professor
  Boston University School of Education
  Boston, Mass.
Van Orden, Dr. Phyllis, Assistant Professor
  Rutgers University
  Graduate School of Library Service
  New Brunswick, New Jersey
Wentworth, Ms. Mary Ann
  Oklahoma Department of Libraries
  Oklahoma City, Oklahoma
Winkel, Ms. Lois
  Graduate School
  Columbia University
  School of Library Service
  New York, New York

Index

A. Philip Randolph Branch, Jackson, Michigan Public Library, 188-93
access to media, 61, 64, 240
accountability, 15, 22, 266, 326, 349-50
Adams County School District #13, Northglenn, Colorado, 82-86
adult participation, 110-11
after school program, 136-40, 191, 249
alternative high school, 93-96
Amelia Street School, Richmond, Virginia, 307-12
American Association of School Librarians (AASL), 31, 51, 141, 200, 232, 347
American Libraries, 343
American Library Association (ALA), 347
animal awareness, 288
arts program, 270-74
Association for Educational Communications and Technology (AECT), 31, 51, 141, 200, 347

Astoria Park Elementary School, Tallahassee, Florida, 120-124
Atlanta, Georgia, 21
attitude for excellence, 353
audio recording, 335
audiovisual collection, 238; equipment, training for use of, 123, (licensing) 175-81, 217, 304; use of, 110-11; presentation, 219; services, 278
awards, The School Library Media Award of the Year Program, 1975, 232
Azalea Middle School, St. Petersburg, Florida, 114-19

basic skills, 35, 49, 50
behavior modification, 115-19
Bicentennial programs, 155, 260, 328, 333-36
bilingual materials, 239
bicultural programs, 211-15
birthday celebrations, 333-36

Bridgeport Public Library, Bridgeport, Connecticut, 92-96
Buchanan Elementary School, Livonia, Michigan, 194-99
budget cuts, 22, 23; outside funding/resources, 153, 228, 255, 272; program, see program budgets, etc. state funding, 170, 212, 303; unified, 194
Bureau of Health Education, 83

Cache Public Library, Logan, Utah, 286-90
California, Huntington Beach, Huntington Beach Public Library, 77-81; Saratoga, Saratoga School, 72-77
career awareness, 265-69; education, 99, 154, 265-69
catalog, computer, 239
censorship, 29
Central Middle School, Newark, Delaware, 97-101
Certification Model for Professional School Media Personnel, 354
change, 64
child development, 212
Chillicothe and Ross County Public Library, Chillicothe, Ohio, 260-264
Churchill, Winston 346
cinematography, 123
Clovis-Carter Public Library, Clovis, New Mexico, 221-25
Colorado, Arvada, Stott Elementary School, 87-91; Northglenn, Adams County School District #13, 82-86
Communication, 79

community cooperation, 159; Garden Project, 75; involvement, 73, 93, 298, 336, 350, in planning, 73, 261, 271; outreach, 53, 104, 155, 191, 248-52, 255, 271, 292, 298, 328; participation, 54, 188; resource coordinator, 278, staff, 137; resources, 155, 261; school, 102-107; support, 188-89, 248
Connecticut, Bridgeport, Bridgeport Public Library, 92-96
consumer education, 170-74
Consumer Survival Kit, 171-74
Coombs, Arthur, 349
cooperation, 280, 330, need for, 57, 64; library school/public library, 257; public library/community, 93, 109-11, 138, 159, 188-89, 248, 280-85; media center/guidance department, 268-69; school/community, 72, 164, 255; school/public library, 13, 14, 15, 50, 60, 79, 94, 228, 237-40, 260-64, 300, 328
cooperative management, 55
creative arts, 190; play, 221, 283; writing, 314-17
criteria for selection of programs, 24-27, 34-37, 357, 362-65

Dallas Texas Public Library, Dallas, Texas, 291-96
day care centers and public library, 300
Delaware, Newark, Central Middle School, 97-101
Dewey, John, 65

INDEX 405

differentiated staffing, 55, 118, 276-78, 324
disadvantaged, programs for, 136, 188, 212, 232-33, 248, 255, 297-301
Disadvantaged and Library Effectiveness, The, 339
discipline in program management, 36
Dixie High School, St. George, Utah, 302-06

early childhood librarianship, 254-59, 297-98
Echo Glen Children's Center, Snoqualmie, Washington, 318-22
Education for Handicapped Children Act, 307
Educational Accountability: Beyond behavioral objectives, 349
educational media associations, unified, 347
Ehrlich, Paul, 30, 31
Eisenhower High School, New Berlin, Wisconsin, 323-27
Elementary and Secondary Education Act (ESEA), 72, 85, 164, 194, 233, 237, 265, 266, 302. *See also* federal funds
Elementary school programs: California, Saratoga, Saratoga School, 72-76; Colorado, Arvada, Stott Elementary School, 87-91, Northglenn, Adams County School District #13, 82-86; Florida, Boca Raton, J.C. Mitchell Elementary School, 102-07, Tallahassee, Astoria Park Elementary School, 120-24; Georgia, Atlanta, Spring Street School, 125-130, Norcross, Peachtree Elementary School, 131-35; Michigan, Livonia, Buchanan Elementary School, 194-99; New Jersey, Sea Girt, Sea Girt Elementary School, 205-10; New York, Rochester, Rochester Public Schools, 231-36, Youngstown, Lewiston-Porter Public Schools, 242-247
Ely, Don, 64
English courses, 94-95
enrichment, 75, 88, 115-17; courses, 88-89, 117; reading, 195, 208
environmental studies, 286-90
equal access, 57
Esperanza Branch, Albuquerque Public Library, Albuquerque, New Mexico, 211-15
evaluation, 224: by parents, 214; by students, 129, 145, 320; in schools, 99, 278, 305, 326, 351; in public library, 15, 192, 273, 351-52; of program, 36, 37, 38, 112, 173, 203-04, 234, 273, 326, 345; of teachers and media specialist, 303
exceptional children, 102, 307
exemplary, definition, 33, 34
exhibit, historical, 260-64
extended hours, 102-07, 148, 167, 250, 304

facilities, 27, 343: audiovisual, 176; award winning, 131; integrated shelving, 267, 323-5; media lab, 144; public

library, 251; school, 74, 131, 144, 154, 165, 183, 203, 234, 275; specially designed, 74, 77, 132, 144, 154, 183, 275; television, 234, 275
faculty participation, 195
family, concern with, 114, 148; involvement, 293
Far West Laboratory for Educational Research and Development, 222
federal funds, 298; Bicentennial Mini-grant, 153; Elementary and Secondary Education Act, Title I, 194, 233, Title II, 72, 86, 89, 164, 237, 302, Title III, 265, 266, Title IV B 265, Title IV C, 85; Emergency School Assistance Act, 291; Federal Career Education Grant, 153; Health, Education and Welfare, Dept. of, 83; Library Services and Construction Act, 112, 136, 137, 175, 178, 188, 189, 248; National Defense Education Act, Title III, 163, 302; National Endowment for the Arts and Humanities, 208, 272; Office of Education, 255, 276
film programs, 80, 150, 299
Finger Lake Library System, Ithaca, New York, 226-230
Fitchburg Youth Library, Fitchburg, Massachusetts, 175-81
Florida: Boca Raton, J.C. Mitchell Elementary School, 102-07; Orlando, Orlando Public Library, 108-113; St. Petersburg, Azalea Middle School, 114-119; Tallahassee, Astoria Park Elementary School 120-24
Forsyth County Public Library, Winston-Salem, North Carolina, 248-53
Fort Worth Public Library, Fort Worth, Texas, 297-301
funding: federal. *See* federal funds; local, 272, 276; public, 23; sources, 153, 222, 272

Gallup, George, 65, 342
George Bruce Branch, New York Public Library, New York, New York, 237-41
Georgia: Atlanta, Spring Street School, 125-30; Norcross, Peachtree Elementary School, 131-35
gifted, programs for, 126-30
Gladding, Walter M., Jr., 315-16
Great Books, 208
Guide to Securing and Installing the Parent Child Lending Library, 222
guidelines, 141, 305

Hawaii, Honolulu, Liliha Community Library, 136-40
Hayakawa, S.I., 24
Health, Education and Welfare, Dept. of 82, 323
health project, 83
history: American, 144; local, 155-56, 260-64; of public libraries, 9 ff.
Huntington Beach Public Library, Huntington Beach, California, 77-81

Illinois, Riverside, Riverside-

INDEX

Brookfield High School, 141-47
Indiana, Indianapolis, Indianapolis-Marion County Public Library, 148-52
individualized instruction, 75, 105-106, 126-29, 132, 166, 246; learning, 56
information control, 59, 61
inquiry method, 142
inservice training, see staff development
institutional programs, 318-22
institutions, impact of 47

J.C. Mitchell Elementary School, Boca Raton, Florida, 102-07
Jackson Randolph Center, 189

Kansas, Topeka, Topeka West High School, 153-57

Larrick, Nancy, 62, 63
Learning: activity packets, 305; centers, classroom, 89; in children, 48, 49; lab, 142-43; objectives, 280; readiness, 212, 254, 257; stations, 105, 132; theory, 44, 46
Lewiston-Porter Public Schools, Youngstown, New York, 242-47
librarians as teachers, 109 see also media specialists as teachers
librarians, training 254-59, 354
library schools, 254-59, 354
library service to the disadvantaged, 136, 188, 212, 232-33, 248, 255, 297-301
Library Services and Construction Act, 112, 136, 137, 175, 178, 188, 189, 248
library skills, teaching of, 100, 103-107, 201-203, 216-20
Liliha Community Library, Honolulu, Hawaii, 136-40
Lipsman, Claire, 339
literature, 94, 108, 207
location, importance of, 77
Louisiana, New Orleans, New Orleans Public Library, 158-62

McLuhan, Marshall, 29
Maine, Waterville, Waterville High School, 163-69
management by objectives, 22, 38, 201, 349
Maryland, Middletown, Middletown High School, 170-74
Maryland Center for Public Broadcasting, 171; State Department of Education, 171
Massachusetts, Fitchburg, Fitchburg Youth Library, 175-81; New Bedford, New Bedford High School, 182-87
materials, commercial, use of, 245; for mentally retarded, 310; professional, 299; selection, 300, 326
Mead, Margaret, 33
Mead Public Library, Sheboygan, Wisconsin, 333-37
media, access, control of, 61; center, 244-45, 344; definition of, 29; fear of, 29; influence, 28, 29, 30, 59, 345-46; lab, 142
Media Programs: District and

School, 31, 51, 61, 141, 163, 200, 277, 354
media programs, role of, 3, 29, 66; skills, 98, 99, 103-07, 121-23, 127, 132-34, 200, 245, 305; specialist as teacher, 97-101, 126, 206, 346, defined, 13, role of, 51, 52, 66, 133, 141, 277, 344; staff as teachers, 154, 217; uses of, 33
mentally retarded, 102, 307-12
Michigan: Jackson, A. Philip Randolph Branch, Jackson Michigan Public Library, 189-93; Livonia, Buchanan Elementary School, 194-99; Spring Lake, Spring Lake Junior-Senior High School, 200-204
Middle School programs: Delaware, Newark, Central Middle School, 97-101; Florida, St. Petersburg, Azalea Middle School, 114-119; Oregon, Beaverton, Mountain View Intermediate School, 275-79
Middletown High School, Middletown, Maryland, 170-74
minority groups, programs for 188-90, 211-15, 292
mobile units, 250
Montgomery County-Norristown Public Library, Norristown, Pa, 280-85
Mountain View Intermediate School, Beaverton, Oregon, 275-79

National Commission on Libraries and Information Science, 61
National Defense Education Act, 163
National Education Association, 347
National Endowment for the Arts and Humanities, 208, 272
Nature appreciation, 287
networks, 56
New Bedford High School, New Bedford, Massachusetts, 182-87
New England Educational Media Association, 347
New Jersey, Sea Girt, Sea Girt Elementary School, 205-10
New Mexico: Albuquerque, Esperanza Branch, Albuquerque, 211-15, Sandia High School, 216-220; Clovis, Clovis-Carter Public Library 221-25
New Orleans Public Library, New Orleans, Louisiana, 158-62
New York: Ithaca, Finger Lake Library System, 226-230; New York, George Bruce Branch, New York Public Library 237-41; Rochester, Rochester Public Schools, 231-36; Youngstown, Lewiston-Porter Public Schools, 242-47
New York City, 21, 237-41
New York Magazine, 23
New York *Times*, 21
non graded, 205, 307-10
non readers, 137
North Carolina: Durham, School of Library Science, North Carolina Central

INDEX

University, 254-59; Winston-Salem, Forsyth County Public Library, 248-53
North Carolina Central University School of Library Science, 254-59

occupational information, 266
Ohio, Chillicothe, Chillicothe and Ross County Library, 260-64
Oklahoma: Oklahoma City, Oklahoma County Libraries, 270-74; Putnam City High School, 265-74
open education, 120-24, 131, 207
Oregon, Beaverton, Mountain View Intermediate School, 275-79
orientation for high school freshmen, 217-19
Orlando Public Library Orlando, Florida, 108-13
outreach programs, 53, 109-11, 155, 159, 164, 181, 191, 248, 267, 271, 292, 298, 328
overhead projector, use of, 110

paraprofessionals, use of, 54, 190, 277
parent/child toy lending library, 221-25
parent involvement, 72, 177, 211-15, 221-23, 255, 256, 293; programs, 213, 280, 284; seminar 158-62
Parent-Teacher Association, 262; support, 72
Peachtree Elementary School, Norcross, Georgia, 131-35
Pennsylvania, Norristown, Montgomery County-Norristown Public Library, 280-85
performing arts, 270-74
pet loan, 287
photography, 292-95; workshop, 123
physically handicapped, 102, 307-12
Piaget, Jean, 44, 46
picture books as basis for preschool program, 281
poetry, Poet in the Classroom, 208
Precious Bane, 28
preschool programs, 211-15, 221-25, 248-53, 258, 280-85, 297-301
prescribed learning program, 83, 195-98
production, audiovisual, 122, 178; facilities, 144, 178, 203; of media, 203, 304, 324, 325
professional associations, 13, 31, 347
professional resource collections, 255-58, 299, 311
program evaluation, see evaluation
program planning and budget systems (PPBS), 349
public libraries, 345; California, Huntington Beach, Huntington Beach Public Library, 77-81; Connecticut, Bridgeport, Bridgeport Public Library, 92-96; Florida, Orlando, Orlando Public Library, 108-13; Hawaii, Honolulu, Liliha Community Library, 136-40; Indiana, Indianapolis, Indianapolis-Marion County Public

Library, 148-52; Louisiana, New Orleans, New Orleans Public Library, 158-62; Massachusetts, Fitchburg, Fitchburg Youth Library, 175-81; Michigan, Jackson, A. Philip Randolph Branch, Jackson Michigan Public Library, 188-93; New Mexico, Albuquerque, Esperanza Branch, Albuquerque Public Library, 211-15, Clovis, Clovis-Carter Public Library, 221-25; New York, Ithaca, Finger Lake Library System, 226-30, New York, George Bruce Branch, New York Public Library, 237-41; North Carolina, Winston-Salem, Forsyth County Public Library, 248-53; Ohio, Chillicothe, Chillicothe and Ross County Public Library, 260-64; Oklahoma, Oklahoma City, Oklahoma County Libraries, 270-74; Pennsylvania, Norristown, Montgomery County-Norristown Public Library, 280-85; Rhode Island, Warwick, Warwick Public Library, 286-90; Texas, Dallas, Dallas Public Library, 291-96, Fort Worth, Fort Worth Public Library, 297-301; Utah, Logan, Cache Public Library, 286-290; Virginia, Richmond, Richmond Public Library, 313-17; Wisconsin, Racine, Racine Public Library, 328-32, Sheboygan, Mead Public Library, 333-37

Public Library Action for Children's Education (PLACE), 248-53
public television, 171-74
publications produced in connection with programs, 79, 80, 111, 112, 156, 291
puppet show, 121
Putnam City High School, Oklahoma City, Oklahoma, 265-9

Racine Public Library, Racine, Wisconsin, 328-32
Randolph Institute, Jackson, Michigan, 188
Rawlings, Marjorie Kinnan, 286
readiness, 254, 281
reading, 35, 156, 191; enrichment, 195
reading programs, public library, 139, 292; school library, 207, 233, 242-47; readiness, 222, 282; relationship of media to, 24; skills, 233, 243, 244, 282; teaching of, 139, 244
realia, use of, 261-62, 282
rehabilitation programs, 318-22
relevance, 49
resource center, 80, 182, 299
rewards, 35
Rhode Island, Warwick, Warwick Public Library 286-90
Richmond Public Library, Richmond, Virginia, 313-17
Right to Read, 108
Riverside-Brookfield High School, Riverside, Illinois, 141-47
Rochester Public Schools, Rochester, New York, 231-36

INDEX **411**

St. Petersburg Independent, 114
Sandia High School,
  Albuquerque, New Mexico,
  216-220
Saratoga School, Saratoga,
  California, 72-76
School Health Curriculum
  Project 82-86
School Library Media Award of
  the Year, 1975, 232
Sea Girt Elementary, Sea Girt,
  New Jersey, 205-10
Secondary school programs, see
  also Middle school programs;
  Illinois, Riverside, Riverside-
  Brookfield High School,
  141-47; Kansas, Topeka,
  Topeka West High School,
  153-57; Maine, Waterville,
  Waterville High School,
  163-69; Maryland,
  Middletown, Middletown
  High School, 170-74;
  Massachusetts, New Bedford,
  New Bedford High School,
  182-87; Michigan, Spring
  Lake, Spring Lake Junior-
  Senior High School, 200-204;
  New Mexico, Albuquerque,
  Sandia High School, 216-220;
  Oklahoma, Oklahoma City,
  Putnam City High School,
  265-69; Utah, St. George,
  Dixie High School, 302-06;
  Wisconsin, New Berlin,
  Eisenhower High School
  323-27
self expression, 282, 293
sensory development, 282
Senior citizens, programs for,
  297-98
skills instruction 35, 122;
  media, 98, 99, 103-107, 121-23,
  127, 132-34, 200, 245; reading,
  35, 243-45, 282
smoking, prevention, 83, 85
Spanish-American, 211-15
special education programs,
  102, 307-12
Spring Lake Junior-Senior High
  School, Spring Lake,
  Michigan, 200-204
Spring Street School, Atlanta,
  Georgia, 125-30
staff development, 58, 84, 111,
  133, 153, 160, 185-86, 255, 305,
  324, 355, career awareness
  program, 268, television
  program supplement, 172-73;
  differentiation, 55, 118,
  276-78, 324; involvement, 37,
  116
staffing, 117-18, 149, 190, 250,
  255-56, 276-78, 298, 346; use
  of community resource
  personnel, 137
*Standards for school media
  programs*, 31, 277
state departments of education,
  171, 303, 305, 323
state funding, 170, 212, 303
state libraries, 263, 300
story hour, 212, 226, 328
storytelling, 121
Stott Elementary School,
  Arvada, Colorado, 87-91
student aides, 320; involvement
  111, 123, 179, 184, 303-04
summer programs, 87-91,
  270-74, 328-31
Sunday programs, 148-51
survey instrument, 27, 339 ff.,
  appendix
Sustained Silent Reading
  Program, 209

tape recorders, use of 293
teacher manual, 268; training, 58, 156, 166
teachers as media specialists, 97-101, 183-84
technology, effect of, 61-62
television, 26, 62-63; commercial, 227; cost, 26; courses for students, 186; program production, 122, 171-74, 226-30, 233, 279; video tape, 122, 160, 278
Texas: Dallas, Dallas Public Library, 291-96; Fort Worth, Fort Worth Public Library, 297-301
Thompson, William, 32
Toffler, Alvin, 32
Topeka West High School, Topeka, Kansas, 153-57
toy collection, 257-58; lending library, 221-24, 257
training of school media specialists, 254-58
transportation, 297-98

ungraded schools, 205; Virginia, Richmond, Amelia Street School, 307-12
unified budget, 194
United States Office of Education, 255, 323
University programs; Hawaii, University of, 138; North Carolina, Durham, North Carolina Central University, 254-59
Utah: St. George, Dixie High School, 302-06; Logan, Cache Public Library, 286-90

Utah State University, 287

videographics, Graphic expression reading improvement system (GERIS), 232-33
video tape, 122, 160, 171-73, 234
Virginia: Richmond, Amelia Street School, 307-12; Richmond Public Library, 313-17
volunteer training, 155, 214, 249-50
volunteers, use of 54, 155, 214, 249, 313-14

Warwick Public Library, Warwick, Rhode Island, 286-90
Washington, Snoqualmie, Echo Glen Children's Center, 318-22
Waterville High School, Waterville, Maine, 163-169
Webb, Mary, 28
wildlife, 287
Wisconsin: New Berlin, Eisenhower High School, 323-27; Racine, Racine Public Library, 328-32; Sheboygan, Mead Public Library, 333-37
workshops for adults, 109-110, 255, 267; for preschool teachers, 299
work/study, 94
writing skills, 314-16

year round school, 87-91
YWCA trust grant, 188, 189

LB
1028.4
.B34

Baker, D. Philip
   School and pub-
lic library media
programs for children
and young adults